Praise for Dr. Will
"Welcome to the Time

"In my more than 30 years as campus chief executive or chief academic officer, I have not met anyone who knows more about motivating today's students, staff, and faculty than does Dr. Will Keim."

Dr. Ronald Eaglin,
President Emeritus
Morehead State University, Kentucky

"I was honored to contribute to the Diversity Perspectives Chapter of *Welcome To The Time of Your Life!* Dr. Keim has presented at our college to rave reviews and his ability to inspire students to achieve success in college and beyond is amazing! This book has the power to inform, inspire, and empower students to make life-giving character-driven decisions. I hope every student in our nation will read it and act on it."

Tondaleya G. Jackson, M.Ed.
Director of Service Learning and Leadership Development
Benedict College, South Carolina

"Will, about your book *Welcome To The Time of Your Life!*, it's fabulous! Our Provost loves it! Thank you for providing us with a great resource. We are using it this year in our Freshman Year Experience Course."

Dewey Knight, Coordinator
Freshman Year Experience Program
The University of Mississippi

"You have a unique ability to relate to students that is incredible in that it gives you the power of a peer but the wisdom of an elder."

D. Kuh, Student
Whitman College, Washington

"Will Keim is one of the best speakers I have heard in holding the attention of college students and coaches today. He is relevant, humorous, empathetic, knowledgeable and entertaining. He is always welcome at our school and in my clubhouse. Will is the best!"

Patrick Murphy
Head Softball Coach
The University of Alabama

"Dr. Will Keim speaks to our new students six times during the Summer Orientation and Advising Program. He touches the hearts of students at California's most ethnically diverse campus with his honesty, love of students, sense of humor. We utilize *Welcome To The Time Of Your Life!* for all of our incoming students and it is having a huge positive impact on our retention and our campus morale!"

Mark Hartley, M.A.
Director of Student Life & Development
California State University, San Bernardino

WELCOME TO THE TIME OF YOUR LIFE!
21 Lessons for the 21st Century

"Make each day
your masterpiece."
John Wooden
1910-2010

Other books from Will Keim, Ph.D.:
Keys to Success in College & Life
*Fan Etiquette: How Did the Burning Desire
  to Win Become the Desire to Burn?*
Why We Hover: Parenting at The Speed of Life
The Education of Character
Spirit Journey
The Tao of Christ
The Truth About College
Life After College
Wit & Wisdom
Demythologizing the Animal House

Co-Author to:
Let Your Leadership Speak: How to Lead and Be Heard
Chicken Soup for the College Soul
Leadership's Greatest Hits
Pillars of Success
Speaking of Success

For information about booking Dr. Will Keim to visit your campus, contact:

Will Keim Speaks!, Inc.
3850 NW Jackson
Corvallis, OR 97330
(541) 740-1318
www.willkeim.com
E-mail ID: willkeim@att.net

This book and other Viaticum Press CDs, DVDs, and VHS resources may be purchased in bulk at discount for educational uses. Contact Viaticum Press. "Ten Strategic Study Success Steps," "Ten Characteristics of Effective Leadership," and "Fifty Stress Busters For Students" were previously published by Viaticum Press. Copyright © 2004 by Will Keim, Ph.D. Reprinted with permission.

Welcome to the Time of Your Life! 21 Lessons for the 21st Century. Copyright © 2010 by Will Keim, Ph.D.; Printed in the United States of America. No part of this book may be used or reproduced or utilized in any form or by any means, electronic or mechanical, including photocopying, recording, or by an information storage and retrieval system, without permission in writing from the publisher. Inquiries should be addressed to:

Viaticum Press
3850 NW Jackson
Corvallis, OR 97330

ISBN 978-0-615-38206-7

WELCOME TO THE TIME OF YOUR LIFE!

21 Lessons for the 21st Century

Dr. Will Keim

VIATICUM PRESS
CORVALLIS, OREGON

"To laugh often and much; to win the respect of intelligent people and the affection of children; to earn the appreciation of honest critics and endure the betrayal of false friends; to appreciate beauty, to find the best in others; to leave the world a little better; whether by a healthy child, a garden patch or a redeemed social condition; to know even one life has breathed easier because you have lived. This is the meaning of success."

—Ralph Waldo Emerson
1803 – 1882
Poet and philosopher

Foreword

In the spring of 1990, I was a first semester graduate student at Miami University in Oxford, Ohio. I had just begun a master's program in college student personnel services, and was extremely pleased with what I was learning. I felt an intellectual awakening that was very exciting to me, one that I felt would lead me to my ultimate goal of becoming a college president.

One morning, I received a call. The person introduced himself as Will Keim, and he wanted to know if I was the person who presented "Black Greek 101" at the Association of Fraternity Advisors Conference that past December in Dearborn, Michigan. I confirmed that I was the person. That December, along with Ron Binder, we presented a session to provide a background on historically Black fraternities and sororities, and techniques for advisors to use. The program was well received, and as an undergraduate, I was just thrilled to be there.

So imagine my excitement that Will Keim was on the phone inviting me to Corvallis, Oregon to participate in an international teleconference targeted at Greek students. There was no way I could pass up this experience, and I agreed to travel there that fall. That last weekend of September 1990 was a defining professional development experience for me. I had a chance to meet and engage with the premier thought leaders in Greek Life. Here I was, a first year graduate student, with this group of exceptional professionals, on stage in front of hundreds of students as part of a teleconference shown to over 100,000 students in 48 states and Canada.

For twenty years I have been able to grow these friendships with this group of colleagues and mentors. We've been at conferences together, served on panels and consulting teams, even been to each others' campuses and organizations. All of this was possible because of the vision of Will to begin to meaningfully address some of the challenges we saw then, and continue to see, on our campuses.

Twenty years later I still call Will my friend. We don't have many opportunities to see each other much, but every now and then we are speaking at the same conference and I have a chance to at least say hello and see what's going on. When I was asked to read his manuscript for *Welcome To The Time Of Your Life!* I jumped at the chance. What I found was classic Will Keim; bringing together a diverse group of people to provide a powerful message to young people on our campuses.

In this new book, Will and friends provide a number of great lessons for students who are navigating the college experience. Some of the lessons are basic skills, like developing a schedule to organize the work for all of your courses. Others are deeper issues that require lots of reflection, reflection that should be continued throughout life. Through a mix of practical wisdom, engaging stories, and structured activities, students will be able to use this book to help make sense of their college experience.

It is my hope that this book will help students seeking to make the most of college so that they can make the most of their lives. In an age when we need more young people to commit to bettering their communities, *Welcome To The Time Of Your Life!* will provide key lessons needed to help them successfully change the world for the better. I am living proof of the power of Will's work. Twenty years ago I learned from the people Will brought together that weekend in Corvallis. Please use this book to learn from the people he has assembled today.

Dr. Walter M. Kimbrough
President, Philander Smith College
Little Rock, AR

Introduction

Welcome!
There are seven thoughts I would like you to consider as the Introduction to this book.

> **"Never give up.
> Never ever give up."**
>
> —Jim Valvano
> 1946 – 1993
> Basketball coach

One. Welcome to the Time of Your Life!

"Welcome To The Time Of Your Life" is an extension of my vocational calling as an Educator. Dr. Martin Buber wrote:

> "Education worthy of the name is essentially the education of character."

Education in Buber's view, and mine, leads students out from the darkness of ignorance, self-absorption, and cynicism, and into the light of knowledge, response ability, and hope. Buber proposed:

> "To educate character we do not need moral geniuses. We do need men and women deeply committed to the creation of authentic interpersonal relationships that prepare students to leave campus and go out into the world and participate in the creation of genuine human community."

Education then, while personal, has at its core the implied assumption that the real good, the true purpose of learning, is to serve the larger good. My greatest hope is that you, the reader, will internalize this truth and act on it. I wrote this book to inspire you to look beyond yourself and I wrote it because students asked me to write it.

This is what this book is. Now, for what it is not.

What this book is not is "product." I have heard this line of thinking from hucksters, self-serving pitchmen, and imposters in the Academy.

"You have to have product in the back of the room. Don't leave any money on the table...give me your money and I will tell you the secret of taking other people's money," they proudly, like peacocks, pontificate.

This book is not about money, profit, or me. It is about you. It is about community, and character-driven decision making. It is my humble attempt to convince you to actualize your full potential for the good of all.

The brilliant, wise Monk Thomas Merton once advised that we must always write and speak for higher causes and not for profit or ourselves, for if we write and speak only for ourselves, then we will read and hear what we have said and written and wish we were dead. It is my fear that if we are the most important thing in our own lives, then we are either narcissists, or dumb asses (see definition of donkey!).

Welcome To The Time Of Your Life! is about Higher Aspirations. I want you to:

Arrive,
Survive, &
Thrive!

on campus and in your life.

> "Arrive, Survive, Thrive! Read, Reflect, Respond"
> —Dr. Will Keim

This book is for you and your journey. Twenty-one lessons to guide you along the way. They are presented as sign-posts along the way to help you progress toward the knowledge of yourself, and your world. It invites you to participate through exercises and questions. Please take time to complete these reflection pieces.

Read,
Reflect, &
Respond

There are no hidden agendas, evasions of purpose, extra pages, or fluff. This is the book that I wish someone would have written and given to me. Now you, and my children, and your children's children's will have it. It is the culmination of my life's work.

Welcome To The Time Of Your Life! is the written response to my student's requests to leave something behind when I leave their collegiate or corporate campuses.

I am not an advocate or believer in the oft-stated orientation mantra:

"These Will Be The Best Four Years Of Your Life"

If I believed that, the book would have been called, "Welcome To The Best Four Years Of Your Life."

That is not the title.

John Mellencamp wrote and sang, "Your Time Is Now" and he is

Introduction

right. This is your moment, your time, your brief streak across the sky. Your chance to blaze a path in the universe. Your time to shine as bright as the sun. Your one ticket ride through life!

The best time of your life is ahead!

The book is entitled, **Welcome To The Time Of Your Life!** because this is your time. Right now. Right here. This is the time where you will:

Set The Banquet Table For The Feast
You Will Eat The Rest Of Your Life

The best four years of your life are somewhere up ahead around the next turn or over the next mountain. Be clear that the only way to make them that way is to set the table well now! Elvis Presley operated under the letters TCB...that is, "Taking Care of Business" and that is precisely what you must now do.

And in reality...everyone knows that the information in the world is growing at such an amazing pace that college takes more than four years for many students. Let's be honest...how can the 5.2 years you might take be the best 4 years of your life?

There will come a time when you are paid and compensated for what you know, rather than paying tuition for what someone else knows. You will eventually find someone to spend your life with and hopefully have a family of your own.

How could the years when you have no money, are often alone, and studying all the time be called "the best four years of your life"? As an undergraduate collegiate myself, I developed a drinking problem, cheated on the love of my life and broke up with her, performed barely above average for two years, and masqueraded my low self esteem with a loud laugh and quick wit.

My "best four years"? Please!

I am more in spirit with John Mayer who said, "I have to believe that the best part of me is somewhere up my sleeve." I have had a number of "four year periods" that were better than college, and I believe the best is still ahead!

> **"I've got to believe that the best part of me is somewhere up my sleeve."**
>
> —*John Mayer*
> *Singer-songwriter, musician*

You are:

Setting The Banquet Table For The Feast You Will Eat For The Rest Of Your Life

> "A warrior is a man or woman not afraid to be their real self."
> —*Chogram Trungpa*
> *1939-1987*
> *Tibetan Buddhist master*

at college or your training institute, community college, or apprenticeship. You likely began setting the banquet table in high school, or even earlier, but now is the moment to seize the day, recognize the opportunity, and create your masterpiece.

I, finally, began my preparation in my Junior year, with the help and assistance of Dr. Don Duns, and Monsignor Robert Silva. We all need mentors. I set the table with their help and guidance. That was my "set the banquet table time" and now I am living the good years with my family. The best four years of your life are ahead. Get ready for them now by setting the table well. This book will help you do just that!

I want you to become a Warrior. Choygram Trungpa, in his book, *Shambala: The Sacred Path Of The Warrior* states that ultimately a Warrior is a man or woman who is not afraid to be their real self. That is, to accept yourself, your strengths and weaknesses, to embrace your past and present without fear, and to find your SISU (more on that in a minute).

This is my hope for you.

1. A Warrior who faces each day with courage, hope, and an acceptance of self.
2. A person who listens to the voices of others but follows the voice within. You are stronger than you think you are.

Will you trust me enough to read on? Thank you.

Two. Three Basic Assumptions About Life

I make Three Basic Assumptions About Life in writing this book. They are:

1. Life is not a dress rehearsal.
2. You have a finite number of days to live and an infinite number of potential experiences.
3. Your time is now!

It is time to enroll and engage. I would encourage you to be a good consumer of the education product and get your money's worth by showing up.

Three. You Can Ignore Labels and Create Your Own Identity

Don't let the college, me, or anyone else label you or your parents as "Generation X"; "Generation Y"; "The Millenials"; The + Generation"; "i.Generation"; or "Helicopter Parents." Stop labeling, being labeled, and stereotyping. One of my fraternity brothers, Kurt Vonnegut, said in a Rolling Stone article: "I am sick and tired of middle aged baby boomers labeling every generation after them. This generation is as much Generation A as Adam and Eve were." What a great line. Don't be categorized, dismissed, or described. Be yourself and find your unique niche. Be who you were always intended to be. A richly complex, one-of-a-kind, unique individual. Go Frost on 'em — take the path less traveled! Resist automazation and dehumanization. Rock On! Make your own journey. Think of **Welcome To The Time Of Your Life!** as 21 Lessons to consider along your way.

> "People will live divided no more when they realize no punishment anyone could lay on them is worse than what they are laying on themselves by conspiring in their own diminishment."
>
> —*Parker Palmer*
> *Author, educator, activist*

Four. Aspire Higher

Aspire Higher! Raise your own bar. You are not in college to get a job — you are in school to find your vocation. What do you love enough to master to the degree that you can get paid to do what you love? Think about it. I think you already know what you want to do. It is in your mind. Don't lowball yourself.

Make sure you are not your own worst enemy, and if you are, get some help and get moving in the right direction for you.

Five. Thank You. Thank You. Thank You!

I want to thank my friends and family who have greatly contributed to this book. It would not have been possible without Editors Kevin Klink and Christa Keim. Thanks to Dr. Tom Hill, Mark Hartley, Dr. Bill Richter, and Tondeleya Jackson for "test driving" the book with all of your new students at Iowa State, California State University, San Bernardino, Lenoir Rhyne University, and Benedict College. Special thanks to Liz Kurt, Sarah Rockwell, Joe Richardson, Rick Barnes, Dr. Walter Kimbrough, Travon Robinson, Tom Durein, Val and Chuck Ross, Kevin Klink, Dr. Gregg Gilles, Dr. Steve Wilhelm, Traci Klink, Laura Klink, Joe Radzvilowicz and Family, Nouveau Vie Eating Disorder Clinic, Dewey Knight, Dr. Mark Nelson, Dr. Bob Witt, Dr. David Jones, Sheryl Garrett, Michael Dunham, David Coleman, John Argeropoulos, Elaine Pasqua. Joe Henley, Delta Air Lines, Manny Hernandez, Jesus

> "No one does anything worthwhile without the help, friendship, and love of others."
> —Dr. Will Keim

Jaime Diaz, Dr. Don Duns, Dr. Tom Stubbs, Dr. Matt Caires, Dr. Michael Beachley, Roosevelt Credit, Lauren Grill, Alaska Air Lines, Amtrak, Hertz, Starbucks, Donna Keim, Sami Keim, Hannah Keim, JJ Keim, Ben Williams, Ford Family Foundation, Sigma Alpha Epsilon, Delta Upsilon, Phi Delta Theta, Lambda Chi Alpha, Connie Clark, Sue Enquist, Pat Summitt, Dr. Bill Sederburg, Dr. Tom Goodale, Sarah and David Patterson, Ashley Armstrong, Cori Hill, Dr. Graham Spanier, Dr. Ed King, Dr. Rod Kirsch, Lyn Culver, Dr. Dick Hage, Tim Keefe, Chief Ken Elwer & Nancy Elwer, Ilaria Pasco, Dr. Tom Stubbs, Steve Good, Char Burgess, Dr. Larry Burgess, Dave and Sandy Bonsall, Mary and Virgil Basham, Dave Maguire, Dr. John and Dr. Sharon McGuire, John Spaulding and Kimber Williams, Dr. Rick Reeder, Dr. Joan Terry, Geoffrey Canada, Dr. Debbie Silver, Dr. Bonnie Davis, Ron Clark, Dr. Sparky Reardon, Tom Durein, Dr. Kent Gardner, Dan Maxwell, Dr. Sally Click, Dan Preston, Dr. Michael Beachley, Coach Don Patterson, Barbara Maxwell, Chuck Cleveland, Dr. Mary Ann Philips, Gary Woehl, Dr. Marcus Borg, Father Robert Silva, Dr. Kathy Cavins, Todd and Marion McKinney, Jesse Marks, Judy Chambers, Des Collado, Dr. Eileen Sullivan, Paul DeWine, Mark Koepsell, Grace Baganu, Rev. Clay Stauffer, John & Amber Duncan, Al Perone, Dr. Tim McMahon, Laurie Prince, Dr. Ray Zarvell, Dr. Cameron Martin, Durwood Owen, Dr. Robert Blaney, Dr. Tom Ambrogi, Dr. David Stephen, Dr. Ed Bryan, Dr. Jo Anne and Dr. Cliff Trow, Dr. Les Wong, Coach Jerry Orlando, Jackson Vaughan, Mike Candrea, Lou Holtz, Jim Tressel, Nick Saban, Patrick Murphy, Marla Looper, Mickie Demoss, Mitch Barnhart, Ross Perot, Joe Mazzola, Peter Ueberroth, Greg Smith and Clare Staton Smith, Dave and Laura Evenson, Dr. William Z. Good, Ed and Mary Konopa, Dennis and Jan Eaton, Tim and Anne Snee, Zac Konopa, Jim and Deb Peacock, Lauren Wickwire, Lily Smith, Britta Evenson, Kendra Strahm, Greg Herman, Ben Blosser, Dan Preston, Katie Reeves, Jeff Martinez, Mawi Asgedom, Dr. Bernard Franklin, Rabbi Bernard Roseberg, Dr. Paul Kopperman, President David Carter, President Tom Bryant, Chancellor Vic Boschini, Ken Keniston, Neil and Cheri Reynolds, Art and Eileen Olson, Merry Crain, Becky Pate, Sun Graphics, Skip Hamilton, Pro Print, Madonna Weathers, President Ronald Eaglin, Mike Garrett, Pete Carrol, Jean Mrasek, Dave Westol, Maureen Syring, Jean Scott, Martha Brown, Brandon Schmeder, Sean Deardorff, Chancellor Gee, Sheryl Garrett, CFP, Principal, Garrett Planning Network, and my students, two million strong, and growing!

Thank you for encouraging me and inspiring me, and for not giving up on me.

Six. The Big Questions ...

The Big Questions, then are:

> *If not now...........when?
> *If not you............whom?

The Answers are clear.....

Now is the time.

You are the one.

It is time to:

> **Arrive** with a positive attitude and with hope.
>
> **Survive** the temptation to shrink away from opportunity.
>
> **Thrive** on your new status as a "Warrior," able to leap tall obstacles with a single thought!

> "No problem can resist the power of sustained thinking."
> —*Voltaire*
> *1694-1778*
> *French writer and philosopher*

Seven. And Now for Something Totally Different: SISU

SISU\sis-su\ "Special strength and STUBBORN DETERMINATION to continue and overcome in the moment of adversity; a combination of STAMINA, COURAGE, AND OBSTINACY held in reserve for hard times."

Returning from what was fondly called the annual "Man Camp" in the woods of the Upper Peninsula ("UP") of Michigan in November, we had sighted the hunting rifles, prepared the deer blinds, sat at fire, consumed beverages of malt and hops, eaten Texas-sized steaks provided by Biggy, and slept nine in a one room Camp (cabin). We were the Brothers Bonsall; Dave, Paul, Steve, and Dan, sons Scott and Adam; and Dean, Josh, and myself. It was a fellowship of men who at one time or another had lived in Michigan, Illinois, California, Oregon, Wyoming, and Montana. I had not had that much fun in 24 hours in a long time. There was the 4:30 a.m. visit to the woods as the boys had failed to tell the new guy where the outhouse was, but we'll save that for another day.

Warm and dry back in Marquette on the shores of Lake Superior, I told Sandy Bonsall, wife of Dave and mother of Scott, that I would need to Man-Up next year for Man Camp as I was exhausted. "I'm always amazed at how hearty you UP'ers are." "We've got Sisu," said Sandy. "What's that?" "It is Finnish," Sandy said. "It is what makes us hearty, firm, and able to cope with the UP." She handed me a piece of paper and on it was written:

> **SISU**
> "... Stamina, Courage, and Obstinancy Held in Reserve for Hard Times."

SISU\sis-su\ Special strength and STUBBORN DETERMINATION to continue and overcome in the moment of adversity; a combination of STAMINA, COURAGE, AND OBSTINACY held in reserve for hard times.

I knew at that very moment that this was the concept I had been trying to find within myself to face my own problems and challenges and more importantly, I had to share it with my students. Sisu is the key to coping with and conquering the challenges discussed in *Welcome To The Time Of Your Life!*

I present my Sisu thoughts for you, with thanks to Sandy Bonsall and the Finnish people. I want you to know that:

> **You have special strength. Accept it and use it for the common good. Be stubborn and determined in your rejection of mediocrity and in your willingness to overcome adversity. Hold stamina, courage, and obstinacy in reserve for there will be hard times. These too will pass, and we will persevere. Sisu!**

Be Strong, Stubborn, Determined, Have Stamina, Courage, and Be Obstinate in your journey toward success in life. You are greater than your moments of adversity and the hard times.

You are greater than your fears.

You have Sisu deep within you.

Welcome To The Time Of Your Life! +
SISU=Success In College & Life

Let's get started!

Blessings,

Dr. Will Keim

Contents

Stage One: Arrive
- Scholarship 3-14
- Writing 15-22
- Speaking 23-28
- Character 29-34
- Relationships 35-52

Stage Two: Survive
- Stress 55-58
- Freedom 59-66
- Health 67-74
- Eating Disorders 75-82
- Letting Go 83-88

Stage Three: Thrive
- Peacemaking 93-98
- Diversity 99-142
- Service 143-148
- Spirituality 149-154
- Financial Literacy 155-168

Stage Four: Aspire Higher
- Leadership 173-182
- Citizenship 183-194
- Sportsmanship 195-202
- Trees of Self-Realization and Self-Defeat . . 203-216
- The Secret 217-222
- 25,000 Days 223-230

STAGE ONE
Arrive

"The best thing about the future is that it comes one day at a time."
Abraham Lincoln

Scholarship ❖ Writing ❖ Speaking ❖ Character ❖ Relationships

STAGE ONE: ARRIVE "CHAPTER SUMMARY"
Scholarship ❖ Writing ❖ Speaking ❖ Character ❖ Relationships

1. SCHOLARSHIP with Mark Hartley, M.A., California State University San Bernardino, & Meagan Denney, University of Texas

"Education worthy of the name is essentially the education of character."
Dr. Martin Buber

"Sit in the front row of class or up close. Take notes in every class and recopy your notes after class in outline form. Get a syllabus from every instructor and make a master syllabus (see options on pages 6-7) of all assignments. Read all of your assignments. Maximize the missing minutes by studying between classes. Pick a study partner or join a study group. Meet every professor, ask questions, and go to the professor's office hours if you need help."

2. WRITING with Nikki Bussey, University of Memphis

"The best time for planning a book is while you're doing the dishes."
Agatha Christie

"This is a good way to describe the thinking process when approaching a huge writing assignment. Don't wait until the last minute to pick a topic, do an outline, or begin writing. Start thinking about the assignment while doing some daily activities like doing the dishes, getting ready in the morning for work or school, or even while exercising. The idea behind this thought is to get you to start thinking about the project early. The earlier you begin the more you can take your time to focus and create something interesting and entertaining."

3. SPEAKING in memory of Dr. Don Duns, University of the Pacific, California

*"When I speak, and every time I speak, I think of three things. I want to be:
Precise in Detail
Passionate in Delivery, and
Persuasive in Appeal"*
Dr. Will Keim

"Every speech consists of an introduction, body, and conclusion. That is, tell them what you are going to tell them, tell them, and tell them what you told them. There are fifteen key elements to every good public speech and they can be achieved with three things: Practice, Practice, and Practice. Great speakers are not born. Rather, they are made with a knowledge of public speaking principles and a desire to communicate clearly and with passion about an idea or concept of great importance to the speaker, the audience, and in the best case scenario, both!"

4. CHARACTER

"Our character is what we do when we think no one is looking."
H. Jackson Browne

"Character is what you are when no one is watching. A world of integrity and character begins with one person at a time knowing and acting on this adage. Say what you mean and do what you say. If you don't, admit it. Make amends and move on. Your personal character will lead you to the discovery of a profession whose values are consistent with your own. Character-driven decision-making is one of the most important skills you can learn and use in your life."

❖ ❖ ❖

5. RELATIONSHIPS with David Coleman, President, Coleman Productions

"Quality interpersonal relationships are essential to human development and growth. This chapter considers these life-shaping interactions and the relationships that students must establish with offices and professionals on campus in order to make a smooth transition into the collegiate community. In this way, I believe the chapter is unique and very helpful to new students."
Dr. Will Keim

(on the value of relationships…)
"The number one factor that will determine whether or not a new student returns for his or her sophomore year is whether or not that particular student forms at least one meaningful relationship with someone on campus. This relationship could be with a roommate, a classmate, a teammate, a co-worker, a professor, a staff member or be more romantic in nature, but if a new student does not feel as if they have "connected" or that they "belong" and are "accepted," odds are they'll be surfing through catalogues to decide upon their next collegiate choice."

Scholarship

> **"**Scholarship is to be created not by compulsion, but by awakening a pure interest in knowledge.**"**
>
> —Ralph Waldo Emerson
> 1803 – 1882
> American essayist, philosopher and poet

Perseverance

We received the following letter from a student who heard Will speak. Will's message about not giving up resonated with this young man. In fact, he had already learned the lesson himself. Read on:

> "My freshman year of high school was the worst year of my life. Instead of doing homework, I was sneaking out to go drinking. By winter break I was taking drugs and drinking nightly. My grades fell to below a 'D' average.
>
> "At the end of the year, most of my friends had been either expelled or sent to military schools. My parents moved me to a new high school where my mother worked so she could keep an eye on me. With the help of my parents and my football coaches, I was able to turn my life around. My grades rose to a 'C+' average, and my parents encouraged me to apply to colleges.
>
> "My guidance counselor, however, told me that I didn't have what it took to succeed at college; she suggested I look into trade schools. I was determined to prove her wrong, and I applied to ten colleges. I was rejected by all ten. I was heartbroken but refused to quit.
>
> "My mom suggested I apply to the University of Redlands, but I was denied again. I appealed the decision. A few weeks later the admission host called and offered me an opportunity. 'Attend community college for 24 units,' he said, 'and if you can maintain a 3.00 GPA, we will admit you.' I took the challenge, succeeded, and was admitted to Redlands where I have done well. I plan to become a high school history teacher.
>
> "I failed many times in my life, but it all made me a stronger person. It took me thirteen applications and a year in community college to be admitted into a four-year university, but with the support of my parents and my mentors, I have persevered.
>
> "One of the greatest delights in my life is that I proved my guidance counselor wrong."
>
> —*Steven Burke*

> "The journey of a thousand miles begins beneath your feet."
> —Lao Tzu
> Sixth century, B.C.
> Father of Taoism

The basic assumption of this character lesson is simple yet profound: **You are setting the banquet table now for the feast you will eat the rest of your life.** Scholarship is the primary key that starts the vehicle in which you will negotiate your post-college plans: graduate school, salary, and career. Or NOT.

You must envision yourself graduating with your diploma in one hand and your self-esteem in the other hand. Students do not plan to fail. Rather, they fail to plan.

Being a good student is the basis on which success must be built. All of us will earn our living with what we learn in the classroom and in co-curricular activities.

Visualization Exercise

Imagine your college graduation day. Is it sunny? What time of day is the ceremony? Where is it? Where would you like to go afterward to celebrate? List the people you want to be there:

_____

_____

_____

_____

_____

Meagan Denney speaks:

"I had big shoulders and I didn't feel good about myself. In addition, I had a learning disability. I could not get the work done as fast as the other children in the class. 'She's in the special class' they would say when I walked by. The I found a teacher who would design tests to help me show my knowledge of the subject matter. My parents never gave up on me. At that time I discovered I could throw a softball and throw it fast. Suddenly, I was popular and began to feel better about myself. My grades improved too. I went to the University of Texas on an athletic scholarship. Now I play professional softball and speak for Dr. Will Keim's Higher Aspirations. Find a mentor. Believe in yourself."
Ask questions. You can do it.

—*Meagan Denney*

> ### Ten Strategic Study Success Steps
>
> 1. Sit in the front row or up close.
> 2. Take notes in every class.
> 3. After class, recopy your notes in outline form.
> 4. Get a syllabus from every instructor.
> 5. Make a master syllabus of all assignments. (See examples on the next two pages.)
> 6. Read all assignments.
> 7. Study on road trips.
> 8. Pick a study partner.
> 9. Study between classes.
> 10. Meet the professor, ask questions, and go to the professor's office hours if you need help.

Keep track

We believe that if you have one place to check on assignments, then there is a much greater chance you can stay on top of what you need to do. On the following two pages, we've provided tables to help you organize your academic workload. Keep track by topic or by assignment — your choice.

> "Education worthy of the name is essentially the education of character."
> —Martin Buber
> 1875-1965
> Philosopher

> **Lou Holtz speaks:**
> "Ability is what you're capable of doing.
> Motivation determines what you do.
> Attitude determines how well you do it."
>
> *Football coach*
> *ESPN Commentator*

Master Syllabus Option #1: By Topic

Write in your assignments for every class.

Day/Week/Month	Reading Assignments	Papers	Presentations & Speeches	Labs	Mid Terms	Final

Stage One: Arrive ... Scholarship 7

Master Syllabus Option #2: By Class
Write in your assignments for every class.

Due	Class 1	Due	Class 2	Due	Class 3	Due	Class 4	Due	Class 5

Mark Hartley is one of my very favorite former students. We are now friends. Setting academic goals absolutely changed Mark Hartley's life for the better…and it all started because he wanted some free pizza. Mark was one of those guys who stepped onto his college campus and proudly proclaimed, "I will never join a fraternity!" You can't blame him for having that opinion because there were only two things he "knew" about Greek Life; 1) they all drank heavily, and 2) their grades were well below the campus average. His expansive knowledge was all changed after attending a "FREE" fraternity rush event. The emphasis is on free because there was no way he was going to go to this event, until the guys said FREE bowling and pizza.

After bowling an unimpressive round the fraternity men found their way to the back dining room where the pizzas and sodas were to be served. Before Mark could get his hands on one of the thick crust slices, a sophomore pulled a chair to the front of the room and climbed up on it. The sophomore's name was Jake. Although Mark had never met this young man it was obvious he was the undisputed leader of this organization. Jake spoke of leaving a legacy over the next four years, standing up to authority figures when an injustice had been created, and setting an example of excellence within the members' desired academic pursuits. Jake's final statement was that each individual in the room had the ability to achieve the objectives laid before the group; however, unless each man was willing to set a goal of a 3.5 GPA, they would not be considered for membership within the fraternity.

> "All successful people, men and women, are big dreamers. They imagine what their future could be, ideal in every respect, and then they work every day toward their distant vision, that goal or purpose."
> —Brian Tracy
> Author, speaker

Have you ever been challenged to reach beyond your capabilities? This is the situation Mark faced on a warm September day in Southern California. What Mark saw in that short speech by Jake was an opportunity to be a part of an organization that wasn't committed to heavy drinking and below-average academic standards. This was a rare opportunity to be a part of something great. The gauntlet was thrown down and Mark bravely picked it up. After four years, that fraternity had the highest Greek GPA for eight semesters in a row, they doubled the number of community service hours completed by their closest competitor, and they had won the Intramural Cup for all four years. Mark, incidentally, graduated with honors and a 3.65 cumulative GPA. This from a man who never broke 1000 on his SAT scores. Anything is possible, when you have a goal and work every day towards it.

Challenge yourself and challenge others

Setting goals involves establishing specific, measurable and time-targeted objectives. Work on the theory of goal-setting suggests that it's an effective tool for making progress by ensuring that participants in a group with a common goal are clearly aware of what is expected from them if an objective is to be achieved. On a personal level, setting goals is a process that allows people to specify then work towards their own objectives. (*Wikipedia.com 2009.*)

Short-Range Goals: What are a few of your goals over the next academic term?
Suggestions: 4.0 GPA. Dean's List. Perfect attendance in all classes.

_____
_____
_____
_____
_____
_____

> "He that can have patience can have what he will."
>
> —*Benjamin Franklin*
> *1706 – 1790*
> *Founding Father of the United States*

Medium-Range Goals: Where do you want to be academically as you begin your senior year of college?
Suggestions: Select a major that suits my skill sets. Become a tutor for others in my major. Acquire an internship. Study abroad.

_____
_____
_____
_____
_____
_____
_____

Long-Range Goals: What do I need to do to set myself up for success after I receive my college diploma?

Suggestions: List five potential companies you would like to work for. Identify three professors who would be willing to write you a letter of recommendation for grad school or a job. Graduate Summa Cum Laude.

> "Behold the turtle: he only progresses when his neck is out."
>
> —Sir Winston Churchill
> 1874 – 1965
> Prime Minister of
> The United Kingdom

_____
_____
_____
_____
_____
_____
_____

Goal Setting as a Lifelong Habit
(The Story of John Goddard)

"One rainy afternoon an inspired 15-year old boy named John Goddard sat down at his kitchen table in Los Angeles and wrote three words at the top of a yellow pad, "My Life List." Under that heading he wrote down 127 goals. Since then he has completed 108 of those goals. These were not simple or easy goals. They included climbing the world's major mountains, exploring from source to mouth the longest rivers of the world, piloting the world's fastest aircraft, running a mile in five minutes and reading the entire *Encyclopedia Britannica*."

Chicken Soup for the Soul
NY Times bestseller

Check out John Goddard's entire list at www.johngoddard.info/life_list.htm.

Start your "Life List" right now!

_____
_____
_____
_____
_____
_____
_____

Expert Advice for Setting Academic Goals

"Every great dream begins with a dreamer. Always remember, you have within you the strength, the patience, and the passion to reach for the stars to change the world."

Harriett Tubman
1822-1903
Abolitionist and Humanitarian

"None of us can change our yesterdays, but all of us can change our tomorrows."

Colin Powell
Retired Four-Star General, United States Army

> **"None of us can change our yesterdays, but all of us can change our tomorrows."**
> —General Colin Powell

"Many of us crucify ourselves between two thieves- regret for the past and fear for the future."

Fulton Oursler
1893-1952
American Journalist and Writer

"I long to accomplish a great and noble task, but it is my chief duty to accomplish humble tasks as though they were great and noble. The world is moved along, not only by the mighty shoves of its heroes, but also by the aggregate of the tiny pushes of each honest worker."

Helen Keller
1880-1968
Political Activist

"Most of the important things in the world have been accomplishments by people who have kept on trying when there seemed to be no hope at all."

Dale Carnegie
1888-1955
American Writer and Lecturer
Author of How to Win Friends and Influence People

"A man who views the world the same at fifty as he did at twenty has wasted thirty years of his life."

Muhammad Ali
World Heavyweight Boxing Champion,
Olympic Gold Medalist and Social Activist

ABOUT THE AUTHOR: Mark Hartley is the author of the highly acclaimed book series *If I Knew Then What I Know Now...* which is used on numerous college campuses. He serves as the Director of Student Leadership & Development at California State University, San Bernardino. Mark speaks on the topics of leadership and academic excellence to students nationwide. He is a former college football and baseball player and has been presented many community service awards for his commitment to education amongst America's youth. Mark heard Dr. Will Keim speak during his new student orientation in 1989 and has been in communication with the good doctor ever since.

WILL'S NOTE: I have known Mark Hartley since his freshman year at the University of Redlands. He is now an excellent young student affairs professional, a great dad, and a loving husband. His growth and development are not only a tribute to his tenacity and work ethic, but to the entire American Higher Education System. Though he is years younger than myself, I consider him not only a friend but a mentor.

Will speaks:
"A few years ago, I visited the University of Tennessee to speak to the student athletes. The women's basketball team was seated in the front row. I asked them, 'How come y'all sit right up front?' One of the players, Semeka Randall, smiled and said, 'Because Coach Pat Summitt tells us to sit in the front of the classroom, in the front of the lecture, in the front of the movies, so we get used to being in front of things like the NCAA.' That basketball team did win the NCAA national championship. Semeka Randall played professional basketball in the WNBA and is an NCAA Head Women's Basketball Coach!"

Sit in the front of the class.

—Dr. Will Keim

Stage One: Arrive ... Scholarship

Assignment: Set your academic goals

At the beginning of the term, write down a realistic goal for each class and an action plan to achieve that goal. At the end of the term, revisit the goals you set. Were you successful? Why? Why not? Be honest with yourself. You are on your way with a plan for academic success.

Class	Desired Grade and Action Plan	Actual Grade	Most Valuable Lesson Learned
Example: Speech 101	*Grade: A. Attend every class. Read all assignments. Practice speeches.*	*A. Accomplished goal!*	*Practice was key to good public speaking.*

> "It is wise to keep in mind that no success or failure is necessarily final."

If you are having academic difficulty, talk to your:

- ❏ Faculty Advisor
- ❏ Resident Assistant
- ❏ Professor
- ❏ Dean of Students
- ❏ Parent
- ❏ Coach
- ❏ Teammate
- ❏ Academic Success Counselor

Tip: Pick more than one.

M&Ms

"Maximize the Missing Minutes" (M&Ms) is our way to help you use your time wisely. Study during the day between classes. You will pick up an additional 2–4 hours of high-quality study time per day. Go to the library, a coffee shop, or wherever you prefer to study. It should be a place where you can focus/concentrate and stay awake!

Combine M&Ms with "Ten Strategic Study Success Tips" (earlier in this chapter), and you will be well on your way to achieving academic success.

Your Passion

We believe that you should choose a major that truly reflects something that you are deeply passionate about. It should lead to a profession that you can willingly and joyfully spend one half of your waking hours pursuing. "The Secret" in Stage Four, near the end of this book, offers you an opportunity to discover your passion and begin the process of selecting a major that becomes your life's work.

> "The world cares very little about what a man or woman knows; it is what the man or woman is able to do that counts."
>
> —*Booker T. Washington*
> *1856 – 1915*
> *Author and activist*

Will you choose:

a Diploma	or	an Education?
a Workout	or	a Healthy Lifestyle?
a Date	or	a Relationship?
an Idea	or	a Dream?
a Job	or	a Vocation?

The first options are good, but the second options are better!

Getting it "Write"

> ❝There is no rule on how to write. Sometimes it comes easily and perfectly; sometimes it's like drilling rock and then blasting it out with charges.❞
>
> —*Ernest Hemingway*
> *1899-1961*
> *Writer and journalist*

It's the night before your ten-page report on Ben Franklin is due, and it isn't finished. You are on page four, and you're stuck, plus your printer isn't working. You're thinking, "How did I get here and who even cares about ole' dead Ben Franklin?" Sound familiar? Everyone has probably experienced this same situation. So, why is writing a paper, essay, or journal entry so difficult and why is it important?

> ❝You have to find your passion with the material first.❞
> —*Nikki Bussey*

It's important because it connects to every career path. Don't think so? Well, unless you don't have to write e-mails, notes, and things of that nature in your future job, then you will probably have to write in some shape, fashion, or form. E-mails, prescriptions, laws, blueprints, tests, and mathematical proofs and theorems all have to be typed or written in a legible language. Good writing opens doors.

Elements of writing well:

You have to find your passion with the material first. Find an aspect of the topic that truly inspires or stirs up your emotions. Next, type every thought that flows from your brain. Now, think about it. Writing something you wanted to write was more fun than writing something you had to write. Only when you have found something that inspires your imagination, is it time to get down to the actual writing.

> ❝Say all you have to say in the fewest possible words, or your reader will be sure to skip them; and in the plainest possible words or he will certainly misunderstand them.❞
>
> —*John Ruskin*
> *1819-1900*
> *English art critic and social thinker*

Basic writing principals: Clear and concise. It's a phrase often used with writing, for several reasons. To write clearly and concisely requires you to think about writing for the reader. If it's a research paper, make sure you explain all the important details to those reading your paper, without overloading them with too much information. If readers want extra information, then they will Google it later. The trick is to give them enough information to get them interested in learning more of the topic. Stick to a clear and concise format and you can't go wrong.

Form and style: There are many ways to format a research paper or essay. The most basic form of writing is the 5-paragraph writing style. It's like a classic novel — timeless and easy to read. Here's how to do it.

Paragraph one is the introduction of your thesis statement, or argument. For example: "Children who grew up having a monthly allowance grow to be better financial planners." That introductory statement should be supported by three main points you will elaborate in the next three paragraphs. "They have to budget their funds earlier than children who are simply given money, learn how to save, and don't usually spend money so freely later in life." Paragraphs two, three, and four develop these points and thereby make your case. The fifth and final paragraph should be restating the introductory sentence with the descriptions bolstered by your argument.

> **"Always tell the truth. It will amaze half the people and astonish the rest."**
> —Mark Twain
> 1835-1910
> Author and humorist

Nikki Speaks:
"The difference between the right word and the almost right word is the difference between lightning and a lightning bug," Mark Twain once said. He was right, too. Simply knowing the right word or the right way to construct a sentence can make a world of a difference.

Punctuation and grammar: The problem with punctuation and grammar today is that our generation has become far too dependent on spell check and Auto Correct. When texting or chatting, we often use abbreviations, numbers or symbols, and partial words. The messages are produced more quickly, but can take more time to decipher and can send the wrong meaning! (hint: consult a chat or messaging guide) Enjoy the text lingo with your friends, but know when to use it and when to not use it.

Punctuation is a special challenge today. Seen anyone use too many exclamation points recently? Point made. Periods end a declarative sentence, and question marks end questions, commas separate different thoughts, colons and semicolons separate thoughts and lists. Use quotations when quoting something. The basic sentence structure is also simple: subject, verb, and predicate. Add adjectives, adverbs, direct/indirect objects, etc. to make it more interesting to read, and put it in active tense whenever possible.

"My dog drank all the water in her bowl."

"After taking a long jog around the block with me, my thirsty dog drank every last drop of water in her bowl."

See the difference?

Vocabulary: A great way to combat that is to challenge yourself with the words you use. Word-a-Day calendars may seem lame, but they are a systematic way to get you to extend your vocabulary. One word at a time can help you sound and eventually become more intelligent. One way to learn punctuation and grammar by osmosis is simply by reading more often. Reading more will expose you to different words and ways to use them.

Plagiarism: **Plagiarism is fraud.** As a writer, I can tell you nothing is more frustrating or maddening than when someone uses your material without citing, quoting, or attributing it to the author. At most high schools and colleges you will receive an automatic F for the course and you could possibly even be suspended from school. You can use other people's work, you just have to quote it and cite it back to the author. Depending on your professor or teacher, you will then cite the quote using whatever format is required. (Usually it is MLA or APA format.) There are so many useful tools on the Internet, not to mention your school, to help you make sure you are correctly citing the material. It doesn't have to be an intentional action either. Sometimes you may be accidentally plagiarizing, and again, there are several websites that can help you avoid this unfortunate situation.

> "Plagiarism is fraud. You can use other people's work only by quoting it, citing it back to the author, and in the case of larger usage, by permission of the author or publisher."
> —*Nikki Bussey*

Write "right" for the situation

Traditional writing: If you wouldn't read it, why should I? Articles, essays, journals and papers should be informative but entertaining. This also carries over into the standard forms of writing you will have to submit at some point in your life, including letters and resumes. Let's take a look at resumes. A **resume** is your way of highlighting your experiences. You list all the work and volunteer work you've done and in a way that best describes your actions. You want it to be eye-catching, but be careful. You don't want to cross the creative line: Resumes should stick to a pretty basic standard. You may think that having a pink-scented resume like Elle Woods in *Legally Blonde* is a good idea, but unless you are applying for a position in the Barbie department of the Mattel toy company, stick to the standard form. With resumes, the best way to make yourself stand out is by using the best descriptions for the work you've done. Reading about someone who "worked well with others" may be good and well, but someone who "worked collaboratively with full-time staff to enhance interpersonal relations with peers" sounds like a much better hire!

Letters should also stick to a more traditional pattern. Letters in themselves are a more traditional form of communicating. However, big things can be announced in letters like a college acceptance, scholarship money, and more. Can you imagine getting a letter announcing your acceptance to a college that said, "Hey Nikki! Congrats on The U of M!!!! See you in the fall, El Presidente Shirley Raines." Your parents would probably rip it up and send you somewhere else. All letters begin with a greeting, "Dear Mrs. Smith." All paragraphs in the letter should be indented with grammatically correct sentences. At the conclusion of the letter, end with a closing such as "Yours truly," or "Sincerely," with your name beneath it.

Hopefully now you feel a bit more confident when it comes to writing!

> "The typos, punctuation, grammer, spelling, sentence and paragraph structure, capitalization? Yeah, that's all important to me. What we write and how it is written is, after all, the first impression we make on this site."
> —2010, Match.com profile

Writing Tips: **Here are some wise words from some unique characters.**

"I used to think those people who sat alone at Starbucks writing on their laptops were pretentious posers. Now I know: they are people who have recently moved in with someone." Carrie Bradshaw, *Sex and the City*.

This quote may have had some other meaning on the show, but here I'd like to stress a different point: the importance of writing somewhere without distractions. Some people can write, carry conversations, listen to an iPod, and eat at the same time, but they aren't truly enveloped or involved with what they are writing. My suggestion is to turn off the music, TV, or ask your roommates, or parents and siblings, to give you some time to write. When you are free from distractions, you are forced to… think. (Gasp!) It's often best to be alone and not surrounded by distraction. For most it's a cubicle in the library. That didn't work for me. I'm too social for a library and I ended up knowing everything about the person beside me instead of learning things about my topic. For some it's a busy coffee shop with just the right level of background noise. Simply stated, find what's best for you.

"The best time for planning a book is while you're doing the dishes." – Agatha Christie, author of numerous murder mysteries.

This is a good way to describe the thinking process when approaching a huge writing assignment. Don't wait until the last minute to pick a topic, do an outline, or begin writing. Start thinking

Stage One: Arrive ... Getting it "Write"

about the assignment while doing some daily activities like doing the dishes, getting ready in the morning for work or school, or even while exercising. The idea behind this thought is to get you to start thinking about the project early. The earlier you begin, the more you can take your time to focus and create something interesting and entertaining.

"The dream begins, most of the time, with a teacher who believes in you, who tugs and pushes and leads you on to the next plateau sometimes poking you with a sharp stick called truth." – Dan Rather, Reporter

Seek input from a teacher or professor you look up to – if you want to do well, ask for their opinion. They're going to be honest. When you realize someone believes in you, writing a paper doesn't seem quite so difficult. Look for that inspiration and thank the person who pushes you to do better instead of letting things slide.

Exercise: List five people you know in your life who believe in you, and to whom you could turn for an honest opinion about yourself, your behavior, your career path or your writing.

_____
_____
_____
_____
_____

Tip: The next time you are facing a difficult writing assignment, an impasse, or what we call a writer's block contact one of these people and let them serve as your WRITING MENTOR.

❖ ❖ ❖

> "Good people are good because they've come to wisdom through failure."
> —William Saroyan
> 1908-1981
> Novelist

> "Please know the difference between their, there, and they're ..."
> —2010, Match.com profile

Contributing Author **Nikki Bussey** participated in the Emerging Leader scholarship program at The University of Memphis, where she graduated in May 2009 with a Bachelor of Arts in Journalism and a concentration in Broadcast Journalism. She has worked for WMC-TV in Memphis, TN; *The Commercial Appeal* Newspaper, also in Memphis, Tenn.; *The Daily Helmsman* Newspaper at The University of Memphis; and WRJB-WFWL Radio Station in Camden, TN. In the summer of 2008, she was awarded a William Randolph Hearst

> **Editor's Note**
> I would recommend that you check out three writing resources to help you write well.
>
> These are:
> *The Elements of Style*
>   by Strunk and White
> *The Copyeditor's Handbook*
>   by Amy Einshon
> *Painless Grammar*
>   by Rebecca Elliott, Ph.D.

Award, 11th in the nation for an article she wrote as a *Daily Helmsman* reporter. After graduation, she hopes to work as a news producer for the 10 'o clock news at a TV news station. In her spare time she enjoys running with her dog, Spunky.

WILL'S NOTE: Nikki Bussey is an emerging star. She did not tell me that during my visit to the University of Memphis – dozens of her friends did. The national media will discover her one day; however, if they knew her now, they would write more positive articles and stories about young people (and offer her immediate employment). Sometimes it is our students who in fact teach us.

> **Will Speaks about Writing**
> "The following lists represent a humorous yet serious approach to good writing. The opinions on just what is good writing are as numerous as the stars in the sky, and perhaps the best advice we can give you is to become familiar with the style your professor is comfortable with because she or he will be grading your writing efforts. If the professor is a disciple of *Elements of Style*, then you should become familiar with that book and its advice.
>
> That said, we wanted to minimize your fear and apprehension of writing by including these two lists that make some excellent points about writing using humor, a bit of sarcasm, and wit.
> **Here's to good writing!**"

> "Paranthetical remarks (however relevant) are unnecessary."
> —Frank L. Visco
> Writer's Digest
> Editor, wordsmith

How to Write Good

The first set of rules below was written by Frank L. Visco and originally published in the June 1986 issue of *Writers' Digest*.

My several years in the word game have learnt me several rules:

1. Avoid Alliteration. Always.
2. Prepositions are not words to end sentences with.
3. Avoid cliches like the plague. (They're old hat.)
4. Employ the vernacular.
5. Eschew ampersands & abbreviations, etc.
6. Parenthetical remarks (however relevant) are unnecessary.
7. It is wrong to ever split an infinitive.

Stage One: Arrive

8. Contractions aren't necessary.
9. Foreign words and phrases are not apropos.
10. One should never generalize.
11. Eliminate quotations. As Ralph Waldo Emerson once said, "I hate quotations. Tell me what you know."
12. Comparisons are as bad as cliches.
13. Don't be redundant; don't use more words than necessary; it's highly superfluous.
14. Profanity sucks.
15. Be more or less specific.
16. Understatement is always best.
17. Exaggeration is a billion times worse than understatement.
18. One word sentences? Eliminate.
19. Analogies in writing are like feathers on a snake.
20. The passive voice is to be avoided.
21. Go around the barn at high noon to avoid colloquialisms.
22. Even if a mixed metaphor sings, it should be derailed.
23. Who needs rhetorical questions?

> "Never use a big word when a diminutive alternative would suffice."
> —William Safire
> "Rules For Writers"
> 1929-2009
> Author, journalist and presidential speechwriter

The second set of rules is derived from William Safire's "Rules for Writers."

1. Parenthetical words however must be enclosed in commas.
2. It behooves you to avoid archaic expressions.
3. Avoid archaeic spellings too.
4. Don't repeat yourself, or say again what you have said before.
5. Don't use commas, that, are not, necessary.
6. Do not use hyperbole; not one in a million can do it effectively.
7. Never use a big word when a diminutive alternative would suffice.
8. Subject and verb always has to agree.
9. Placing a comma between subject and predicate, is not correct.
10. Use youre spell chekker to avoid mispeling and to catch typograhpical errers.
11. Don't repeat yourself, or say again what you have said before.
12. Use the apostrophe in it's proper place and omit it when its not needed.

> "Have you ever read a book and cried when you finished it because you were so sad it had ended? I hope so. If you have, you are now thinking of that book. If not, I hope you will find a book to read that you literally cannot put down. There is a depth of character in writing that movies, however good, cannot approach."
>
> —Dr. Will Keim

13. Don't never use no double negatives.
14. Poofread carefully to see if you any words out.
15. Hopefully, you will use words correctly, irregardless of how others use them.
16. Eschew obfuscation.
17. No sentence fragments.
18. Don't indulge in sesquipedalian lexicological constructions.
19. A writer must not shift your point of view.
20. Don't overuse exclamation marks!!
21. Place pronouns as close as possible, especially in long sentences, as of 10 or more words, to their antecedents.
22. Writing carefully, dangling participles must be avoided.
23. If any word is improper at the end of a sentence, a linking verb is.
24. Avoid trendy locutions that sound flaky.
25. Everyone should be careful to use a singular pronoun with singular nouns in their writing.
26. Always pick on the correct idiom.
27. The adverb always follows the verb.
28. Take the bull by the hand and avoid mixing metaphors.
29. If you reread your work, you can find on rereading a great deal of repetition can be by rereading and editing.
30. And always be sure to finish what you ....

Do not fear the written, emailed, or texted word.
Practice in writing is essential.
Writing well is a tremendous key to success in almost every endeavor.

Tips for Writing Well

1. Use short sentences.
2. Use short first paragraphs.
3. Use vigorous English.
4. Be positive, not negative.

—*Kansas City Star Guide* adopted by 18 year-old cub reporter Ernest Hemingway

Speaking 3

❝Public speaking is a learned skill that with great practice can become an art.❞

—Will Keim, Ph.D.

Success is a widely defined term and yet I find the words of legendary UCLA basketball coach John Wooden the most poignant. Paraphrasing the greatest coach and one of the finest Americans ever, Coach Wooden said that success is the peace of mind that comes from knowing that you did the best you are capable of doing and that you would be the only person who could ever know that. It is the internal recognition of a job or paper or presentation done to the best of one's ability. The world thrives on external evaluation, analysis, and frankly, criticism. Real success in life comes from within with the self knowledge that you laid it all on the line, left it all on the field of play, that you went "all in" in life, and therefore have peace of mind.

> ❝Be sincere, be brief, be seated.❞
> —Franklin D. Roosevelt
> 1882-1945
> 32nd President of
> the United States

Every great insight, discovery, or solution to a problem has to be communicated. The greatest love in the world has to enter language to be known. As a matter of fact, Dr. Martin Buber, the great Jewish existentialist and philosopher, said that human beings feel addressed by nature and by God, but the relation—the address if you will—does not enter language. Our ability to speak and our opposable thumbs have brought us upright and have given us the possibility to use language as a tool along with the tools our hands can grasp. Between one person and another, the address enters language.

Language is what our brains use to enter into relationships, communicate, and commiserate with one another. It is hard to believe someone could be successful to his or her ultimate potential without the ability so speak with words, signs, or gestures.

I must relate one of my most memorable speaking experiences. I was at Gallaudet University in Washington, D.C., which is a great university for the deaf. Frankly, it is a great university. But my audience could not hear.

I had three people taking turns interpreting in sign language for my speech because I talk so fast. In preparing for the presentations, I asked myself, "Who is a great speaker that speaks to audiences who do not or cannot know his language and yet is able to reach them?"

> "When I speak, I want to be...
> • Precise In Detail
> • Passionate in Delivery, and
> • Persuasive in Appeal."
>
> —Dr. Will Keim

The answer came immediately—Billy Graham. He speaks a sentence in English, the translator puts the sentence in the audience's native tongue, and then Mr. Graham picks up the sentence in exactly the right place and with the right intonation and pitch. He is amazing, as a speaker and as a person.

I would start my sentence or thought, then the signer would sign it to the audience. I would wait what I thought was an appropriate amount of time for them to decode the sign and grasp my thought or joke and then continue. When I finished, the woman who had booked me said she had never had a hearing speaker adapt his message to their audience as well as I had. And I owed it all to Billy Graham. We all need mentors like Coach Wooden and Billy Graham, even from afar, to help us actualize our gifts.

When I speak, and every time I speak, I think of three things. I want to be:

- Precise In Detail,
- Passionate In Delivery, and
- Persuasive In Appeal.

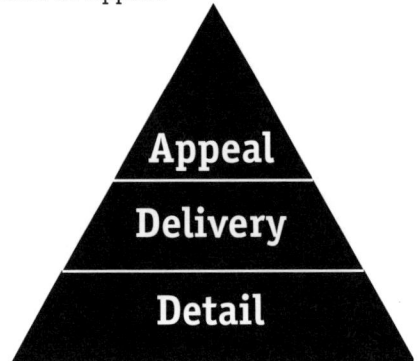

```
     /\
    /  \
   /Appeal\
  /--------\
 / Delivery \
/------------\
/   Detail    \
----------------
```

Every public presentation should include:

- *An Introduction:* Tell Them What You Are Going To Tell Them,
- *The Body:* Tell Them, and
- *The Conclusion:* Tell Them What You Told Them.

Dr. Donald Duns shared that with me at the University of the Pacific in 1971. He was my favorite professor and a great public orator and debater. He is gone now, but not forgotten. To learn more about this outstanding human being, teacher, husband, and father, read the Dedication to Donald Frederick Duns in my book *The Tao of Christ: The Way of Love for a World of Hurt*. I owe nearly everything good that has happened in my life to the lessons he taught me as my mentor.

Stage One: Arrive ... Speaking

Exercise:
- Identify someone you believe is a great public speaker.

  _____

  _____

- List three charateristics of his or her speaking style.

  _____

  _____

  _____

> "Tell them what you are going to tell them; Tell them; and Tell them what you told them.
> Introduction
> Body
> Conclusion."
> —Dr. Will Keim

The Introduction should include:
- *A welcome and introductory comment* on the speaker's pleasure in being present,
- *An attention-getter*—An amazing fact, rhetorical question, or visual aid,
- *A credibility appeal*—Why the audience should listen to the speaker,
- *A forecast*—What is going to happen in the speech, the verbal outline,
- *A segue/transition*— "Let's move on to the topic at hand", or "Point One ..."

The Body should include:
- *The main point(s)*—Engage the audience immediately in the topic.
- *Evidence/support*—The main point is supported by the following evidence ...
- *Supporting/secondary point(s)*—Further evidence is provided by ...
- *Evidence/expert testimony*—Utilize evidence from widely accepted or known sources. For example, "On the topic of success, Stephen Covey states—"
- *Segue/transition*—This moves us in an obvious manner towards the conclusion.

The Conclusion should include:
- *Refocus the assertion*—Reinforce the audience's attention on your main point(s).

- *Remind/redirect*—If you have given two sides to the argument or issue, redirect them to your point of view or assertion.
- *Call to action*—Tell them what you want them to do (i.e., no one should leave saying to themselves, "What can I do?" or "So What?").
- *Brake light*—As with a car, people like to know when you are going to stop. Say, "In conclusion ..." or "Please, remember to ..."
- *A parting thought and thanks*—Quotes work great here, amazing factoids, and statistics. And always thank the audience for giving you their time and attention.

My children will tell you that they often say to me, "What Dad?" And I will say, "Sorry, I was rehearsing a speech."

Everything I see in life falls into two categories for me: things that are topics for a speech or sermon, and things that need a caption such as "*The Far Side* cartoon." I don't know why this is, but I can never remember a time when I did not look at the world like this. The old adage is that people do not plan to fail; rather they fail to plan. Most great oratory looks effortless, but only because the speaker has practiced and practiced and practiced some more.

Every successful speaker should remember **"The Five Always"**:

1. Always gather as much information about the group you are speaking to as possible.

2. Always adapt your speech to your audience and their demographics.

3. Always put yourself in the place of the listener and learner.

4. Always have fewer points and more evidence to support them.

5. Always remember it is about the audience, not you.

> "I have seen the "Speaking Divas" come and go—those who threw a tantrum about not having water at the podium or being picked up at the airport by a student in a small car. I have a one-page contract with no special requests. I need a podium and a microphone. I have, however, worked without either. What I need most though is an audience. Some speakers forget that and they are not successful for long, if ever."
>
> —Dr. Will Keim

Stage One: Arrive ... Speaking

> *"Life's real failure is when you do not realize how close you were to success when you gave up."*

How important is public speaking and communication to your ability to get hired after graduation? One shining example is the University of California, at San Diego. UCSD is a powerful research and teaching university and when they received feedback that the employers of their students reported "good communication and public speaking skills" as the missing attributes among job-seeking graduates, they did something about it!

They created the *Express To Success Program,* offering their students an opportunity to learn about interpersonal skills, public speaking, and leadership. Their goal is to empower their students to "Communicate With Confidence." The program is described on the next page and you may learn more about it by contacting Grace A. Baganu at the web address below. Does your campus have a similar program? If so, enroll. If not, help create one.

> "The Reverend Dennis Savage once said, 'The purpose of a good sermon is to comfort the afflicted, and afflict the comfortable.' I think the same is true of a good public speech. If you don't ruffle a few feathers when you speak, then you probably haven't said anything of much importance or something worth thinking about."
>
> —*Dr. Will Keim*

> "Dialogue is to the relationship as blood is to the body."
> —Dr. Reuel L. Howe
> *The Miracle of Dialogue*
> Author, Professor of pastoral theology

UCSD
Express to Success
Programs

Did you know that employers of UCSD students report "good communication and public speaking skills" as the missing attributes among job-seeking graduates?

Communicate with Confidence!

ETS Interpersonal Communication Seminars
Enhance your interpersonal communication skills and social self-confidence, and establish new friendships!

ETS Public Speaking Seminars
Develop your confidence in preparing and delivering quality speeches and presentations with an audience of supportive peers!

Triton Success Program
Designed for emerging leaders, this yearlong program provides an opportunity for a select group of students to develop confidence in interpersonal communication, public speaking and leadership skills through interactive workshops and experiential learning activities!

CommunicateUCSD!
This collection of communication and public speaking workshops provides a flexible alternative to the quarterly seminars or yearlong programs. Attend 12 seminars to earn a Certificate of Completion!

ADVANCE! *Leadership at the Next Level*
Designed for upper division and graduate students, this yearlong program offers a unique opportunity for students to take their leadership to the next level through advanced communication, public speaking and leadership training and a community project.

ETS Peer Educator Program
Looking to build your resume? This one-year voluntary internship includes advanced public speaking training and many opportunities to practice. Peer Educators coordinate all Friend*Express* events and promote ETS programs to the campus community!

PRONTO:
Professional Communication Training for College Students
Explore new friendships with other college students from UCSD and Southern California during this 2.5 day conference designed to provide professional communication training *on the go!*

http://ets.ucsd.edu

UCSD Express to Success Programs
9500 Gilman Drive, MC0078, La Jolla, CA 92093-0078
(858) 822-0181 or esuccess@ucsd.edu
3rd Floor, Price Center East

Communicate With Confidence

Character   4

> **"**I hope I shall always possess firmness and virtue enough to maintain what I consider the most enviable of all titles: the character of an honest man.**"**
>
> —George Washington
> 1732 – 1799
> First President of the United States

When no one is looking

"Our character is what we do when we think no one is looking," said the author and philosopher H. Jackson Browne. While lecturing at the University of Kentucky, Will mentioned that Megan Jones, one of the gymnasts at Oregon State University, had been hit and seriously injured by a drunk driver. Will asked the Kentucky gymnasts if they would have the time to send her a get-well card. One of them said, "We already did, Dr. Keim. Gymnastics is like a family, and we prayed for Megan and sent her a card." This didn't make the Lexington newspapers but it did make an impression on Will.

> **"**The best and most beautiful things in the world cannot be seen or even touched. They must be felt within the heart.**"**
>
> — Helen Keller
> 1880-1968
> Blind and deaf social activist, author, and lecturer

Dr. Keim writes:
"There is a great voice within you that moves you toward persons, ideas, and things with strong feelings, affect, and fervor. The voice stirs your heart, stimulates your mind, and calls you passionately into relationships with others."
Are you too busy or unwilling to hear the voice?

—Dr. Will Keim, 1990
The Education of Character

> **Will speaks:**
> Dr. Martin Buber said that "Education worthy of the name is essentially the education of charater." I wrote in my first book in 1990, *The Education of Character: Lessons For Beginners*:
>
> You spend a lifetime making ethical decisions, living in community, and developing a sense of purpose and self-worth that helps others discover the goodness in themselves. Simply put, the more involved you become in and out of class, the greater chance you stand of leaving the campus as a more educated person...Education will prove to be the way to a better self and ultimately to a way of improving everything you touch. It is your most important investment in your self. The character you develop through education is truly your own!
>
> **I still believe that to this day! What is important about higher education is what kind of person you become as a result.**
>
> —*Dr. Will Keim*

Character is who you are when no one is watching. A world of integrity and character begins with one person at a time knowing and acting on this adage:

**Say what you mean. Do what you say.
If you don't, admit it. Make amends, and move on.**

Your own model

Let's build your own model for character: Fill in each line with a word that begins with the letters of "character." Take your pick from the list below or come up with your own words. Your list will represent what character means to you.

C_____
H _____
A _____
R _____
A _____
C _____
T_____
E _____
R _____

Some suggestions:
Caring. Coaching. Cooperative. Courageous. Charismatic. Compassionate. Committed. Candid. Humourous. Humble. Hearing. Helpful. Happy. Action-oriented. Accommodating. Appreciative. Respectful. Responsible. Renowned. Responsive. Relatable. Teaching. Trusting. Tutor. Team-focused. Empathic. Empowering. Energetic. Exciting.
Be creative!

> "All of your scholarship, all your study of Shakespeare and Wordsworth would be in vain if at the same time you did not build your character and attain mastery over your thoughts and your actions."
>
> — *Mahatma Gandhi*
> *1869 – 1948*
> *Idealist, political and spiritual leader of India*

Character in person

Name someone you know who has a good character and list his or her characteristics:

I admire _____ because
_____
_____
_____

> "Never doubt that a small group of committed citizens can change the world. Indeed it's the only thing that ever has."
>
> —Margaret Mead
> 1901 – 1978
> Anthropologist, writer, speaker

Character in the workplace

List your desired professions or jobs in Column 1. Write down three to five. In Column 2, write down the characteristics needed to do those jobs well. In Column 3, list the characteristics of successful organizations that would offer these jobs. What are the connections?

Profession of Job	Charateristics Needed to Do this Profession or Job	Characteristics of a Successful Organization
Example: Newspaper foreign correspondent	Courageous. Curious. Honest. Good listener. Observant. Open-minded.	Honest. Cooperative. Committed. Responsible. Team focused. Appreciative.

LEADERSHIP BY CHARACTER

You can buy a person's time. You can buy a person's presence at a given place. You can buy a measured number of skilled muscular motions per hour a day. But you cannot buy enthusiasm. You cannot buy initiative. You cannot buy loyalty. You cannot buy the devotion of hearts, minds and souls. You have to earn these things. To do this, the leader must believe that the greatest assets are human assets and that improvement of their value is both a matter of material advantage and moral obligation. The leader must believe that workers must be treated as honorable individuals, justly rewarded, encouraged in their own progress, fully informed and properly assigned, and that their lives and work must be given meaning and dignity on and off the job. If a leader has supervision of so much as one person, he must try to honor these principles in practice.

Clarence Francis
1888-1985
General Foods chairman, Secretary of the Interior

> "It is in your moments of decision that your destiny is shaped."
>
> — Tony Robbins
> *American self-help author and motivational speaker*

Character involves Enthusiasm, Initiative, Loyalty, and Devotion in Francis view. How would you rate yourself on these criteria.

- **ENTHUSIASM** _____

- **INITATIVE** _____

- **LOYALTY** _____

- **DEVOTION** _____

The United States Airforce Academy annually convenes the National Symposium on Character and Leadership. I was honored to follow John Wooden and Ross Perot to deliver a keynote address. You may wish to contact the Josephson Institute of Ethics and their Character Counts program or The National Character Partnership and learn more about their Schools of Character program. Character matters in college and in life.

Stage One: Arrive ... Character

A GREAT "BIG QUESTIONS" CHARACTER IDEA

"One of my favorite college visits each year is Elmhurst College in Illinois. Their Program, *Big Questions: What Will You Stand For?* encourages students to think about their principles and values and how they will impact their character-driven decision making. One student said, 'Big Questions reminded us to be aware of our values and allow them to guide our steps in college.' Big Questions offers five action-packed days of in-depth discussions, service opportunities and activities aimed at:

1. Easing transition to college life, and
2. Getting students to think about their principles and values

You may contact my dear friend Desiree Collado at www.dcollado@elmhurst.edu to learn more about how colleges can address the concept of character. It's a great program."

Dr. Will Keim

"I am only one, but still I am one.
I cannot do everything, but still I can do something;
and because I cannot do everything,
I will not refuse to do something that I can do."

— Helen Keller
1880-1968
Blind and deaf social activist,
author and lecturer

Relationships   5

> **"You can go to class every day and eventually earn a degree or you can get involved on campus and receive a true education."**
>
> —Mr. Gregg DeCrane, Retired,
> Bowling Green State University
> Dean of Students
> Assistant Vice President, Student Affairs

THE VALUE OF RELATIONSHIPS

The number one factor that will determine whether or not a new student returns for his or her sophomore year is whether or not that particular student forms at least one meaningful relationship with someone on campus. This relationship could be with a roommate, a classmate, a teammate, a co-worker, a professor, a staff member or could be more romantic in nature. If a new student does not feel as if he or she have "connected" or that they "belong" and are "accepted," odds are they'll be surfing through catalogues to decide upon their next collegiate choice.

> **"A sense of belonging is an essential human need."**
>
> —Abraham Maslow
> 1908-1970
> Founder of humanistic psychology

According to Denny Ryberg, Founder of YoungLife, as adults we face "three necessary losses" that we must deal with and process during our lifetime. The first is the death and burial of our own parents. The second is our children heading off to attend college. The third is seeing our children get married and have a family of their own. Some students and families are more than ready for the college experience to begin. They've enjoyed the high school years, but are glad to see them come to an end as they realize that new and exciting challenges lie ahead. But there are other students and families that are not nearly as prepared or accepting that life is moving on in a natural way. They have become so dependent upon one another that cutting the cord and letting go is difficult at best and traumatic at worst. If a local romantic relationship for the student exists that may become long distance in nature, then the transition to college may be even more stressful.

MEETING OTHERS

Depending on how socially gifted you were prior to attending college, meeting others may be effortless for you and a non-issue or may be troublesome and disconcerting.

Here are some simple tips for meeting others:

SMILE
HAVE THEM SPELL THEIR NAME (if appropriate)
ASK OPEN-ENDED QUESTIONS
LISTEN TWICE AS MUCH AS YOU TALK
SINCERELY BELIEVE IN YOURSELF

> "People seldom remember who broke the ice, they're just happy to be standing in a puddle!"
> —David Coleman

- **Smile,** make eye contact, and say hello. If you shake hands, be firm, be brief and be confident without becoming over-bearing.

- **When they tell you their name, if appropriate, ask them to spell it for you.** You are much more likely to remember their name if you see it transcribed in your mind. Often, we are so excited to meet someone, or are so attracted to them that mere moments after they tell us their name, we have forgotten it already.

- **Ask open-ended questions.** These require a response beyond a "yes" or "no." Instead of asking, "Do you like movies?" Ask, "What is your favorite movie you have seen recently and why?" This will spark more conversation and lead other topics to surface.

- **Listen twice as much as you talk** and actually focus on what he or she is saying, not on what your response will be the moment they stop speaking. The latter is called "Trigger Listening". When you do this people can often tell that you have "checked out" and they are left to feel insignificant or frustrated. Listen all the way through before you respond and then keep your comment brief, on topic and to the point. Then, give them a chance to respond.

- **Sincerely believe in yourself and the other person,** and that having an opportunity to meet each other is a great honor. Why? If you don't believe that you are a great catch, how can you expect them to feel that way? If you face only one obstacle in life, and you doubt yourself, you are already outnumbered. Relationships are hard enough without living a self-fulfilling prophecy whereby you place added and undue pressure on yourself. Believe in yourself, choose to have a great attitude and give life your best effort. That is the best you can do and the most you can ask of yourself.

Get involved on and off campus! The more people you interact with, the more likely you are to make new friends and even meet someone special. If you play an intramural sport, join a co-ed team too. Join a community-based activity as well and get to know and become more comfortable within the city in which you are now residing.

CAMPUS RELATIONSHIPS
12 Relationships to Foster in the First 12 Weeks of School!

Feeling connected is the key to a rewarding first year experience and there is no better way to build a sense of belonging than to foster friendships and relationships with those who can and will make your first year an enlightening and exciting time. Below is a suggestion of 12 relationships to foster in your first twelve weeks on campus and how to begin the process.

> "Students who are involved on campus, students who engage with the campus community early in their careers are more likely to make successful transitions and graduate."
>
> —Eric Hartman
> Dean of Students
> The University of the South

1. **Your Roommate(s):** You will probably spend more time with your roommate(s) than any other relationship you develop during your first year on campus. Knowing each other's likes and dislikes, habits, belief systems, study habits, hobbies, eating patterns, dreams, goals, desires and motivations can help you live in a teamwork-like harmony. Each of you should share three minimum standards that you live by and that you expect the other person to respect as well. Introduce each other to your own personal friends and use this as a friend multiplier effect. The more people you meet the more people you get to know! And remember … if you are living at home while going to college, you and your parents or guardians need to sit down and discuss the new ground rules for living together as parents and a college student.

2. **Your Professors:** First, remember, they are human and want you to succeed. Sometimes the student to staff ratio is enormous, but you can still get to know your professors by visiting them during their office hours, taking advantage of extra credit opportunities and asking for ideas on how to better prepare for each and every class. At some point before you graduate, you will be asking these same professors to be references for you. Wouldn't this be easier if they actually knew who you were?

> "Faculty members want to see students who are stuggling early in the term while there is still time for mentorship, clarification, and grade enhancing study."
>
> —Dr. Will Keim

3. **Student Affairs Staff:** You can go to class every day, study and ultimately earn a degree or you can get involved on campus and receive a true education. We prefer an educational blend of curricular (in class) and co-curricular (out-of-class) learning experiences. It is a proven fact that students who get actively involved on campus get better grades, feel more accepted, and experience an increased level of personal satisfaction with college in general. Your Vice President of Student Life, Dean of Students, and Student Activities Director can and will help you connect to the people who run the programs and events that can meet your needs. You will get to know students, just like yourself, who have involved themselves in campus life and who have made the campus culture and environment better.

4. **The Health and Counseling Center Staff:** College life can be a real challenge. Classes can be more difficult than you thought. You are adjusting to living away from home. You are dealing with homesickness and perhaps for the first time in your life, making important decisions on your own. There are times when it is nice to have someone objective to talk to who can also help you prepare to combat common college life challenges for new students like: the cold and flu season, potential weight gain or loss, and sleep deprivation. They might not be Mom and Dad, but they will be friendly faces who sincerely care for you when you need them most.

5. **The Classified and Custodial Staff:** I know, you are reading this and thinking…. "Huh?" But, who did you go search out at home when you were out of something or needed something special? Mom and Dad! Mom and Dad are not around but your classified and custodial staff are. Treat them well. Get to know them by name. Stop and take a moment to talk to them and treat them like the wonderful people they are. Believe me, they will remember you over all the other students who treat them as if they are invisible.

6. **The Campus Safety and Security Staff:** They are not just the parking police. They are not simply on campus to bust you doing something wrong. In this age of escalating and senseless campus violence, knowing your campus police by face and name can never be considered a bad thing. Often,

Campus Safety offers special workshops and services. Attend them. Take advantage of them. If they have a ride along program, go along one night. Experience the campus world through their eyes and they may much more easily see the world of college through your eyes.

7. **The Food Service Staff:** Everyone loves to eat and outside of your roommate, the door monitors and line servers might be the people you interact with most often. They will get to know you and your tastes and let you know when exciting new delicacies or changes are on the way. On days when you can't make certain meals, they may reach out and offer you the help you need to eat healthy meals that day. The food on campus won't be just like home, but they will do their best to make your on campus dining experience one that keeps you coming back for more.

> "You never hear anyone who has visited a third world country complain about dining hall food."
>
> —Dr. Will Keim

8. **Your Resident Advisor (RA):** Although they are heavily trained to uphold the policies and procedures of your living environment, they can also become a close friend, confidant and ally, especially when you are having problems adjusting or simply missing home. They often plan activities for their residents to partake in and attend, so ask if you can assist them with any of their endeavors. Working together is a great way to form a new friendship and relieve the awkward moments of getting to know one another.

9. **Your Hall Director:** Hall Directors are chosen for their ability to build cohesion within their staff, and to provide an outstanding living and learning environment that meets the needs of their residents. As such, they are fabulous people to encounter and get to know. They are often uplifting, inspirational and give solid advice that many new students need early in their college careers. Most are exceptional people who place students high on their priority list and want you to feel that living in their environment is as close to home as possible for you. Stop in their office and say hello. Offer to get involved in the hall council or even apply for an RA position in the years to come.

10. **Your Hall Council Officers or Commuter Council if you commute to school:** Many years ago, my first leadership

> "There are over 18 million college students in America and I believe there is something for each of them on every campus if they will take the initiative and show up."
>
> —Dr. Will Keim

position was on my hall council. It is the primary reason that I felt less homesick and adapted to college as easily as I did. You get to know most of the residents of your building, program activities that create interest and excitement and you become one of the people who are "in the know." Hall councils are a wonderful first step to getting involved on your campus. Attend one of their initial meetings and express your interest in getting involved. Believe me, they will be thrilled to have your energy and input.

11. **The Director of Greek Life:** Joining a fraternity or sorority can be one of the wisest and most fulfilling decisions a student can make. Learning about a chapter's rich history and tradition and then going through recruitment and installation with members of your pledge class forms bonds and friendships that will last a lifetime. You'll grow as a person, as a friend and as a leader, while involving yourself in philanthropies that will help people and places you may never know or visit. Keep an eye out for informal and formal recruitment events on your campus. It doesn't hurt to show up and simply see and hear what Greek Life has to offer.

12. **Campus Ministry Staff:** Many campuses have Chaplains, Campus Ministers or Coordinators of Religious Life. If you have a faith tradition or want to learn more about the world's religions, Chaplains, Campus Ministers or Coordinators of Religious Life would be great resources for you. Very few colleges and universities have mandatory Chapels anymore, but you can find many voluntary opportunities for worship in many traditions including Christian, Jewish, Muslim, Buddhist and other traditions on or near campus. If you are interested in doing community service, helping those in need or finding a support group of friends in your religious tradition, these campus religious leaders would be valuable relationships for you.

Remember, if you are living on campus in a residence hall then you will form relationships with your RA, Hall Director and Residence Hall Counsel earlier in the term. If you live at home you may not meet these people until you visit your on-campus friends. There are literally hundreds or maybe thousands of potential relationships on campus. We have identified 12 special groups of people who can generally help you on almost every campus. **THE POINT IS: GET INVOLVED EARLY AND ESTABLISH RELATIONSHIPS ON CAMPUS.** If you form, mend and sustain these relationship in your first 12 weeks, you'll probably find that you are helping other students adapt to college life in your second twelve weeks.

P.S. – If you want to get anything done on a college campus, you need to get to know the Administrative Assistants, Registrar's Professionals and the Cashier's Office. We want to make this perfectly clear – if the guy or gal serving you in the Dining Hall "feels the love" and your respect, you will get more food!

> "Get involved early and establish relationships on campus!"
> —David Coleman

Exercise: *Building a Sense of Belonging.*
Pick three of the relationship categories above, write them down and set a meeting with a member of the organization. Write the person's name, contact information and time of the appointment below. Make sure to set an actual appointment, time with a date so you remember to arrive on time.

_____

_____

_____

_____

_____

_____

_____

INTERPERSONAL RELATIONSHIPS
The ABC & D's of Dating with David Coleman, M.A.

Whether you are charismatic and outgoing or a bit more shy and reserved, you can discern whether you are interested in someone and they are interested in you. This is a very complex decision-making process and we will provide for you our thinking on interpersonal relationships, in particular dating. Below, you will find the four important factors to focus on when you meet someone:

>**A**TTRACTION
>**B**ELIEVABILITY
>**C**HEMISTRY
>**D**ESIRE

> "These are the ABC & D's of Dating:
> Attraction
> Believability
> Chemistry
> Desire."
> —David Coleman

Attraction: Is there a Hmm… factor? Do you find them physically attractive or appealing? Is there a charming presence to them? The attraction does not have to be jaw dropping, but you should not consider them repulsive or a "creeper" either.

Believability: Do their words seem sincere and true and genuine to you, or does it feel as if they are fabricating their responses, trying to impress you or attempting to top everything you say? It is hard for a person to feign sincerity. Look into their eyes as you talk with them and attempt to get a sense of who they are and their true intentions.

Chemistry: This encompasses every attraction you feel toward them EXCEPT physical. Did they make you smile? Laugh? Were they easy to be around? Were they interesting and intelligent? Did you share any mutual interests? Did the time pass by rapidly when you were in their presence? Did you find yourself wanting to learn more about them? If you answered yes to most of the questions above, that is a very good sign!

Desire: This is not in the physical sense, but in the feeling that you would like to get to know them better. Physical desire may exist as well, but if that is the only positive factor you felt for them a "friendship or relationship" is probably not in the cards.

So, if after spending quality time in someone's presence you are able to answer…Am I attracted to them? **Yes!** Do I believe them? **So far!** Do I feel a sense of chemistry with them? **I think so!** Do I have a desire to get to know them better? **For sure!** Then it is time to spend some social time together. So many people get hung up on the word dating, that I encourage a new couple to just spend some social time together. Don't even give the interaction a title. Your first mutually agreed upon social encounter should be scheduled for no more than one hour. This way, if the (shhh…Date!) is not going well, there is a finite time limit that simply must be lived through. However, if things are progressing well and the time simply "disappears," you can always agree to "do something else" and you may get to hear the three most reassuring words in early dating, "I'd love to!"

Exercise: *Picking your ABC and D.*
Prioritize attraction, believability, chemistry and desire in order of their importance to you.

_____

_____

_____

_____

> "I understand and affirm the role technology can play in facilitating relationships today.
>
> Facebook, twitter, texting, skyping, and online dating services are a reality of the 21st Century and the speed and pace at which we live.
>
> I have also been on three campuses where students were missing who accepted money from 'suitors' to go and meet them somewhere.
>
> Please be smart, trust your instincts, use the technology, and do not get used by it.
>
> *Take care and beware.*"
>
> —Dr. Will Keim

Basic Principles for Initial Relationship Success

1. **Be Yourself**
2. **Quickly Ascertain: Am I an option for them or a priority to them?**
3. **Remember that the person least invested controls a relationship.**

Be yourself! If you pretend to be someone else, you won't be able to keep up that facade for long and the person interested in you won't know which version of "you" they are with at any given point in time. If they fall for the "real you," and vice-versa, that should bode well for you as a couple over time.

Quickly ascertain: Am I an option for them or a priority to them? No matter what your early feelings are for someone else, you cannot let them blind you as to the truth of the entire situation. You are either an option for someone or a priority to them. Knowing which one is true will help you keep a proper balance whereby you are both investing equally into the relationship.

Remember that the person least invested controls a relationship. The person who likes, loves, cares, or tries the least has all the control in a relationship as it makes the person who is more invested work twice as hard to keep the relationship going and to keep the other person interested. There is nothing worse than finding out that you have been making excuses for someone who simply doesn't care for you or for the success of your relationship.

The Five Stages of Relationships

Remember that relationships progress in stages, and they are:

1. **Infatuation**
2. **Discovery**
3. **Reality**
4. **Decision**
5. **Commitment**

> "The person who likes, loves, or cares the least has all the control in a relationship, as it makes the person who is more invested work twice as hard to keep the relationship going."
>
> —David Coleman

Infatuation: Infatuation is immediate, demanding and exciting. The object of your affection can do little wrong and you could not be more attracted to them. You are oblivious to their faults and can't stop thinking about them. You've "never met anyone quite like them before."

Discovery: You begin to realize that the object of your affection is a human being after all, will not ever be perfect and will make mistakes as they have flaws and faults like everyone else. Your true feelings for them become a bit clearer.

Reality: You have known this person long enough to know exactly who they are and they you. There are no facades. No one is playing games. The truth is clearly evident and this allows you both to make an informed decision regarding your future.

Decision: Should you stay or should you go? Should the relationship move forward or should you both call it quits? It is at this point where some couples stay together out of obligation and that rarely leads to long-term relationship success.

Commitment: As a couple, you work in harmony to form a connection that is meaningful and real. One of three things will happen. The relationship will grow and improve, hit a plateau, or wane.

A common mistake people make in the early stages of a relationship is to get themselves in way too deep, way too fast and then panic when they realize they don't have the same feelings they once had for this new person in their life. Additionally, they don't want to reject them as they feel they led them on and are now "responsible" for their unhappiness. Take a deep breath, stay in the moment, and take things slowly. Let the relationship pass naturally through the stages, and your decisions should be much clearer and easier to make.

The Three Types of Love

Whether a couple is straight, gay or unclassified, to maintain a healthy and meaningful relationship that can and will stand the test of time, they need to regularly practice the three types of love. The three types of love are:

> "I would rather have thirty minutes of wonderful, than a lifetime of nothing special."
>
> —From Steel Magnolias, the movie

1. **Eros Love**
2. **Agape Love**
3. **Philia Love**

Eros Love: Eros is the root of the word "Erotic" and means I'm attracted to you and I'm pretty sure you're attracted to me!" It is a primal, attraction-based love where we instantly feel "different" when in their presence. Our heart beats a bit faster, our blood courses more rapidly through our veins and our neurons fire a bit more efficiently. There is an excitement involved that is involuntary and different than we have felt for anyone else.

Agape Love: This is a heartfelt type of love that grows stronger every day. When we can look into another person's eyes and express to them, "I love you; I am so in love with you" and mean it, we have achieved Agape Love. This love also manifests when they are not being all that lovable and we choose to love them anyway!

Philia Love: This the love shared between friends who enjoy each other's company and have no preconceived notions as to where the relationship will eventually lead. See True Friends later in this chapter.

How Can You Tell If You Are "Just Friends?"

It is not always easy to ascertain your status with someone to whom you've grown quite close. Are you "just friends" or is there something deeper that transcends friendship? Often, it is hard for former romantic couples to maintain a close friendship. It is not because they don't want to remain friends, but because the factors involved and their sense of personal history and physical intimacy make it difficult. Here is how to tell if someone is your friend or if there are ulterior motives at work.

If you are…

1. Physically attracted to them (or they are to you)
2. Romantically interested in them (or they are to you)
3. Or they can make you jealous by what they say or do (or you can make them)

…you are **NOT** "just friends!"

If you cannot envision them with someone else or someone new without feeling as if your insides are turning upside down, then, in all likelihood, you are not just friends. You feel, sense and desire something more intimate with them.

True friends are rare. Time spent with them is effortless. Nobody keeps score. There is no jealousy and there is no gossip involved whatsoever. True friends are not judgmental toward one another, can talk about anything face-to-face and can be separated for long periods of time and simply pick up from where they left off the last time they saw one another. The time they spend in each other's presence is precious and they are cognizant of the appreciation and respect they feel for one another.

Long Distance Relationships (LDR's)

A long distance relationship is defined as one in which the couple involved lives at least a two hour drive apart from one another and does not have the time, means or wherewithal to drive to each other and meet face-to-face every time a problem or longing arises. As they are trying to stay connected, they are doing so from different locations, with hectic schedules, different friends, varying circumstances and ever-changing responsibilities. Long distance relationships can be tough to successfully navigate but are not impossible! Here are some of the more common obstacles that LDR couples face and several suggestions and strategies to help make them work.

> "There are no shortcuts in life to anywhere worth going."
>
> —Beverly Sills
> 1929-2007
> Opera Singer

Obstacles Faced in Long Distance Relationships

- **People force communication to occur every day.** Due to the instant gratification associated with our electronic era, students can actually begin to smother one another from afar. An over abundance of text messages, email, phone calls, instant messages, video chats, winks, nods, pokes and tweets can leave us feeling overwhelmed and disinterested. If this happens, we may begin to wonder whether or not our partner misses us, doesn't trust us or doesn't quite have what it takes to survive the separation period.

- **People simply miss being together.** Seeing each other every day in high school or during the summer period prior to leaving for college, and having that come to an abrupt end, has left an interpersonal void in their life. People can actually become "addicted" to seeing one another or physically being together and feel a tremendous emptiness and loneliness when their partner is not around as often as they once were.

- **The Hmm… Factor.** A Hmm is someone who catches your attention and causes you to take notice. They might be physically attractive, charming, witty, humorous or have that certain intangible quality that you find appealing, but you begin to notice that there are other people walking the planet that have wonderful qualities to offer as well.

- **We adapt to our dilemma.** As human beings we have learned to be adaptable and versatile when faced with adversity. Sometimes a couple adapts so well to being apart that they are not quite as close as they once were when they reunite.

- **Short-term memory issues.** With our partner no longer around on a regular basis, we begin to lose sight of what caused us to fall for them in the first place, until we see them again and then the memories and feelings come rushing back…usually!

Here are some strategies to give your long distance relationship a fighting chance:

- **Communicate in moderation!** Do not force communication to occur every day. If your schedules are full or you have begun to feel as if you "must communicate" instead of feeling a "desire to communicate" it may be time to let a day or two pass so that you once again look forward to hearing each other's voice or reading each other's words. College life can be so repetitive. Allowing a day or two to pass between extended conversations can lead to more meaningful phone calls, more interesting email, more thoughtful texts and even take pressure off the couple involved to always be entertaining and compassionate.

> **"Good communication is the key to good relationships."**
> —David Coleman
> "The Dating Doctor"

- **Alternate your methods of communication.** Keep your partner off-balance and interested. Send an email one day, text the next, hand write a letter and mail it, drop them a note on a social networking site, video chat, mail them a care package or card…variety truly can be the spice of life. When someone or something becomes easily predictable it can also lose some or all of its luster.

- **Try to see each other at least once every two months.** I realize that for many, this may be impossible due to distance, time, money or a myriad of other factors, but nothing can compare to reconnecting in person at precisely the time it is needed most.

- **Believe in each other, your relationship, and trust one another.** No LDR can survive if a couple does not completely trust one another. It is the cornerstone of all relationships but is highly accentuated in LDR's because of the inability to validate what you hear about or read about from your significant other. Plus, you both must believe in the final outcome (staying together… growing closer) or only one of you will be working to achieve that goal, and that won't fly!

- **Avoid arguing on line.** Why? Because it is permanent! You can read their words over and over again and get more and more angry or disillusioned with every word. The same is true for leaving hurtful, painful, or thoughtless messages on another person's voice mail. They can be (and will be) listened to over and over again!

- **Don't play out your relationship on Facebook.** It is no one's business but your own regarding how well your relationship is progressing. Sometimes jealousy may become a factor from others not involved with someone and envious of the success you are having, or attempt to "grease the wheels" a bit to get your relationship to fall apart so that they can reap the benefits of the break-up.

Exercise: *Long Distance Relationships.*
Think of an LDR that you or someone close to you have been involved in. Why did it work? Or, why did it fail? Be honest with yourself.

_____

_____

_____

_____

_____

MILITARY RELATIONSHIPS

Military Relationships need specific and very special help to ease the time and distance relationship challenges. Depending on where a person is stationed, for how long they may have been deployed or how specialized their mission is, other factors may certainly apply. There are several options available to you:

- Visit www.Hand2HandContact.org. It is a top rate website and shares cutting edge information on the intricacies of being involved with someone serving in our Military Services.

- Visit www.Sgt.Brandi.com. His mission is to change and save lives by mentoring combat warriors and empowering positive futures. This is simply a fabulous website for anyone involved in a military relationship.

> "Victory has a thousand fathers; Defeat is an orphan."
>
> —President John F. Kennedy
> 1917-1963
> 35th President of the United States

- Visit **www.DatingDoctor.com** and look under Relationship Advice. David has written several blogs on the topics of Military Relationships that you may find beneficial. David travels the world talking to our Soldiers, Sailors, Airmen, Marines and Coast Guard to give them hope for the future and tips to strengthen their relationships.

- Visit **TheDatingDoctor@Facebook.com** and look under the NOTES section. Several blogs exist on the pro's and con's of dating someone in the military. You can also search under David Coleman, Cincinnati, Ohio or visit **www.DatingDoctor.com** to be connected to David's profile.

Exercise: *Describe the Perfect Date:*
(hint: think of person, place, time, event and locale)

_____

_____

_____

_____

_____

❖ ❖ ❖

ABOUT THE AUTHOR: David Coleman is known worldwide as "The Dating Doctor" and "America's Real-Life Hitch"! He has been honored 12 times as The National Campus Speaker of the Year and has over 2,500 appearances in all 50 states and numerous foreign countries speaking to more than two million people. He has authored or co-authored eight books and has released a DVD and CD on forming, mending and sustaining healthy relationships. David is a former newspaper columnist, radio talk show host and college administrator. He holds a Master's Degree in College Student Personnel from Bowling Green State University (OH) where he was also named an Outstanding Alumnus. David received The Patriotic Citizenship Medal from the United States Army, which is one of the highest honors bestowed upon a civilian and he now travels the world bringing hope, encouragement, laughter and the promise of stronger relationships to our troops. His website, www.DatingDoctor.com

receives over one million visitors annually and David blogs for numerous websites and publications. He is the father of two delightful daughters, Shannon and Natalie.

WILL'S NOTE: David Coleman and I have been friends and brothers for 20 years. We were recently featured in an article on campus speakers in the *Chronicle of Higher Education*. He is a gifted presenter, a great dad and a colleague I can trust to give you tremendous insights on relationships and dating. Make sure to catch him when he comes to your campus. He will help you feel good about yourself.

David and I have recently created "SpeakeRevolution" to educate and train speakers for the collegiate market. We want to make sure that speakers who present to college students understand their role as educators and mentors. SpeakeRevolution holds conferences annually, and college students who are interested in public speaking as a success skill or a career can attend at a deeply reduced rate. Students are also able to join The National Collegiate Speaker's Association and be mentored by educational speaking mentors. Visit www.willkeim.com for more information or visit www.higheraspirations.net and www.thencsa.org.

"The Relationships chapter features information regarding interpersonal, long distance, military, and campus relationships. If you would be interested in working professionally on community college, college, and university campuses, then here are a few organizations of Student Affairs and Student Services professionals for your consideration."

- National Association of Student Personnel Administrators
  www.naspa.org/

- ACPA College Student Educators International
  www.myacpa.org/ac/a

- National Orientation Directors Association
  www.nodaweb.org/

- National Association of Campus Activities
  www.naca.org/

- Association of Fraternity Advisors
  www.fraternityadvisors.org

- Association of College and University Housing Officers International
  www.acuho-i.org

- Association of College Unions International
  www.acui.org

There are many more excellent organizations and opportunities to interact. Remember to look for state and provincial regional chapters of these national and international organizations."

— *Dr. Will Keim*

STAGE TWO
Survive

"There's no such thing as making the miracle happen spontaneously and on the spot. You've got to work."
Martina Arroyo

Stress ❖ Freedom ❖ Health ❖ Eating Disorder ❖ Letting Go

STAGE TWO: SURVIVE "CHAPTER SUMMARY"
Stress ❖ Freedom ❖ Health ❖ Eating Disorder ❖ Letting Go

6. STRESS

> *"The sun will set without your assistance."*
> **Yiddish Proverb**

Fifty Stress-Busters for Students includes practical suggestions on academic, co-curricular, personal, and family life that encourage students to seek wellness and a balanced life while in the collegiate environment. Stress Busters include (1) Be a scholar; (21) Focus on one thing at a time. Do the least attractive stuff first; (39) See a counselor if you need or want to see one, (43) Find something you love to do and learn to do it well enough that someone will pay you to do it and forty-six other practical and philosophical ideas for coping with stress.

❖ ❖ ❖

7. FREEDOM with Elaine Pasqua and Rick Barnes

> *"I quit drinking because I didn't want to be 'that guy.' That guy who was a jerk. That guy who woke up each morning thinking, 'Whom do I have to apologize to today?' That guy nice women avoid."*
> **Senior, University of North Dakota**

"This chapter deals with developing freedom from dependence on alcohol, other drugs, tobacco, and gambling. Why do so many of our citizens choose to live their lives in dependency on alcohol and other drugs? We are asking for personal honesty and offering a Personal Drinking Inventory that will guide you as you make alcohol-related choices in college. Studies have shown an amazing relationship between drinks per week and grade point average. If you have problems when you drink, then you are a problem drinker. Let's talk about it."

❖ ❖ ❖

8. HEALTH

> *"Be more concerned with your character than your reputation. Your character is what you really are while your reputation is merely what others think you are."*
> **John Wooden**

Here is a *Prescription for Healthy Living.* Take Seven Goals: Drink alcohol responsibly or not at all; live other drug free; practice responsible sexuality or abstain; perform at your academic best; promote personal wellness; exhibit community-minded behavior; be tolerant of others; and mix them with Seven Success Tips: respect yourself and others; set your academic and personal agenda early; don't be afraid to fail or succeed; take care of yourself and others; accept the challenge college offers; listen to the 'voice' within; find something you love to do and learn to do it well enough that someone will pay you to do it, and *Refine, Personalize, and Take Daily.*"

❖ ❖ ❖

9. EATING DISORDERS with Joe Radzvilowicz, Kevin Klink, and Laura Klink

> *"I constantly crave exercise."*
> **Laura Klink**

"Just a few months ago, I spent every hour of the day exercising. Most evenings, I could hear my family laughing as they watched movies downstairs in the living room. I was always on the verge of crying because I missed being able to sit with them. No matter how badly I wanted to go and relax with them though, I didn't have a choice. I had to stay thin. The hours would grow later, everyone would go to bed, and I would continue to exercise in my room. I worked out until I collapsed in my bed, then I'd sleep for four or five hours and get up to workout again. I'd hide food in my pockets at meals, stand up in class or just skip class altogether to run around the neighborhoods, and when I was forced to sit, I would hold myself up on my legs so I wasn't actually touching the seat. I felt a sick satisfaction with my disintegrating body.

After being sent away for three months to Remuda Ranch treatment center in Arizona, I've had to repeatedly ask myself one question: if I spent the rest of my life feeding these obsessions, losing my relationships, my personality, my health, my lifelong sport (gymnastics), and everything else in my life, would I die thinking "at least I had a thin body?" With each day that passed, the behaviors seemed more and more irrational. Although I still crave my eating disorder horribly, I feel like I am in the process of finding my life again, and I love being kissed goodnight and then actually going to sleep."

❖ ❖ ❖

10. LETTING GO

> *"When I was 14 I thought my father was ignorant. By the time I was 21 I was amazed how much he had learned in seven years."*
> **Mark Twain**

"Are you majoring in something because of your parents, because of a trend, or because you love it? Do the right thing for the right reason. Both students and parents have to let go at some point and allow each other to live their lives. You must either learn to forgive your parents for not being perfect or thank them for a job well done. You cannot fly with wings like eagles if you have a weight on your back because you still hold a grudge or anger because your parents split up when you were young. One day your parents will evolve into your children and you will be the caregiver. Begin the process now of appreciating the fact that the very least your parents did was give you life. In best cases, they gave you love and a sense of life's goodness."

Stress

> **"I have found a direct correlation between student stress and being behind academically. Calm and contentment come with completed assignments. The Tao Te Ching says, 'Do your work, then step back.' So do your work, step back, relax, and enjoy."**
>
> —Dr. Will Keim

Dr. Don Duns once said, "A growing person is always a freshman at something." The President of a major insurance company told me, "Tell your students that I will never ask them to tell me about their successes. Rather I will ask them to tell me about their failures." Taken together, we believe that you must always set your goals just beyond your grasp and that to be fully human means to constantly be endeavoring to try new things. It is not the number of times that you get knocked down that matters, it is the number of times that you get back up.

> **"Tell your students that I will never ask them to tell me about their successes. Rather, I will ask them to tell me about their failures. If they tell me they have never failed, then they have never set their goals beyond their grasp."**
>
> —President, Penn America Insurance to Dr. Will Keim

Stress is the most normal occurrence for a growing person trying new things. We cannot, nor should we try to eliminate stress. Jean Piaget even suggested that it is essential to our willingness and readiness to achieve. Therefore, we present you with 50 stress busters; that is 50 ways you can begin to cope with stress and use it to motivate yourself to change and grow.

Fifty Stress Busters for Students

1. **Be a scholar.** Read all your assignments.
2. **Go to class.** Life goes better if you show up.
3. **Re-copy your notes** every night in outline form to eliminate the unimportant stuff.
4. **Make a master syllabus.** Combine course syllabi into a megalist of all assignments.
5. **Maximize the missing minutes.** Study between classes during the day.
6. **See all your professors** at least once during office hours. Then, they can grade a person, not a number.
7. **See your advisor** at least once a term.
8. **Get involved.** Check out opportunities at the student center.

9. **Work out** in the campus rec center for thirty minutes every day.
10. **Play intramurals.** It's a great way to relax and meet people.
11. **Sleep 6-8 hours a night.** No one says you have to stay up all night.
12. **Eat breakfast every day.** Get it … Break(the)fast.
13. **Get up 15 minutes** earlier each day. Avoid starting your day in a rush.
14. **Keep a to-do list** and daily planner. Structure gives freedom—really!
15. **Avoid procrastination.** Now!
16. **Think before you speak.** Be nice to your roommate.
17. **Don't sweat** the small stuff.
18. **Do good,** and be good to yourself and others.
19. **Listen more,** talk less.
20. **Set a realistic schedule** (daily/weekly/semester) and plan in rest breaks and time off.
21. **Focus on one thing** at a time. Do the least attractive stuff first.
22. **Volunteer some time** to charity or community service.
23. **Make friends** with a diverse group of people.
24. **Be kind** to unkind people; they need kindness the most.
25. **Cut people some slack.** Remember that everyone on campus is carrying some kind of heavy burden.
26. **When stressed, breathe** from your abdomen, not your chest. Deep and slow.
27. **Learn from the past;** live in the present; prepare for the future.
28. **Laugh** easily and often.
29. **Check your e-mail once** a day, not on the hour.
30. **Eat sensibly.** Only one third of your calories should come from fat.
31. **Say what you mean** and do what you say. When you don't, admit it.
32. **Make promises sparingly** and keep the ones you make.
33. **Be yourself.** Trends come and go.
34. **Delegate.** Let people help you and choose to help others.
35. **Eliminate or moderate** your intake of alcohol, caffeine, tobacco, and other drugs.
36. **Replace the word "problem"** with "opportunity."
37. **Do your best.** This will give you peace of mind.
38. **Practice humility** and random acts of kindness.
39. **See a counselor** if you need or want to see one.
40. **Forgive your parents** for not being perfect.

> "In order to succeed, you must fail, so that you know what not to do the next time."

Stage Two: Survive ... Stress

41. **Thank your parents** if they did a good job.
42. **Dream big dreams** about your success.
43. **Find something you love to do** and learn to do it well enough that you can get paid to do it.
44. **Go to the Career Planning** and Placement Services Center now! Avoid the rush.
45. **Keep a journal** with your victories and concerns.
46. **Keep a book by your bed**—one you read for pleasure before you go to sleep each night.
47. **Attend the spiritual service** of your choice or practice reflective quietude regularly.
48. **Be patient** with yourself and others.
49. **Be enthusiastic** and develop your sense of humor.
50. **Celebrate your attendance** at the university by smiling at people on campus.

The most important stress buster is to be kind to yourself and know your limitations. If you find campus related stress unbearable or debilitating please do yourself a favor and talk to a friend, an RA, or counselor. Think of a teapot ... it functions because it lets off steam. You can also vent stress through regular workouts at the campus recreation center. Rarely, if ever, has the consumption of alcohol or use of other drugs provided a long-term resolution to stress or other problems.

> "I tried and failed. I tried again and didn't fail."
>
> —*Gail Borden Jr.*
> *1801-1874*
> *Inventor and co-founder*
> *Borden Dairy Products*

Stress Test

The number one cause of stress in my life is:

_____

_____

_____

Identify three of the Stress Buster suggestions that might help you manage or reduce stress:

1. _____

2. _____

3. _____

Freedom

7

> "I quit drinking because I didn't want to be 'that guy.' That guy who was a jerk. That guy who woke up each morning thinking, 'Whom do I have to apologize to today?' That guy nice women avoided."
>
> —Senior
> University of North Dakota

Be free from dependence

Will stood in front of 2,000 students at Oregon State University to conduct a memorial service for a young fraternity man who died after falling, drunk, and hitting his head on a boat at Lake Shasta, California. His fraternity brothers tried to save him, but by the time they found him on the bottom of the lake, he was gone.

This event and others like it have prompted Will to speak out strongly to students: "I ask you to be free from dependence on alcohol and other drugs. I affirm your right not to drink, but I ask that, if you do drink, please be responsible and safe. When you are not, then people like me—ministers, priests, rabbis, imans—stand in sadness. No parent should outlive their child. No friend should be haunted with such a memory. Please, be free from dependence. Practice low- or no-risk drinking. Your life and the lives of your precious, wonderful friends depend on it."

Will speaks:

My stepfather Jack Wilhelm raised me from age three as if I where his own. My biological father Will Keim, Jr., died months before I was born. Jack was a great Dad and an alcoholic. He loved me unconditionally. He drank himself to death one month before my first child Christa, was born. I miss him every day and he would have loved his granddaughter so much. Do you know a story like mine? Share it with me at www.willkeim@att.net.

—Dr. Will Keim

Finding freedom

Many nations struggle with freedom from tyranny, despots, autocratic rulers, or brutal repression. For some, freedom of speech, assembly, religion, and even the choice of your own occupation or spouse are dream-like fantasies. Freedom draws a significant percentage of the world's immigrants to the shores of North America.

In North America, freedom is a basic right. Why then do so many of our own citizens choose to live their lives in dependency on alcohol and other drugs? They surrender their freedom and give up control of their lives to something outside of themselves. Do you come from a home where alcohol or other drug abuse has damaged relationships, caused misery or even death? Many of us have.

Who are you fooling?

Abraham Lincoln said, "You can't fool all the people all the time." Ultimately the one person you cannot fool is yourself. Please do not feel that we are judging you. That is not our intent. Do feel invited to take an honest look at what you put into your body—particularly in terms of alcohol and other drugs.

Personal honesty

In his book *Sick and Tired of Being Sick and Tired,* author Philip L. Hansen writes, "It seems in this country whenever someone mentions alcohol, people either get mad or thirsty."

Do you get mad or thirsty? Some of you can drink socially and some of you can't. We are not advocating Prohibition II. We are asking for personal honesty, and we are offering a Personal Drinking Inventory that will guide you as you make alcohol-related choices in college.

> "Twenty-five percent of college students (age 18-24) have alcohol-related academic problems."
> —*National Institute on Alcohol Abuse and Alcoholism*

Personal Drinking Inventory

How many drinks do you have per week?

- ❏ 0 drinks per week
- ❏ 1–5 drinks per week
- ❏ 6–10 drinks per week
- ❏ 11–15 drinks per week
- ❏ 16+ drinks per week

Stage Two: Survive ... Freedom

Why include a Personal Drinking Inventory (PDI) in a character lesson on freedom? Because by "freedom" we mean:

Freedom from dependence on alcohol and other drugs.
Freedom from addictions to nicotine and gambling.

So take a look at your PDI above.

Studies have shown an amazing relationship between drinks per week and grade point average: the higher the PDI drinks per week, the lower the grade point average. Higher PDIs are also related to missed classes and dropout rates.

You may say "I can handle it." All that should tell you is that you have built up a high tolerance—which isn't necessarily all that good either.

If you are drunk every weekend, you have a problem with alcohol.

The Good Book says that money is not the root of all evil. Rather, the love of money is the root of evil. Likewise, alcohol is not the cause of most student problems. *The abuse of alcohol* is the problem.

> **"An American monkey after getting drunk on brandy would never touch it again, and thus is much wiser than most men."**
> —Charles Darwin
> 1809 – 1882
> Father of evolutionary biology

> **Will speaks:**
> "I can't think of a single big mistake I made in college that wasn't alcohol related. I never missed a class in college because I was too sober. I never yelled an obscenity at the fraternity next door because I was too sober. I never cheated on my girlfriend because I was too sober. Every once in a while I think about all the time, and perhaps friends, I lost because of alcohol."
> **If you have problems when you drink, you are a problem drinker.**
> —*Dr. Will Keim*

Question: Do you frequently or ever pass an entire day without a drink?

Answer: _____
_____
_____

The SAD Facts
(The Sex, Alcohol and Drug Connection)

The following numbers represent the percentage of these crimes or tragedies that are caused by alcohol and/or other drugs.

- 66% of all date/acquaintance rapes
- 41% of assaults
- 64% of homicides
- 60% of mental cruelty divorce cases
- 60% of suicide attempts
- 80% of college dropouts

In addition:

- Alcohol-related car crashes kill 22,000 per year
- Alcohol is the #1 killer of men and women 18–24

Myth: Everyone drinks all the time.
Fact: 55% of students either don't drink or drink only 1–5 drinks per week.

Another way to look at the statistics that might help your friends think about their behavior related to alcohol would be the following information provided by Elaine Pasqua, a frequent speaker on alcohol, other drugs and sexuality on campus.

1,825 deaths per year from alcohol-related accidents
97,000 victims of sexual assault or rape
595,000 injuries
696,000 assaults
300 alcohol poisoning deaths

The brain does not fully develop until one is 25 years old. Studies show that alcohol is very harmful to the developing brain. A binge drinking episode can shrink the memory center of the brain and arrest cognitive development. Underage drinkers test poorly on cognitive and verbal testing compared with students who abstain from alcohol.

One night of binge drinking negatively affects your mental and physical function for the next three days. If you drink like this for two nights in a row it will be negatively affected for five days.

> "[Social Norming Theory] holds that if students perceive something to be the norm, they tend to alter their behavior to fit that norm, even if it isn't reality. If, however, they are presented with the actual norm, they will conform to it. So, if students think heavy drinking is normal, they'll drink more. If they think responsible drinking is normal, they'll drink more responsibly."
> —Michael Haines
> Director National Social Norms Center

Stage Two: Survive ... Freedom

Elaine Pasqua advises, "Girls do not clear alcohol as quickly from their body as guys. Alcohol is stored in body fat. Girls have more body fat than guys and also less of the enzyme that breaks down the alcohol. **Don't try to keep up with the guys!"**

Your blood alcohol level will continue to climb for an hour and a half after you consume your last drink. The best rule of thumb: Do not consume more than one alcoholic beverage per hour and alternate it with a non-alcoholic drink. You will give the body a chance to clear the alcohol and you are rehydrating yourself so you will feel much better the next day!

A special thank you to Elaine Pasqua for making a clear case for response-ability when it comes to drinking. **And remember ... if you are under 21, it is legal not to drink.**

> "If we burn ourselves out with drugs or alcohol, we won't have long to go in this business."
> —John Belushi
> 1949 – 1982
> Comic actor who died of a drug overdose

Social Norming Theory makes the strong case that if students think "Everyone drinks. Everyone is having sex," the students will more likely behave in this perceived "norm." But the reality is that most students drink responsibly or not at all; and a significant percentage of students abstain from sex for religious, health, and personal safety and self-esteem issues.

Question:
Do you know which of your friends drink too much?

Bigger Question:
How many of you know someone who has been killed in an alcohol- or drug-related accident?

Answer:
Too many of you.

Know the law.
Know your limit.
Know yourself.

> "ThisAmericanLife.org identified the University of Nebraska, Lincoln as a university which has significantly reduced the amount of underage and binge drinking through an aggressive partnership of the University, City of Lincoln, students, police, neighbors, and alcohol prevention specialists. Check it out! Go Huskers!"

The National Council on Alcoholism and Drug Dependence - NCADD - can be researched at www.ncadd.org. Toll free HOPE line number is 800.NCA.CALL.

> RAINN stands for the Rape, Abuse, & Incest National Network. You can contact them at www.rainn.org/. 800.656.HOPE(4673) is the National Sexual Assault Hotline.

Designer or club drugs

Methylenedioxymethamphetamin (MDMA or Ecstasy), gamma-hydroxybutyric acid (GHB), Rohypnol, ketamine, methamphetamine. Big names for some serious drugs. They are just a few of the designer or club drugs showing up on campus, at "raves," dance clubs, and bars. These drugs can cause serious health problems and, in some cases, death. Used in combination with alcohol, they can be even more dangerous.

Date rape

You need to be aware of the horrific use of these drugs on campus. GHB and Rohypnol, for example, have been used in cases of date rape. Because you can't taste or smell GHB, it can be slipped into your drink or even put on your food without detection. Rohypnol, when mixed with alcohol, can incapacitate and prevent you from resisting sexual assault. Take care of yourself and your friends.

Important: Do not leave food or a beverage of any kind unattended at a party. If you feel light-headed, warm, or nauseous, find a same-sex friend to take you home.

Designer or club drugs adversely affect memory. If you can't remember the party, your date, what happened, or where your keys are, seek professional help.

> "Alcohol abuse and other drug use are Equal Opportunity Unemployment Facilitators! They will take even the very best minds down."
> —Dr. Will Keim

Marijuana

The rules all changed in 1990 when Congress passed a law called the 1990 Drug Free Campus and Community Act, which says any drugs used within a mile of any school doubles the penalty upon conviction. What was a misdemeanor for our generation is a felony for your generation. That means on all your future job applications you will have to check the "YES" box when asked:

> **Have you been convicted of a drug-related offense or a felony?**

DRUGS: The Equal Opportunity Unemployment Facilitator
YOU ARE SMARTER THAN THAT!

Up in smoke

While we're talking about drugs, we can't forget nicotine. College students are the leading users of tobacco products today, with the number of smokers continuing to increase. According to a survey from the Core Institute, 35.5 percent of college students in the United States reported using tobacco within a one-month period. Many students identify themselves as "social smokers." Social smokers? Give us a break. Cigarettes contain nicotine, a drug that is as addictive as heroin or cocaine, according to the Royal College of Physicians. Just ask someone who has ever tried to quit. We have sympathy for people who got hooked fifty years ago — before the long-term health consequences of tobacco were known. But today, you have no excuse. If you choose to smoke or chew tobacco, you are putting a cancer-causing substance in your body. Pure and simple. And besides, tobacco makes you smell bad. Who wants to kiss an ash tray?

> "A cigarette hanging from the lips ... is as sexy as a missing tooth [in a] smile."
> —Paul Carvel
> Author and writer

Hold 'em or fold 'em?

We came across the following statement from a college freshman at Syracuse University: "Each month, my parents give me $300, and right afterwards you can find me online gambling or at a casino. All in all, I would say **I've lost at least $2,500, which more than emptied my graduation savings account.**"

Losing your graduation savings account to gambling is a sure-fire sign that you have a gambling problem. Rick Barnes, an expert in college student affairs and a well-known speaker, offers this insight:

Rick speaks:

"For most, gambling can be fun and entertaining. For some, it can be a devastating illness that negatively affects every aspect of their lives. Referred to as 'the hidden addiction,' compulsive gambling is a challenge for some gamblers, carrying the same kinds of negative consequences as drug or alcohol addiction. Compulsive gamblers come from all walks of life. One cannot be too smart, too old, too young, too successful, too religious, or too good of a student to develop a gambling problem."

—*Rick Barnes*

Barnes has these suggestions if you choose to gamble:

- **Pre-determine the amount of money you plan to gamble prior to the outing.**
- **Take breaks at least every thirty minutes during a gambling outing.**
- **Avoid taking ATM or credit cards into the casino.**
- **Remain focused on why you are in college in the first place — make grades, pass classes, and graduate.**

Problem Gambling Quiz

If you are concerned about your gambling, take this short quiz:

YES NO
- ❏ ❏ Do you have an inability to stop gambling once you start?
- ❏ ❏ Do you set "loss limits" for the day and then routinely exceed them?
- ❏ ❏ Do you borrow money to pay gambling debts?
- ❏ ❏ Do you lie to friends or family about your gambling frequency or the extent of your losses?
- ❏ ❏ Do you neglect other responsibilities, such as school, because of a preoccupation with gambling?
- ❏ ❏ Do you constantly worry about your gambling?

If you answered "YES" to any of these questions, it's time to get some help.

If you or someone you know needs help, contact the National Helpline for the National Council on Problem Gambling, (800) 522-4700 or www.ncpgambling.org. Rick Barnes can be contacted at rick@rickbarnespresents.com or by calling: 817-788-5109.

> "[Problem gambling is a] progressive addiction characterized by an increasing preoccupation with gambling, a need to bet more money more frequently, restlessness or irritability when attempting to stop, 'chasing' losses, and loss of control manifested by continuation of the gambling behavior in spite of mounting, serious, negative consequences."
>
> —*National Council on Problem Gambling*

Health

> **"If you want to solve the world's problems, you have to put your own household, your own individual life in order first."**
>
> —*Chögyam Trungpa*
> *1939 – 1987*
> *Teacher and meditation master*

Gold medals for sex?

Dr. Robin Sawyer is a wonderful teacher and researcher at the University of Maryland. His expertise is public health, with a focus on human sexuality. Dr. Sawyer is English, witty, and the husband and father that wives and children dream of having. He says, "If sex were an Olympic sport, the United States would have all the gold medals."

Before Americans gloat about medals, Dr. Sawyer goes on to clarify. Of the 13 industrialized nations, the United States is ranked:
- #1 in unwanted pregnancies
- #1 in sexually transmitted diseases (STDs)
- #1 in acquisition of HIV
- #1 in genital herpes

We really don't want those gold medals after all.

Will speaks:

Dr. Martin Buber wrote hundreds of essays and books on the human condition. He once talked about Response Ability; that is, one's ability to respond to his or her own needs, the needs and desires of friends and family, as well as city, state, nation, and world. When it comes to intimate human contact, we must surely seek to be response able and care for one another with the ultimate respect for the humanity we share.

—*Will Keim*

> "Never continue in a job you don't enjoy. If you're happy in what you're doing, you'll like yourself, you'll have inner peace. And if you have that, along with physical health, you will have had more success than you could possibly have imagined."
>
> —Johnny Carson
> 1925 – 2005
> Television host and comedian

Dr. Keim's Prescription for Healthy Living

Take seven goals:
1. Drink alcohol Response-Ably*
2. Live drug free*
3. Practice Response-Able sexuality*
4. Perform at your academic best
5. Promote personal wellness
6. Exhibit community-minded behavior
7. Be tolerant and respectful

*Understand that saying "no" is often the most Response-Able thing to do.

Mix with seven success tips:
1. Respect yourself and others.
2. Set your academic and personal agenda early.
3. Don't be afraid to fail or succeed.
4. Take care of yourself and others.
5. Accept the challenge college offers.
6. Listen to the "Voice" within.
7. Find something you love to do and learn to do it well enough that someone will pay you to do it.

Refine • Personalize • Take daily

Making the case for abstention

We've known a lot of great relationships ruined by sex and some bad relationships prolonged by it. Be honest with yourself. Virginity and self-control are not a curse. If you choose to be sexually active, consult a campus health educator, and practice safer sex. Sex is never safe. Call us old-fashioned, but we would like to make the case for abstention. Not having sex is a great way *not* to get pregnant. You have little chance of acquiring HIV, and it limits the acquisition of herpes and other sexually transmitted diseases.

Men should treat women the way they would like their little sisters treated. And women should treat men the way they would like their little brothers treated.

Remember:

A night of unprotected sex can be a life-altering evening. However, a night of abstaining from sex rarely creates regrets.

Sex is one of the most powerful human behaviors. It can give life, dramatically alter your life, and potentially take away your life. It is not to be taken lightly or advantage of.

> "True friendship is like sound health. The value of it is seldom known until it be lost."
> —Rev. Charles Caleb Colton
> 1780 – 1832
> Author

Will speaks:
My colleague Dr. Alan Berkowitz has worked tirelessly on challenging and eliminating bystander mentality. We worked together at the United States Air Force Symposium on Character and Leadership. Alan works with students all over the nation to engage them in the process of not standing by and letting someone be hurt or hurt themselves. He is a powerful ally to people who believe in the inherent value and worth of each human being. We challenged second hand-smoke and the damage it did. We are working to eliminate abuse enablers - those who stand by and do nothing when others are being abused or are abusing themselves. We must all rally around the elimination of bystanderism and get involved in protecting the rights of all people to life, liberty, and the pursuit of happiness.

—Will Keim

The emotional connection that makes sex so much more gratifying and healthy is missing when sex is treated as a sport or conducted outside of a meaningful relationship or marriage. If you don't want someone practicing with your future wife, husband, partner or significant other, then don't practice with someone else's.

It is OK not to have sex!

~ And Now A Word From Our Friend Elaine Pasqua ~
Nationally Known Speaker

If you can't sit across the table from a person and talk to them about sex, about the responsibility that you are taking on, and what you are ready to do or not do, you aren't ready to share yourself with them physically. Communication is essential! So is relationship.

Abstinence doesn't mean that you can't be intimate with someone, you just won't engage in activities where you will share infected bodily

> **Something to think about …**
>
> There is really no such thing as "safe sex." Nothing as powerful emotionally, psychologically, physically, and spiritually as sex could ever be called safe. It might be "safer" with proper preparation, but safe is not an accurate descriptor.
>
> Many of you belong to Spiritual Communities, such as the Jewish Synagogue, Roman Catholic Church, Latter Day Saints, Islamic Mosques, Buddhist Temples, Protestant Churches, and many other contemplative places for your spiritual expression …
>
> What do these communities tell you about the role of human sexuality from their traditions? It would make sense to us that if you identify yourself with one of these value and belief groups then you would want your life to be lived in concert and in consistency with these beliefs.
>
> We have primarily encouraged abstention, and mentioned "safer sex", but in the short and long term, perhaps our best advice would be to talk with a mentor or spiritual advisor about what your group believes about human sexuality, relationships, and marriage before engaging in a powerful experience, sex, that has definitive consequences.
>
> Rabbis, Ministers, Imans, Priests, Monks, Bishops and other religious vocationalists have great training and wisdom in the human condition and its relationship to faith. Perhaps this would be a good time and a good issue to discuss with a spiritual mentor.
>
> If you are an agnostic, or an atheist, it would still be good advice to discuss your thoughts about human sexuality with a well-intentioned mentor.
>
> —Dr. Will Keim

fluids such as intercourse or oral sex. Be creative! Kissing for a long time is very sensual; there is massage, caressing…all of these things will provide safe intimacy!

The Center for Disease Control and Prevention (CDC) stated that the spread of sexually transmitted infections is one of the most under-recognized health problems in the United States.

We are tempted to gauge our sexual experience by whether we get pregnant or not. However, there are other consideratons:

1. Chlamydia can cause pelvic inflammatory disease which can lead to sterility.
2. One has herpes for the rest of their life and has to worry about infecting their partner.
3. Certain strains of HPV can cause cervical cancer.
4. HIV/AIDS can take your life away.
5. How will I feel about myself in the morning?

How difficult would it be for you to reveal to your partner that you are infected with a sexually transmitted infection?

If you choose to engage in sex then you need to protect yourself each and every time! I know people who know the one night that they let their guard down and contracted a sexually transmitted infection. **Remember…it only takes one time!**

65 million people in the US are living with an incurable sexually-transmitted infection

Don't judge a book by its cover! Many who are infected with a sexually transmitted infection look healthy!

Unprotected oral sex can lead to herpes in the back of the throat, gonorrhea tonsillitis, syphilis & transmission of HIV through the mucous membranes of the mouth.

A new trend has emerged in cases of throat cancer. Many teens and young adults are now presenting with throat cancer from Human Papillomavirus strain 16, the same strain that causes cervical cancer.

One should always use protection during oral sex to avoid contact with infected bodily fluids.

Alcohol and sex often go hand in hand, with devastating outcomes. If you find yourself at a party and you think you might hook up with someone, step out of the situation and ask yourself a few quick questions:

1. Does this person respect me the same way that I respect myself?
2. Am I certain that they don't have a sexually transmitted infection?
3. Will they make eye-contact with me tomorrow on campus, or will they walk by acting like they don't know me?
4. Will I regret this tomorrow, one year from now, or five years from now?
5. Does this go against the parameters that I set for keeping myself safe and healthy?

> "It's OK not to have sex. Respect and take care of yourself. You're worth it!"
> —Dr. Will Keim
> *Message to his children*

If you are not comfortable with any of the answers, step back, THINK, and come up with a different game plan.

People even cycle back to a more responsible sexual behavior. I once had a senior female athlete from a campus come up to me and say, "I went through my crazy phase in my freshman and sophomore years. I slept with a lot of different guys. Now I have totally backed off of that behavior and I have a much higher regard for my body than I ever had for it. I feel so much better about myself and I respect myself so much more!"

Respect yourself and others will respect you!

We went to our friend Elaine Pasqua to speak to you clearly, honestly and directly about sex on campus. We thank her for her candor and willingness to share her knowledge with us.

Authors Note: Elaine Pasqua and I speak every year to the new students at the University of Redlands. She and her husband Jeff have become good friends of mine. Their residence on the East Coast renders them direct, pointed, and refreshingly honest. Elaine's message empowers students; inspiring women and challenging men to be good people, and to be good to one another.

Thank You Elaine!

> **LOVE YOUR FRIENDS**
>
> "A prophet said, 'Greater love has no person than he or she lay down their lives for their friends!' This doesn't mean you have to die. It does mean you have to put it on the line so that your friends don't get hurt or die. 'Putting it on the line' means being there, not leaving them behind, watching out for them. This is true love of a friend. Love is an action, and sometimes it means talking to your friend about a problem, not ignoring it."
>
> —*Dr. Will Keim*

Respect yourself. Respect others.

- Women and men should know that they will get the respect they command.
- Men and women who sleep around generally don't go home with anyone for Thanksgiving.
- Sex doesn't always include love and intimacy.
- Practice respect, and you'll get it right back 'atcha!

Making healthy choices is a matter of life and death

Based on several studies, the National Institute on Alcohol Abuse and Alcoholism estimates the following consequences of excessive and underage drinking for college students ages 18-24:

- 1,400 deaths per year
- 70,000 victims of sexual assault or rape
- 110,000 arrests related to alcohol
- 150,000 people with alcohol-related health problems
- 500,000 injuries
- 600,000 assaults
- 400,000 students had unprotected sex
- 100,000 students were too drunk to know if they consented to sex
- 2.1 million students drove while drunk
- 1.2% of students attempted suicide while drunk
- 11% committed acts of vandalism while drunk

Don't be a statistic. Be a graduate.

> ### Will speaks:
> "I am an intercollegiate chaplain. Most students I've had the misfortune to bury were victims of alcohol- and drug-related incidents. Until you've seen the pain you cannot imagine the suffering."
> **Think. Abstain. Remember.**
>
> —*Will Keim*

Stage Two: Survive ... Health

Practicing wellness is a smart lifestyle choice, perhaps your most important short- and long-term decision.

Club and designer drugs

Club and designer drugs sound quite benign, when in reality students are dropping dead and dropping their standards because of them. Medical doctor Michael Finley advises, "Even one use of club or designer drugs, especially Ecstasy, severely limits the brain's ability to produce serotonin, which is essential to the brain's ability to remember things. These drugs are not benign, they are neurotoxins."

- If you don't know what these drugs are: Great!
- If you don't know what they can do: Great Danger!
- It is time for you to educate yourself about Rohypnol, GHB, DXM, Ecstasy, and Ketamine.

Do not leave a drink unattended at a social gathering at college.

Because some club drugs are colorless, tasteless, and odorless, individuals who want to intoxicate or sedate others can add them unobtrusively to beverages or food. In recent years, there has been an increase in reports of club drugs used to commit sexual assaults, and for that reason they are referred to as "date rape drugs."
Source: National Institute on Drug Abuse

> "The healthy, the strong individual, is the one who asks for help when he needs it —whether he has an abscess on his knee or in his soul."
>
> —Rona Barrett
> *Gossip columnist and businesswoman*

> "There is a connection on campus between abuses in sex, alcohol, and other drugs. I call this the 'S.A.D.' Connection. Break this life-threatening triad by respecting yourself and others. Choose a well and healthy lifestyle. The world needs you and your many gifts."
>
> *Dr. Will Keim*

Name four people to whom you could bring a problem (Sister? Step Mom or Dad? Brother? Best friend? Teammate? Mom? Dad? Grandma? Counselor? Resident assistant? Coach? Professor? Guardian?)

_____   _____

_____   _____

List a few healthy choices you'd like to make this year:

_____

_____

_____

_____

Healthy mind + Healthy body = Healthy spirit
Let your spirit soar.

Eating Disorders

> **"The wise man should consider that health is the greatest of human blessings. Let food be your medicine."**
>
> —*Hippocrates*
> *Fourth Century, B.C.*
> *Greek physician, Western father of medicine*

What is an eating disorder?

Wikipedia defines an eating disorder as the need "to eat, or avoid eating, which negatively affects both one's physical and mental health." Eating disorders can be all encompassing. They can affect every part of the person's life. Eating disorders are not a fad, phase, or a lifestyle. They are a life-threatening mental illness, that, if untreated, can lead to multiple physical and mental complications as well as death. The most common eating disorders are anorexia and bulimia. It is estimated that there are over 10,000,000 people in the United States suffering from eating disorders. Although historically eating disorders affect women, a growing percentage of those affected are now male. Eating disorders can begin at a very young age, with diagnosed cases as young as five years of age. It is not a choice to have an eating disorder just as it is not a choice to have cancer or diabetes. In America eating disorders are two times more prevalent than Alzheimer's disease, and 10 times more prevalent than autism.

Alexis speaks:

"Although I've lived a seemingly short 16 years, I have experiences and hardships to last me a lifetime. I have been battling a demon called anorexia nervosa since the age of 10. While most spend their adolescence celebrating with friends and exploring the wonders that life has to offer, I have been a prisoner in my mind, held captive by my own self-hatred. Hospital stays, crying, and a feeling of general darkness are the memories that will be forever etched in my mind, in place of what should have been the best years of my life. However, with much prayer and hard work, as well as effective treatment, I have been able to fight this disease, and am proud and thankful to say that I am in recovery now."

> "Funny how we think the key to happiness is being thin, so we throw our happiness away in search of the key."
> —Anorexia sufferer

Statistics about eating disorders:

- According to the Eating Disorder Coalition for Research, Policy, and Action, 13% of high school and college girls purge.
- It is estimated that 45% of boys and girls in grades 3-6 have a desire to be thinner.
- 9% of 9 year old girls have already vomited to lose weight.
- Within the last 30 days it is estimated that 5% of high school and college students have taken laxatives or vomited to keep from gaining weight.
- Bulimics on average binge 11 times per week, yet 64% of the bulimic population are at a healthy weight range.
- While anorexics struggle to starve themselves, often consuming minimal calories a day, a bulimic can consume excessive calories in a sitting.
- 40% of newly identified cases of anorexia are in girls 15-19 years old.
- The incidence of anorexia in young women 15-19 has increased each decade since 1930.

Why did this happen to me, my sibling, or my friend?

There is no one cause for a person having developed an eating disorder. It is important to stop blaming and work together.

**NEDA stands for the National Eating Disorder Association.
For more information, contact
www.info@NationalEatingDisorders.org, 800.931.2237**

> **Do these thoughts or statements sound familiar?**
> "I always wanted to be the most popular girl; the thinner I am the more people will find me attractive."
> "If I lose weight I will be a better athlete, gymnast, wrestler or swimmer. I have already improved by losing some weight, so losing more can only make me better."
> "I was always unpopular and overweight, I finally started a diet and everyone has noticed. If I keep losing weight I will be healthier, happier, and more accepted."
> "I want to be a model or a dancer; the thinner I am the better my career will be."
> "I am sad and have no control over my life. Others have abused or hurt me, and I will take control of the one thing only I can effect - my eating."
> "I'm not good enough for anyone including myself. I'm sad and don't care if I die. If starving brings me to that goal, then that is the tool I'll use."

Thought-altering Exercise: Think of the times you or someone you know has had one of these distorted thoughts. List three things that you could tell yourself or your friend to change this thinking pattern to a more realistic and healthy thought process.

_____
_____
_____

> "He that takes medicine and neglects diet, wastes the skill of the physician."
> —Chinese Proverb

Health Concerns Associated with eating Disorders
Osteoporosis, osteopenia
Kidney/renal failure
Ruptured stomach and esophagus
Damage to stomach lining
Infertility
Loss of period in women
Anemia
Electrolyte imbalances
Life-threatening lowering of potassium levels

Liver damage and non-alcoholic fatty liver disease
Irregular heart beat or dangerously low heart beat, leading to long-term heart damage and failure

Eating Disorders: Not Just for females anymore:

A recent Harvard study found that the male population affected by eating disorders is growing at an alarming rate. It is estimated that 10-25% of the 10,000,000 people diagnosed with eating disorders are now male. Males are under similar social stresses to be thin, to be the best athletes, to get the best jobs, to get the best girlfriends, and to be the most popular.

Take care of your body and your mind will follow.
Starve your body and your mind will perish.

Male Eating Disorder facts:

As many as 2,500,000 men and boys may suffer from eating disorders. Because of their lower body fat stores it is more dangerous for boys and men to have eating disorders. A study done in 1995 indicates that 5-14% of adolescent boys have intentionally vomited after eating. Athletes such as wrestlers, gymnasts, swimmers, rowers, and skiers are at higher risk.

There are now both inpatient and outpatient facilities that focus on the treatment of boys and men with eating disorders. Historically there have been few options to help men and boys.

Character Check:

Even though eating disorders are life-threatening mental illnesses, they are often maligned by those who are not intimately familiar with them.

> "What lies behind us and what lies before us are small matters compared to what lies within us."
> —Ralph Waldo Emerson
> 1803-1882
> American essayist, philosopher and poet

Have you heard a fellow student make fun of the thin child or make insulting statements about the "anorexic." Maybe a TV show or movie has joked about an eating disorder, or a specific person suffering. Would you make fun of a child with cancer, autism, or diabetes?

The next time you hear or are a part of a conversation making light of this disease, do a character check. 10,000,000 people are suffering

Stage Two: Survive ... Eating Disorders

from these disorders. They can be hurt and negatively affected by your words and actions.

Show character and compassion, it may just change a life.

Action Exercise: Find five examples of media that you feel projects a negative or unrealistic influence on the thoughts of young people. For each of the examples, list the effects you believe these messages can have on your thought process. Compare real life to the illusion of each of these false images and messages.

> "Young men and young women are affected by eating disorders."
> —*Harvard University study*

_____

_____

_____

_____

_____

_____

Be Aware of the signs:
- Intense fear of becoming fat
- Compulsive exercising
- Follows own diet preoccupation with food
- Unusual food rituals
- Long periods of time in the bathroom after meals
- Reluctance to eat in front of people
- Eats rapidly, without control
- Large weight loss in a short period of time
- Exhibits strange weight fluctuations
- Looks unhealthy
- Low self-esteem
- Unrealistic, perfectionist standards
- Attributes successes or failures to weight
- Makes statements about being fat although not
- Hides food
- Misuses laxatives
- Wears loose, baggy clothing
- Seems depressed, isolated or lonely
- Demonstrates fatigue and muscle weakness

- Developes downy hair on face and arms
- Thinning hair/hair loss
- Denies problem with food or eating
- Has dental erosion
- Feels undeserving of life's pleasures

The Profile:
Athletes
Perfectionists
Overachievers
Models or actors
People-pleasers
Abuse victims

> "The need for my eating disorder and inability to restrict or over-exercise like I used to led to a horrific chain of destructive habits ..."
> —Laura Klink

Help and Intervention
1) **Outpatient treatment**
   Therapists
   Counselors
   Nutritionists
   Nurses
   Dieticians
2) **Inpatient Care**
   Combines all of the above and more into an intense residential program
3) **Hospitalization programs**
   For the medically-compromised

Treatment of eating disorders calls for a specific program that involves three main phases:

- Restoring the patient to a healthy weight and keeping them physically stable is the most critical step. One approach used is to empower the patients to take control of food choices, exercise, and food quantities while learning a weight restoration and management program that can be used to support recovery on an ongoing basis.
- Treating psychological disturbances such as distortion of body image, low self-esteem, and interpersonal conflicts using individual therapy, group therapy, art therapy, equine therapy, self-awareness and esteem workshops are all important to changing body image and removing fear of weight gain.

- Giving the patient an ongoing plan to manage their life and recovery.

Laura Speaks:

Me at 15:

I constantly crave exercise.

Just a few months ago, I spent every hour of the day exercising. Most evenings, I could hear my family laughing as they watched movies downstairs in the living room. I was always on the verge of crying because I missed being able to sit with them. No matter how badly I wanted to go and relax with them though, I didn't have a choice. I had to stay thin. The hours would grow later, everyone would go to bed, and I would continue to exercise in my room. I worked out until I collapsed in my bed, then I'd sleep for four or five hours and get up to workout again. I'd hide food in my pockets at meals, stand up in class or just skip class altogether to run around the neighborhoods, and when I was forced to sit, I would hold myself up on my legs so I wasn't actually touching the seat. I felt a sick satisfaction with my disintegrating body.

After being sent away for three months to Remuda Ranch treatment center in Arizona, I've had to repeatedly ask myself one question: if I spent the rest of my life feeding these obsessions, losing my relationships, my personality, my health, my lifelong sport (gymnastics), and everything else in my life, would I die thinking "at least I had a thin body?" With each day that passed, the behaviors seemed more and more irrational. Although I still crave my eating disorder horribly, I feel like I am in the process of finding my life again, and I love being kissed goodnight and then actually going to sleep.

Me at 19:

I originally wrote an excerpt for this book almost five years ago, when I was 15. At the time, I was fresh out of treatment for anorexia nervosa and hoping that this new life free from the control of my miserable and tormenting eating disorder meant the end of my worst problems. Unfortunately, I was terribly wrong.

The need for my eating disorder and inability to restrict or over-exercise like I used to led to a horrific chain of destructive habits, beginning with methamphetamine addiction, followed by purging and laxative abuse, then alcohol abuse, and then heroin addiction.

> "As the arguments got worse the family split further apart. I didn't want to watch my sister die. It wasn't something either of us could control - it's just I couldn't handle it and she couldn't help it."
>
> —*Kayla*
> *Younger sibling of an eating disorder sufferer*

> "Low self-esteem, relentless self-criticism, and especially anxiety were the root issues of everything I went through."
> —Laura Klink

Seven months ago, I overdosed shooting up heroin and may very well have died had I not been in a public bathroom where I was found in time.

The reason I'm sharing this in a section about eating disorders is because of how closely my eating disorder and substance addiction are related. Low self-esteem, relentless self-criticism, and especially anxiety were the root issues of everything I went through. One of the things I believe is most important to understand is to never ignore what may seem like a "small" issue, such as anxiety, because such problems are what lead to life-threatening obsessions and addictions.

Most importantly, whatever your problems are, I believe nobody should ever give up on themselves or their lives. I know I never will.

❖ ❖ ❖

WILL'S NOTE: I met Joe Radzvilowicz in Nevada at the Noveau Vie Eating Disorder clinic at the invitation of my friend Kevin Klink. Kevin and Joe shared the common experience of having daughters who wrestled with eating disorders. Kevin's daughter Laura wrote the deeply moving narration above. The Radzvilowicz and Klink families remain committed to helping others with this disease by sharing their personal triumphs and tragedies. Their work is changing lives.

In Memorium

Joe Radzvilowicz passed away in February 2010. His love for his family and his friendship, kind-heartedness, optimism, business/technical excellence, humor, directness, and incredible drive to battle eating disorders will not be forgotten. You are in our hearts Joe.

Letting Go 10

> ❝When I was 14 I thought my father was ignorant. By the time I was 21 I was amazed how much he had learned in seven years.❞
>
> —*Mark Twain*
> *1835 – 1910*
> *Author and humorist*

Living your own life

"I hate chemistry," the student said to her counselor. "I hate it, and I have failed it three times. But I have to take it to be a dietician." Her counselor looked puzzled. "Is that what you want to be?" he asked. "No. But my mom was a dietician, and I don't want to disappoint her."

"Does she want you to be one?" he asked. The student's face crinkled up as she pondered the question. "I think so."

"Why don't you call her? Now." He handed his phone to the student who punched in her mom's number. The tears started to fall. She told her mom thanks and hung up. The student turned to her counselor. "My mom said she just wants me to be happy. Whatever major makes me happy is fine with her."

Are you majoring in something because of your parents, because of a trend, or because you love it? Do the right thing for the right reason. Both students and parents have to let go at some point and allow each other to live their lives.

Will speaks:
"I know a soccer player from the University of New Hampshire whose father went to all her games. Watching their exchange of love and respect after a game was great. She is blessed. So here it is: Your parents did the best they could. Most of them parented you the way they were parented by their folks. Perhaps that New Hampshire dad had a father who went to all of his games."
What kind of parents do you have?

—*Will Keim*

> "There are two lasting bequests we can give our children. One is roots. The other is wings."
> —Hodding Carter, Jr.
> 1907 – 1972
> Journalist

Walls

The Great Wall of China was built to keep marauding armies and unwanted cultures out. The Berlin Wall was built to separate East Germany and West Germany; it also separated brothers and sisters, parents and children. The goodness or badness of a wall largely rests in the eye of the beholder.

Here is some information that generally gets left out of the collegiate educational experience:

- **Some of you were blessed with great parents.**
- **Some of you were not.**

It is time to make a "Big Choice" regarding your parents. You have two choices:

Choice 1

If you are angry at your parents, begin the healing and forgiving process by letting go of your anger. If you let it eat you up, then the anger wins. Their problem becomes your problem.

Choice 2

If you have a good relationship, thank your parents for doing a great job—especially if you have a single parent who did a great job. Those parents are saints. For single parents or guardians, this is the picture: WORK • WORK • CARE GIVE • PARENT • WORK • COOK • SLEEP • WORK SOME MORE • PARENT • SLEEP

Tear down the wall between you and your parents or figure out a way around it. Let people - friends, siblings, advisors, counselors - help you do this. Life is short and as Dr. Martin Luther King, Jr., said, "Hate is the most ineffective emotion. Half the people you hate don't know. The other half don't care. The only person hate destroys is you."

Stage Two: Survive ... Letting Go

Assignment:

Write a letter to your parents. Share the most important lesson they have taught you. Pretend that after this letter, for whatever reason, you will not be able to speak directly with them again. Please handwrite the letter after five minutes of quiet reflection.

> "Children begin by loving their parents. As they grow older, they judge them. Sometimes they forgive them."

Dear _____

Sincerely,

_____

The wise path

Your parents will, in the best-case scenario, become your friends and trusted mentors or advisors. As you have your own family, your parents will become grandparents and valuable assistants in the raising of your own children.

Then one day it will dawn on you that you are taking care of your parents, or not. The quality of their health care and later years will largely be determined by their relationship to you. It makes good sense to make peace with them now. Thank them if you can. Forgive them if you can't. Let go of the past, and get on with the present. This is the wise path to take with your parents.

Remember: Going to college is not just a big step for you, but also for your parents.

> **"There can be no gain without loss. No redemption without forgiveness."**
> —Lindsey Buckingham
> *Singer-songwriter, guitarist, producer*

> **Will speaks**:
> Students tell me that they will not make the same mistakes that their parents made. I always tell them, "You are right. You will invent mistakes we never thought of." Each generation creates problems all its own and inherits the problems of the generations before it. You must not be limited by the mistakes, or accomplishments for that matter, of the past. You must not seek to "find" yourself. Rather, in the words of Mary Catherine Bateson in *Composing A Life*, you must seek to invent yourself. This means accepting your strengths and weaknesses while reinforcing the former and working to minimize the latter. What would you change if you could?
> **(Because...you can!!!)**

> **Will speaks:**
> There were so many things I wish I would have said to my Mom and Dad. First among those would have been, "I am sorry for so harshly judging your lives and your performance as my parents." It is so easy for me to look at what others are doing and see a better way, while overlooking the things I could be doing to be a better me. Perhaps that is what was meant by the Great Teacher who advised, "Take the log out of your own eye before you try to take the speck out of your brother's eye". Talk to your parents, and either thank them or begin the process of letting go of the bad stuff and getting on with your life.

List a few things that you'd like to let go:

_____
_____
_____
_____
_____
_____
_____
_____
_____

> "I talk and talk and talk, and I haven't taught people in 50 years what my father taught by example in one week."
>
> —*Mario Cuomo*
> *Former governor of New York*

STAGE THREE
Thrive

"Love is that condition in the human spirit so profound that it allows me to survive, and better than that, to thrive with passion, compassion, and style."

Maya Angelou

Peacemaking ❖ Diversity ❖ Service ❖ Spirituality ❖ Financial Literacy

STAGE THREE: THRIVE "CHAPTER SUMMARY"
Peacemaking ❖ Diversity ❖ Service ❖ Spirituality ❖ Financial Literacy

11. <u>PEACEMAKING</u> with Dr. J. Wesley Robb, USC, Professor Emeritus

"People will live divided no more when they realize that no punishment they could lay on them is worse than what they are laying on themselves by conspiring in their own diminishment."
                    Dr. Parker Palmer

"From reading the title of this chapter you may have thought that this lesson was about making peace in the world. That is certainly a good idea, and it is much needed today. We, however, are talking about making peace with your self.

Our goal is simple: Civility between people, groups, religions, and nations - civility on earth - doing what's right. We would like to help by offering A Four Step Model For Ethical Decision Making: (1) Motive: Why am I doing this? (2) The Law: Is it legal? (3) What are the potential Consequences?, and (4) Moral Principles? Is this action consistent with whom I see myself to be?"

❖ ❖ ❖

12. <u>DIVERSITY</u> with Joe Richardson, Esq.; Tray Robinson, California State University, Chico; Tondaleya Jackson, Benedict College, SC; Jesus Jaime Diaz, Oregon State University; Valerie and Dr. Charles Ross, University of Mississippi; Samantha Keim, Linfield College, John Graham, The Giraffe Project; & Tom Durein, Delta Upsilon Educational Foundation

"Complacency is a far more dangerous attitude than outrage."
                    Naomi Little Bear

A. Joe Richardson, Esq. …
"Diversity Is A Strength"
"I am an African-American lawyer in a diverse state (California). Yet, not even 5 percent of lawyers in California are African-American. I rarely see another African-American lawyer in Court, even when the docket has 20 or more cases to be heard (usually meaning 40 or more lawyers). I was prepared for this because I had to be. My parents believed that I needed to be around all types of people, and so my "culture shock" began relatively early, in 7th grade……"

B. Tray Robinson, Director of University Diversity Programs, CSU Chico
"Growing up in an environment that was consumed with gangs, drugs, prostitution and killings did not allow me to deal with being gay, so I thought Chico would provide me with a new start in doing so. Bouts of depression, anxiety attacks, and being fed up with lying to my friends and loved ones forced me to finally come out of the closet in 1995. I felt liberated. Those were some of the most trying times of my life, but my faith, friends, and love for humanity allowed me to prevail. My motivation to complete my undergraduate degree was to prove my eleventh grade high school English teacher wrong, who laughed at me when I told her I wanted to go to college. I also wanted to be the first person in my immediate family to graduate from college."

C. Jesus Jaime-Diaz, M.A. Candidate, Ethnic Studies and Communication..
"The Fight To Achieve Full Potential"
"I remember a wonderful lady by the name of Jeannie Lockwood at Blue Mountain Community College in Hermiston, Oregon. She was one of my GED teachers that gave me so much positive reinforcement. I remember she would say to me, "go to school to wake up everyday in the morning loving what you do. Don't see life as a job." I remember she said I had the life experience to make a difference in many people's lives. This lady I believe was an angel. She got me through the hardest days I have had to face in life….."

D. Sami Keim's College Admission Essay: *"Diversity Is More Than Color"*
"Growing up, Tommy D. and I remained close. Every time my dad was speaking at an event that Tommy was attending, I would beg to travel with him so we could set out on another incredible dinner adventure with Tommy. Having him as such a dear friend definitely shaped the way I looked at the world around me. Every single time I heard homophobic slurs, or saw graffiti of hate and intolerance on the bathroom stall walls, memories of Tommy and his wonderful personality flooded into my mind. I would recall his kindhearted gestures, humble ways, and the phenomenal dinners we had shared. I could not apprehend how anyone could be so malicious. Tommy was the most amazing person I had ever met, and yet daily I was reminded of all the hate that was associated with the simple fact that he was gay."

From Tom Durein's response:
"I believe one of the things I'm most thankful for in Sami's essay was the reminder that learning comes in the most unexpected of situations. Just like life. Sami not only reminds us that diversity isn't just about race, color, or creed, but that much of this world still has a long journey to travel around issues of sexual orientation, civil rights, and basic human understanding."

E. John Graham, Vietnam Veteran, Founder of The Giraffe Project
"Life is an adventure - sometimes a risky one. The key is knowing what to take risks for and how to take them well. We've told the stories of over 1,100 Giraffe Heroes over the last quarter-century. Our strategy is simple: others see or hear the stories of these remarkable people and are moved to stick their own necks out to help solve the public problems *they* care about. Giraffe Heroes are models and catalysts for the rest of us."

F. Tondaleya Jackson, Benedict College, South Carolina,
Founder of Total Learning Concepts

"I don't know if it was fear or inner strength from a source beyond me, but for a brief moment I dared to look at these men and caught the eye of the driver. I'll never know if he saw a human being or a young lady no different than any in his family. Maybe he realized that a prank was suddenly turning into much more for his friends. For you see, I caught the eye of his front seat passenger too; and all I saw was hate. I will always remember the hatred in this young man's eyes. Whatever the driver saw in my eyes, he instantly turned his head away from me. He no longer laughed and yelled with his passengers; instead after a few brief moments more he passed my vehicle and drove ahead of me, out of sight."

❖ ❖ ❖

13. SERVICE

"No matter what accomplishments you make, somebody helps you."
Wilma Rudolf

"By now it should be obvious that we believe good character includes service, and that great learning takes place in the act of giving assistance to others. Mentoring is just one way to be of service. As Mother Theresa said, we can do 'small things with great love' and inspire others to join us in the effort. Nothing puts your problems in perspective better than helping others in their time of need. It is always wise to follow the Golden Rule because what you 'do unto others' may eventually be 'done unto you'."

❖ ❖ ❖

14. SPIRITUALITY

"I've always found one's tolerance of another's spirituality to be a direct barometer of that person's own spiritual security."
Rabbi Lawrence Kushner

"Billy Mills, the Native American Olympic gold medalist, tells us about a Lakota tradition of holding a child up facing the heavens and saying to the little one, **'Behold the only thing greater than yourself'**. Professor Diana Eck of Harvard University defines 'spirituality' as **'real religion that touches the heart'**. Sister Joan Chittister proposes, **'Religion is for people that are afraid to go to hell. Spirituality is for those of us who have already been there."** When we talk of spirituality, we are talking about solid values and beliefs that will help every student grow and achieve his or her own peace. We are talking about compassion, love, tolerance, patience, and kindness."

❖ ❖ ❖

15. FINANCIAL LITERACY with Sheryl Garrett, The Garrett Planning Network

"Watch the pennies - the dollars will take care of themselves."
Aunt Mary Keim

(from start saving/investing early example) "… Notice in the end, Bill only invested $16,000 toward his retirement, yet Phil saved $78,000 and never caught up with Bill. Start or increase your savings now. Let the miracle of compound interest through time let you reach financial security the easiest way possible."

(from car purchase example) "… So, what have you given up? The new car smell! By simply choosing to buy gently used cars and driving them for 5 years the positive impact on your wallet is actually much greater than it appears. With the new car you would go through this routine 2 ½ times (every 2 years verses every 5 years) as compared with the lost value on the used car. Projecting this cost out over your driving lifetime can result in a total cost of $300,000 to $500,000. Are you absolutely certain that driving fresh new cars is worth this much to you? That money could have been used to buy a nice house or would make a significant investment portfolio. It's ALL about choices. *Your choices matter!"*

Peacemaking   11

> **"An eye for an eye and a tooth for a tooth results in a blind, toothless world."**
>
> —*Golda Meier*
> *1898 – 1978*
> *Israeli political leader*

Putting the 'Civil' back in Civil War

The annual in-state rivalry football game between the University of Oregon and Oregon State University is called the Civil War. The crowd behavior, however, had a history of being anything but civil. After two years of extraordinarily rude and obnoxious home crowds at the popular event, Dr. Will Keim and Shelley Sutherland along with the fraternities and sororities at both schools founded "Put the Civil Back in Civil War." Students, athletes, cheerleaders, and student leaders from both schools began to visit elementary schools together in each town. Side by side, they talk about resolving conflict without violence. Each elementary school receives a $500 check for school supplies from the rival university. The mascots shake hands, and the children see cooperation and friendship. Since the inception of the program, civility has increased and the crowds have respected each other with little or no problems. Peacemaking can be taught and can be learned. Would a program like this work at your school and its rival?

> **Will speaks:**
> From reading the title of this chapter, you may have thought that this lesson was about making peace in the world. That is certainly a good idea, and it is much needed today. We, however, are talking about making peace with yourself.
>
> In 1998 I heard Dr. Parker Palmer, a well-known writer, teacher, and activist, speak in St. Louis. He said something so profound that I carry it with me to this day. What he said was this: "People will live divided no more when they realize that no punishment anyone could lay on them is worse than what they are laying on themselves by conspiring in their own diminishment."
> **Make peace with yourself.**
>
> —Dr. Will Keim

Are you a conspirator in your own diminishment? Do your actions bring people closer to you, or push them away? Do you live divided between the person you wish you were or want to be and the person you really are?

We believe it is completely possible to "live divided no more." You can change, become integrated, and be at peace with yourself.

Albert Einstein observed, "One definition of insanity is doing the same thing over and over again and expecting a different result."

Change is not the enemy. You are not the enemy. In order to make peace with yourself, you must ask yourself some serious questions in moments of quiet reflection.

Good starter questions:

- Who am I?
- Why am I here?
- What is my purpose?
- What are my greatest gifts?
- What do I have to offer?
- What gives my life meaning?
- What do I believe in?

THE BIG QUESTIONS!

> "If there is to be peace in the world,
> There must be peace in the nations.
> If there is to be peace in the nations,
> There must be peace in the cities.
> If there is to be peace in the cities,
> There must be peace between neighbors.
> If there is to be peace between neighbors,
> There must be peace in the home.
> If there is to be peace in the home,
> There must be peace in the heart."
>
> —Lao Tzu
> Sixth century, B.C.
> Father of Taoism

These questions rest in every soul, and sadly, some people never ask them nor search for the answers.

Once you begin on the path of making peace with yourself, then you may desire to make peace and resolve conflict with others.

Our goal is simple: civility between people, groups, religions, nations—civility on earth—doing what's right. Civility is treating others as you would like to be treated. Let's look at ways to reach ethical decisions and a methodology to handle conflict interpersonally, rather than angrily or violently.

> "Peace gives victory to both sides."
> —Ralph Waldo Emerson
> 1803 – 1882
> Poet and philosopher

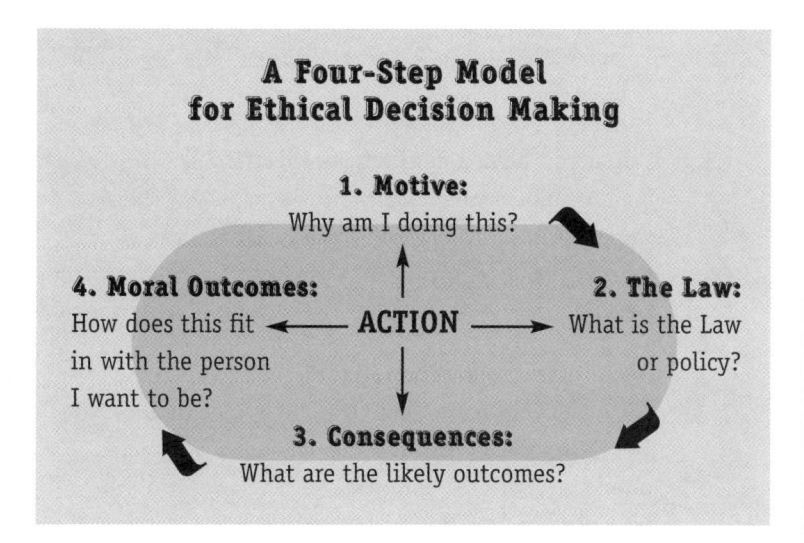

A Four-Step Model for Ethical Decision Making

1. **Motive:** Why am I doing this?
2. **The Law:** What is the Law or policy?
3. **Consequences:** What are the likely outcomes?
4. **Moral Outcomes:** How does this fit in with the person I want to be?

→ ACTION

Author's Note:
I wish to thank Dr. J. Wesley Robb for giving me the permission to use the model. We met at an Order of Omega Retreat for The University of Southern California on Catalina Island. He told me he was retiring and that I could make of the model what I deemed appropriate. I am pleased to share The Four Step Model for Ethical Decision Making. Dr. Robb's teachings live on ... 25 years and going strong!

Dr. Will Keim

Ask:
1. Why?
2. Is it legal?
3. What could happen?
4. Is it moral?

Think before you act.

Bottom line: Is it right? Is this action consistent with my values and beliefs? Then, and only then, do the deed.

Conflicts are a normal part of life. Sporting events are organized conflict within a set of established rules and plays. It is how we handle conflict that matters most.

If you have a disagreement with a parent, professor, boyfriend, or girlfriend, then follow this five-step model to resolve conflict interpersonally:

A Five-Step Model for Handling Conflict Interpersonally

Step 1: Be specific.
Step 2: Avoid blaming and moralizing.
Step 3: Talk one to one.
Step 4: Talk in a nonstressful place and time.
Step 5: Leave an open door.

> "All humanity is one undivided and indivisible family, and each one of us is responsible for the misdeeds of all the others."
>
> — *Mahatma Gandhi*
> *1869 – 1948*
> *Political and spiritual leader of India*

1. When you have a conflict, be specific. "You were a flaming idiot" is interesting but not helpful. "When we stopped them on fourth down and one, and you got a taunting penalty, it really hurt the team" is very direct and specific.

2. Avoid blaming and moralizing. "We lost because of you," "It's your fault," and "If you continue to drink you, will burn in hell" are not bridge-builders. "I have a problem." "What's your problem?" "I have a problem with your drinking" works much better.

3. Talk one to one. Public arguments turn into theater, and we often say things we don't mean just to "win" the argument in front of others. It's quite possible to "win" an argument and lose a friend.

4. Talk in a nonstressful place and time. Calm down before you heat up. Call a personal "time out," walk away, agree to disagree. Rarely has stress, alcohol, or anger helped resolve anything. Stress, alcohol, and anger can dissolve, not resolve, relationships.

5. Leave an open door. That means never bringing the disagreement to an end with statements like: "That's it. We're done. It's over." "Get out of here. I never want to see you again." Or "I'll never change my mind, so we should just go our separate ways." Instead, tell your friend you will talk about it later.

Stage Three: Thrive ... Peacemaking

Think about a conflict in your life. It could be with a roommate, a parent, a professor, or a friend. Using the list below, describe how you might handle the situation. Refer to the list at left for examples.

> "Blessed are the peacemakers."
> —*Jesus of Nazareth*
> *First century, A.D.*

1 Describe the conflict in specific terms:
_____
_____
_____

2 Write a statement about the conflict that does not blame or moralize:
_____
_____
_____

3 Specify a setting where you could discuss the conflict privately:
_____
_____
_____

4 Describe how this setting and time will not contribute to the stress of the discussion:
_____
_____
_____

5 Write an example of a statement that will leave an open door between the two of you:
_____
_____
_____

Diversity 12

> **"We all should know that diversity makes for a rich tapestry, and we must understand that all the threads of the tapestry are equal in value no matter what their color."**
>
> —Maya Angelou
> Autobiographer and
> Pulitzer winning poet

PERSPECTIVES

When author John Grisham addressed the 2007 graduating class from The University of Virginia, his commencement speech called for three abilities from the students in order to be successful. They were:

TALENT:	The ability to find your passion
PERSERVERANCE:	The ability to handle rejection, and
LUCK:	The ability to spot an opportunity you weren't looking for

It was a brilliant and humorous address delivered with Grisham's beautiful humility.

I want you to carry these abilities with you as you read this chapter.

Talent: Find the passion in one of the perspectives to help yourself feel welcome and develop a sense of belonging essential to going the distance. You have the ability to find your unique talent, your passion. Let one of the Perspective "Guides" I have asked you to write mentor you toward your goals.

Perserverance: Each of my friends who have contributed mightily to this chapter have faced rejection and have risen above it. Let their stories give your perspective and enhance your ability to perservere and rise above rejection or disappointment.

Luck: I do not know what you are expecting in the Diversity chapter. I ask you to be open to the opportunity to grow that you may not have originally been looking for. Maybe you had to read it as a class assignment. Perhaps you are tired of diversity as a topic. It could be you think nobody really understands your struggle. Read on! Please. Be open to the possibility that with a little luck, we might all just learn something here about one another.

> **"We all have culture. It's just that some folks don't think they do."**
>
> —Mona Jones
> Poet and educator

Different perspectives.
Different voices.
Different races, genders, and orientation.

ONE UNIFIED CALL FOR UNDERSTANDING & RESPECT

You are humbly invited into this chapter to meet some amazing people and hear their unique stories.

❖ ❖ ❖

> "I feel my heart break to see a nation ripped apart by it's greatest strength - it's diversity."
> —*Melissa Etheridge*
> *Singer, songwriter, & activist*

WILL'S NOTE: I met Joe when he was an undergraduate student at the University of Redlands in California. We have been friends for over 20 years. I have watched him grow from a young, extremely bright teenager with a thousand questions into a husband, father, civic servant, and lawyer with great insight. I am proud of him, and his words will inspire and challenge you. When I asked him to help with the Diversity chapter he said, "Absolutely. Whatever I can do to help students find their way."

Joe encourages us in "Diversity Is A Strength" to:
  I. **Have a positive self-image.**
  II. **Listen to ourselves and each other better.**
  III. **Seek dialogue with the rest of the world.**

We can all be proud of our culture, homelands, and ethnicity, <u>AND</u> find our greatest strength in the understanding and appreciation of diversity as a strength. *Thank you, Joe!*

DIVERSITY IS A STRENGTH
By Joe Richardson, Esq.

America, in becoming more and more diverse, is just following the reality of the rest of the world. The definition of diverse in the *Merriam-Webster's Dictionary* is "differing from one another." As people, it is a natural instinct to want to categorize. We do it at home with our clothes and our things (i.e. now, where does this *belong?*), and since the beginning of time, we have done it with each other. Right or wrong, categories underlie most conflicts you see, be it in Congress or on the battlefields during war. We see each other in ways that we think will protect and shield us. Now, that may be fine when we're talking about obvious extremes. For instance, when you see someone who is walking down a city street with a gun drawn and pointing it at people, then you know you aren't supposed to be "hanging out." However, that is not fine when we are talking about other human beings who look different, come from different places, speak with an accent (related to region, culture or otherwise), worship differently or who otherwise make us uncomfortable just because they represent "something else." It's somewhat ironic, but we can free ourselves to recognize and embrace differences because the exercise teaches us that we are so much the same. Here are some steps for us to embrace diversity as strength, both in school and in life:

I. **HAVE A POSITIVE SELF-IMAGE**

   A. Once you see that you are a powerful, positive, principled person, you can visualize yourself in the role of a participant, and a leader, in the *whole world,* while still remembering, and prioritizing, issues that concern and move you related to race, culture, or class. I am an African-American lawyer in a diverse state (California). Yet, not even 5 percent of lawyers in California are African-American. I rarely see another African-American lawyer in Court, even when the docket has 20 or more cases to be heard (usually meaning 40 or more lawyers). I was prepared for this because I had to be. My parents believed that I needed to be around all types of people, and so my "culture shock" began relatively early, in 7th grade. In weeks, I met a pal who would become my best friend and is to this day. When Steve invited me to his bar mitzvah, I had to get some info on what it was. What did we have in common? Many things: we both loved basketball and we were huge USC fans (no offense whatever school you may be reading this from). We also liked all kinds of people, were open to other points of view, and were good listeners.

   Many people could not imagine being in a situation where only 4% of the students looked like you, as I was in college. But the key was that, by then, I knew to look past the differences of how people looked. I knew there was much to learn by listening and confirming what we had in common. I went on to be student body president and on to law school and into the practice of law. I owe a debt I could never repay to my University; they provided the environment that I was fortunate enough to see my way clear to participate in and contribute to. But I had to make a decision to take advantage of the environment, just like you do. And you do that by taking part, rooted with a self-image that does not react to diversity with timidity, insecurity, dislike, or hatred.

> "Many people could not imagine being in a situation where only 4% of the students looked like you, like I was in college. But the key was that, by then, I knew to look past how people looked."
>
> —Joe Richardson, Esq.
> Attorney at Law

> "True understanding can only begin when we recognize that other points of view exist."
>
> —Joe Richardson
> Attorney at Law

Money could not buy the lessons that I learned about people being fundamentally very alike, while different, going back now more than 25 years. To this day, I love and enjoy being around all types of people. You can embrace both the similarities and the differences. In being able to do so in your own educational and life experiences, you will find that this is the essence of thinking and conducting yourself as a leader.

II.   LISTEN TO OURSELVES AND EACH OTHER BETTER

We often get in trouble because of our tendency to outright demonize any point of view that we do not understand. Of course, we have to believe that our individual feelings and opinions are valid, as based on personal experiences, observations, and reflections. However, we must also realize that the feelings of others are no less valid, as they are likewise based on experiences, observations, and reflections. While I had a good childhood growing up in South-Central Los Angeles, my environment and experiences have naturally influenced issues that I am passionate about. However, that is no less true for my friends from West Los Angeles, from the farm in Oklahoma, or from the suburbs of the east coast.

One of the most interesting times I had in law school was when the (first) O.J. Simpson case was being played out on television. While we were a friendly law school environment filled with students and professors with mutual respect for one another, I never saw such diametric opposition when the case came to be decided. It amazed me that individuals that were taking the same law school classes, eating and living together could look at the case and not only disagree, but react with amazement and shock that any other viewpoint than theirs even existed.

Remember the "Amphitheatre Theory." I remember going to a concert with a friend and my best friend's mom Janis more than 20 years ago. (My best buddy Steve liked music, but not enough to go the concert.) My friend and I sat together in the upper left corner of the amphitheater, while Janis had a seat in the lower level, dead center. (And if you want to know, it was the Beastie Boys and Run-DMC.) After the concert, we were amazed that Janis saw some different things than what we'd seen. It was literally like she was at another concert.

How you see things will often begin with where you sit. If you are in the theater on the left side of the stage, you have to look to the right to see the action. If you are on the right side, you have to look to the left. Each of our views can be valid, while they are different.

True understanding can only begin when we recognize that other points of view exist. That is, it should not hurt at all for you to recognize that another person in your class, fraternity, or student government sits somewhere else in the amphitheatre of life. This is a strength and benefit because you can use them to solidify your own point of view, or to even modify your thoughts in some ways. In fact, most of the time, some of both will end up occurring. With recognition comes sensitivity; when you recognize another view point exists, you can be sensitive to that viewpoint and start to more objectively examine it "on the merits" (as we say in law). With sensitivity comes progress; suddenly, or more often over time, you have become sensitive enough to a point of view where you embrace it and act on it. Most great accomplishments in civil and human rights have come about because people that were outside of the situation came to understand the plight of people in the situation. What underlies this progress, again, is the recognition of this concept of "sameness through diversity." When we get to the point where we recognize that "helping him, her, or them is helping me," we have set ourselves up for the next great chapter in our individual and collective stories for our college campus, our community, our country and our world.

> **A QUESTION**
> Where do you sit in the "Amphitheatre of Life"?
> —*Dr. Will Keim*

III. SEEK DIALOGUE WITH THE REST OF THE WORLD

If we have a positive self-image and listen to ourselves and each other better, we are free to seek dialogue with the rest of the world in everything that we do. In essence, we will find ourselves more equipped to contribute to our community, country and world. This expectation will allow you to broaden your horizons by thinking of involvement opportunities in school, career, and other opportunities after the school years that will allow you to maximize your contribution to the world around you. I am absolutely thrilled that I get to use my "gift for gab" and love of speaking in convincing judges and juries that they should find for my client. The recognition and understanding of the different points of view that are represented in that judge or that jury, however, gives me great insight as to what may or may not be successful, and how to approach my case.

Think of your life as Marketing 101. While you have thought to yourself (hopefully) what you may be passionate about and what college major can help facilitate that, also ask yourself , "How do I sell myself to everyone who needs to 'buy'?" People need to be convinced of your objectivity, your ability to understand (and perhaps even persuade) others, and your passion in being a good representative in who you work for, volunteer for, and of what you believe in.

> "Think of your life as 'Marketing 101' ... embracing and understanding diversity is key. People need to be convinced of your objectivity, your ability to understand others, and your passion in being a good representative of who you work for, volunteer for, and of what you believe in."
>
> —Joe Richardson
> Attorney At Law

In all of this, embracing and understanding diversity is key. Responsible individuals weigh in on the things that are happening around them. That's how bad things are made good, and good things are made better. I have been privileged to be part of a local Rotary club, where the motto is "service above self." In this pursuit, Rotary International has nearly eradicated polio all over the world. Having a positive self-image, listening to oneself and others, and seeking a dialogue with the world are three keys to living successfully in a diverse world.

The Amphitheatre Theory Exercise: Identify an experience you have had where "where you sat" or your perspective altered the way you heard or saw the event. Was it a concert, class, accident, family dinner, sporting event, etc.

List five things that might have impacted your perspective and contributed to the Ampitheatre Theory (we've listed some possibilities upside down at the end ... don't look until you're done). **Reflect • Remember • Write Them Down:**

_____
_____
_____ = **FACTORS THAT ALTER YOUR PERSPECTIVE**
_____
_____

physical distance from event • amplification • line of site • physical fatigue • alcohol • prejudices • previous experience • time of day • hunger • pain • stress • the way you were brought up • news media • age • ethnicity • socioeconomics • preconceived notions • education

DIVERSITY IS NOT JUST ABOUT RACE
Sami Keim, College Student
Linfield College, OR

> "Diversity is not just about race."
> —Sami Keim

WILL'S NOTE: I have known Samantha Keim all of her life. In fact, I was present at her birth! You see, she is my daughter. When asked to write an essay on Diversity for her college admission to Linfield College in Oregon, she decided to write about her friend Tom Durein. Tommy D. as she calls him, is a successful businessman. He is also my fraternity brother. Sami's essay follows.

Sami Keim
Ms. Egan
College Writing
October 11, 2007

Linfield College Admission Essay

Diversity is not just about race. My parents taught my siblings and me to accept people no matter their race, creed, color, national orientation, or sexual orientation. I have lived by this message. My father's profession was always a key tool in teaching me to embrace others and their differences. He has lectured to students all over the world, and I have been fortunate to travel with him. By the time I was twelve I had been to 49 states, encountered a variety of people, and been submerged in cultures very different from my own. The people that I met while traveling with my dad taught me to believe in equality. Though I have bonded with thousands of people over the years, there is one encounter that truly changed my life, and helped me to establish my own views and beliefs about the world around me.

I met Tommy D. when I was nine years old. Sitting by myself after my dad's speech, waiting for him to finish answering questions, was nothing new to me. Through years of practice, I had mastered the art of entertaining myself; folding the programs into intricate designs or coloring hearts on my dad's business cards always seemed to keep me occupied. As I completed my design, a tall man came and sat next to me. His bubbly personality was obvious right away; indeed anyone who wore a bright pink tie had to be outgoing. People regularly came to tell me how great my dad was, but this was different. Tommy asked questions about me, and quickly we became friends. He was a fraternity brother of Dad, and I fell in love with him right away.

That night after my Dad's speech we all went to dinner. Tommy pulled out my chair for me, and joked about all the boys who would be chasing after me soon. I was in awe of Tommy the entire night. His confident manner, and genuine concern for everyone around him made me respect him even more. He lit up a room, yet was humble at the same time. It was not until the next day after Tommy had left, and we were on our way back home, that my dad delivered the news. Tommy was gay. I had heard this word, but its concept was unfamiliar. My dad explained that Tommy didn't date girls, but instead dated boys. At nine years old, my first response was simple, as I blurted out, "Ok, so I can't marry him?" My dad laughed and called Tommy right away.

Growing up, Tommy D. and I remained close. Every time my dad was speaking at an event that Tommy was attending, I would beg to travel with him so we could set out on another incredible dinner adventure with Tommy. Having him as such a dear friend definitely shaped the way I looked at the world around me. Every single time I heard homophobic slurs, or saw graffiti of hate and intolerance on the bathroom stall walls, memories of Tommy and his wonderful personality flooded into my mind. I would recall his kindhearted gestures, humble ways, and the phenomenal dinners we had shared. I could not apprehend how anyone could be so malicious. Tommy was the most amazing person I had ever met, and yet daily I was reminded of all the hate that was associated with the simple fact that he was gay. I found the phrase "that's gay" offensive, and I noticed a considerable number of people using it in their daily lives. Through my experiences with Tommy I became more aware of just how much homophobia there was not only in my school or my town, but in the world around me as well.

As I got older, I decided that I wanted to sit down and converse with Tommy about his experiences, and what it was like to be gay in our society. He was more than willing to discuss the topic, and once again astonished me with the calm way he approached the conversation. I inquired what it was like to be gay; a question I figured had a simple answer. Tommy smiled and proceeded to respond to that one question for half an hour. It became evident that there were many elements in my life that I took for granted, because I was not gay, that Tommy had to struggle with daily in his. Being glared at in public, made fun of, or loathed by strangers for no reason, were incidents that I never had to experience in my life. Tommy had to live with events such as these almost every single day. I was furious, and I began to feel a mild hate for everyone who didn't believe like I

> "Every single time I heard homophobic slurs, or saw graffiti of hate and intolerance on the bathroom stall walls, memories of Tommy and his wonderful personality flooded into my mind."
> —Samantha Keim

did. I couldn't comprehend why it was such a big deal he was gay. Tommy explained that he wasn't furious, because hating other people for hating him would not resolve the problem. This advice opened my eyes. In one sentence he had summarized the concept of tolerance, a message my parents and teachers had spent my entire life trying to convey to me. Tommy inspired me, and he continues to do so today.

I am now a senior, ready to proceed to college. I am ready to experience a brand-new place, with many dissimilar people who may not have the same views or beliefs that I do. My experiences with Tommy have taught me many important lessons. They have demonstrated the importance of diversity in our lives, and also the key role that tolerance plays in order to keep peace with the people around us. I am prepared to abandon the place I know, and immerse myself into a new place, and different culture. My experiences through the years have readied me to take on a variety of challenges, including accepting everyone around me. Diversity has been extremely meaningful in life, and I will sustain the lessons I've learned wherever I go.

❖ ❖ ❖

Tom Durein's Response:
"When I was given the opportunity to provide response to Sami Keim's reflections of the onset of our very important friendship, I recalled immediately my initial feelings of embarrassment and humility, and then my overwhelming sense of pride and good fortune.

You see, I always believed I'd had it easy growing up. In fact, I knew from a young age that I had it better than most. I was a white male, born to an upper-middle class family, and afforded a well-rounded education that adequately prepared me for personal and professional success early on in life.

I also knew very early on that I was gay.

Early in my professional career, I was able to meet Sami's Dad, Will, who also reminded me that I'm human, and a glaring example of one of our nation's, and higher education's, most important and ongoing cultural and diversity wars.

As I mentioned, when I was fortunate to read Sami reflections, I initially felt embarrassed. Not because I felt undeserving of her

> "Early in my professional life I was able to meet Sami's dad, Will, who also reminded me that I'm human, and a glaring example of one of our nation's, and higher education's, most important and ongoing cultural and diversity wars."
>
> —Tom Durein

admiration and appreciation, but because she found value in something about my life I guess I'd always taken for granted, and yet clearly could have taken me for granted.

Sami is right. Diversity is not just about race. I never really considered myself to be different, or diverse. But Sami helped to remind us that even the most unexpected of life's 'gifts' can be a lesson, and the way in which one copes with being gay, or 'diverse', can be another parable altogether for someone else.

> "Sami is right. Diversity is not just about race."
> —Tom Durein

I was indeed humbled that my ability to overlook challenges typically associated with being gay inspired Sami. From an early age I had little time or energy for things I couldn't control. I grew stronger with each insult or confrontation, addressing circumstances head-in that were beyond my control. And it always reinforced in me that if anyone was going to take responsibility for my future, positive or negative, it was going to have to be me.

I believe one of the things I'm most thankful for in Sami's essay was the reminder that learning comes in the most unexpected of situations. Just like life. Sami not only reminds us that diversity isn't just about race, color or creed, but that much of this world still has a long journey to travel around issues of sexual orientation, civil rights, and basic human understanding.

Her essay helped to remind me of my own good fortune, and the hazard of forgetting where we come from, and who helped us get there. Without Sami, her Dad and Mom, and my own family and mentors, I wouldn't have the strength to remain solid in my own convictions, demonstrating pride and never shame for who I am and how we can make a difference.

And I'm grateful to be living a life that brings me into contact with opportunities to share that strength, potential, and hope each and every day."

> "Diversity affects us all. At times in our nations history, we have all been what I have come to call the 'Group Of The Week'. That is, a group of people looked down upon, put down, or excluded. You could include Italians, Irish, Polish, African, Hispanic, Chinese in that 'Group' to name just a few. The GLBT (QQAI) group receives harsh treatment, taunting, exclusion, and unequal protection under the law. A great prophet once said, 'None of us are free until all of us are free.' Tommy said, 'Hating others for hating me will not resolve the problem.' His words changed Sami's life and I hope they will soften your heart."
>
> — Dr. Will Keim

> "As a black woman I have experienced the thoughtless, bitter words from others because of race and gender. Often I worked hard to keep my tongue from becoming a weapon and prevent my actions from inflicting pain."
>
> —Tondaleya Jackson

Exercise: *From Theory to Practice*

Write about a situation like Sami's where something that had been a concept became real. That is, for Sami, someone being gay was an idea and hating someone was something she had not done. Meeting Tommy D. made it personal and she felt hate for those who despised him. Briefly relate the dynamics of a situation where you learned a life lesson from personal experience and not from a book.

_____
_____
_____
_____
_____
_____
_____
_____
_____
_____
_____
_____

Tondaleya Green Jackson
Thoughts On Diversity
Director of Service Learning & Leadership Development
Benedict College, SC

WILL'S NOTE: Tondaleya is one of the most positive professional friends I know. She has a quick wit, an inviting smile, and a true commitment to her students. I did not know Tondaleya's whole story when I asked her for her "Thoughts On Diversity," but I am so glad I did. She writes with passion and honesty of her own journey and offers students encouragement to respect each other and live a life of dignity, equity, and honor. I was at Benedict College last year with my son J.J., age 16. I asked him, "How did it feel to be in a room with 300 black students and you and me?" He said, "What do you mean?" I honestly don't think he thought about it. I know we are making progress and not without great personal pain. Let Tondaleya take you with her on her journey and learn from it.

> "Our Father, with a chart in Heaven ..."
>
> —Tondaleya Jackson's daughter, during her bedtime prayers

THOUGHTS ON DIVERSITY
by Tondaleya Green Jackson

Every night before bed, my daughter recites the Lord's Prayer. She begins *Our Father with a chart in heaven.* On varying occasions through the years I have attempted to correct my sweet child's misunderstanding of what she hears in this often cited verse. The Lord's Prayer actually begins "Our Father, which art in heaven." *(King James Version Bible, Matthew 6: 9-13).* But night after night before she lies down for the evening, she offers the Lord her unchanging version; *Our Father with a chart in heaven.*

My daughter is six years old, and these days as I find myself correcting her misinterpretation less and less; I find myself thinking more and more about her words long after she has gone to sleep. In fact, each night my child's prayer evokes different thoughts and images that return to the same central theme for me. I openly wonder what would happen if *"Our Father"* truly did sit on the heavenly throne with a chart and recorded all of our daily thoughts, deeds, successes, and missteps. What would our chart say about the person we are? The person we used to be? Or even the person we are becoming? I cannot help but wonder how differently we would behave if we knew all of our actions would be replayed during a daily meeting with *"Our Father?"*

Stage Three: Thrive ... Diversity

The thought of a daily meeting with a higher power to discuss my actions has significance to me. I replay my actions daily, oftentimes analyzing each and every one of my thoughts and deeds, well before and long after they are said and done. I cannot really tell you if I do this because of or in spite of the fact that each and every day I wake up as a black woman in America. As a black woman I have experienced the thoughtless, bitter words from others because of race and gender. These attributes heighten my awareness and make me sensitive to the fact that words and actions have the potential for longstanding impact which can be either positive or negative. Often I work hard to keep my tongue from becoming a weapon and prevent my actions from inflicting pain. Taking into consideration the long, arduous history of both blacks and women in the United States, I consider this fact again, each and every day I wake up as a black woman in America. Born and raised in the Coastal regions of South Carolina where plantations still abound and remnants of the slave/master hierarchy still exists to a degree, I grew up vividly aware of the differences between blacks and whites.

> "To give you perspective, I'm not speaking of a time in the Civil Rights era in the '60s. No, the time I refer to is the late 80's and early 90's."
> —*Tondaleya Jackson*

As a teenager, jobs in the local restaurants and retail stores were hard to come by. In fact rarely, if ever, did you see a young woman of color holding a job in my hometown. Instead black people, woman mostly and some men, boarded buses and rode 45 minutes in the best case and two hours in the worst to serve as maids and housekeepers in hotels and motels in Myrtle Beach, South Carolina. To give you some perspective, I am not speaking of a time in the civil rights era. No, the time I refer to is the late '80s and early '90s. I was one of those people who spent a portion of my youth riding those buses to work. Those long trips up and down the highway to work made me determined to earn a college education and serve as an encouragement to others. While I respect and appreciate the fact that these individuals; family members, friends, and neighbors, worked hard and sacrificed much to make a living wage, I knew I would not spend my adult years working that way.

With the full support of my family, years passed and I completed high school and successfully enrolled in college in 1994 with an academic scholarship. I recall driving home from college in 1995. I was alone, and against my parents' wishes, driving down country roads at night. I had finished up my work earlier than expected on a Friday evening. Instead of waiting until Saturday morning, I decided to get a head start on my weekend. I was young and enjoying the freedom of having a car and setting my own schedule. That night I was driving about 65 mph on a 55 mph road, enjoying the fresh air and listening to the radio. The night was clear and traffic was minimal. About 30 minutes into my drive, I saw a vehicle that seemed to be rapidly approaching. I decided to slow down slightly so they could safely pass on the two lane road. Instead of passing however, the vehicle seemed to inch closer and closer to my bumper. My heart began to pound. No other car was in sight and I had no phone. During those days, the phone would have been pointless because cellular service was extremely limited in this rural area. I started to become even more concerned as the car got closer and closer. I sped up again. The vehicle behind me then sped up as well. Suddenly, the car veered from behind me and proceeded as if it was going to pass; but instead they jerked from behind me and pulled up on my driver side. In the vehicle I could clearly make out three white males. They were yelling racial epithets and gender slurs that could clearly be heard. They were also making sexual gestures with their hands and motioning wildly. That night these young men didn't see a young college student determined to make a difference. No, they saw a "nigger girl" (their words of course, not mine).

At that moment, my life didn't pass before my eyes. Instead, horrible images and physical pain took over me. I quickly realized the nearest town was miles away and we were the only ones on the road. I recalled the horrible, true stories family members had told of how racial hate resulted in hangings, rapes, tortured souls, and even death. I was consumed with a fear so powerful it transcends words. That night I drove like the proverbial bat out of hell and both hands bore into the steering wheel because I did not want my story to end that way.

> "Whatever the driver saw in my eyes, he instantly turned his head away from me ..."
> —Tondaleya Jackson

I don't know if it was fear or inner strength from a source beyond me, but for a brief moment I dared to look at these men and caught the eye of the driver. I'll never know if he saw a human being or a young lady no different than any in his family. Maybe he realized that a prank was suddenly turning into much more for his friends. For you see, I caught the eye of his front seat passenger too; and all I saw was hate. I will always remember the hatred in this young man's eyes. Whatever the driver saw in my eyes, he instantly turned his head away from me. He no longer laughed and yelled with his passengers; instead, after a few brief moments more, he passed my vehicle and drove ahead of me, out of sight. I continued to drive at a record pace, my heart waiting, anxiously anticipating their return. I reduced 90 remaining minutes of drive time to less than 50 minutes. I didn't see or hear anything else that night. When I arrived home, I remained in my driveway, emotionally rattled for a considerable amount of time. I now wonder what *Our Father* would say to these gentlemen at their daily meeting. I also wonder what he would have said to me.

The highway incident while seeming like an eternity was probably about 5 to 10 minutes in actuality. I would later be asked why I didn't stop at the nearest town and call the police, why didn't I file a report. I would replay this incident over and over in mind and I came to the same conclusion: the only thing I wanted to do was get home. Home, not the police, represented safety in mind. The images of that night are indelible and will be with me forever. I can still hear the words and feel the hatred. You see that night my only 'crime' was being a black female driving along a South Carolina highway alone. Unless you share both of those birth traits and have walked a mile in my shoes, I do not fully expect you to realize how difficult a day in the life really can be. I do not ask for pity, sympathy, or admiration; only an acknowledgement of what being both black and female entails in the United States.

With the image of a black female; imagine if you will what it feels like to walk past a table in a restaurant and be stopped by other patrons asking you - a guest like them - "When will you be back for our drink order?" Have you ever been openly followed by a clerk, who stares and never offers his/her assistance? Have you ever been the next in line only to have the cashier look directly past you to the next guest and say, "May I help you?" Have you ever been told by a clerk in an upscale retail store, "This is very expensive. Are you sure you can afford it? We don't accept returns on used merchandise". Do you know what it feels like to be the only person of color or the only person with a particular gender in a classroom, workshop, seminar, lecture hall, etc. and asked, "How do you all feel about (fill in the blank with any subject that requires me to speak for an entire race or gender of people)?" The examples are endless, but I feel certain that by now you get the point.

What matters more than my response in these situations is the pain that I was left to bear long after the situation transpired. In each case, the "offender" was a caucasian or a male who immediately made an assumption about me solely because of my race and/or gender. I place "offender" in quotes because in some of these instances I do not believe it was the intent to offend; some of the statements and actions resulted from the individual's biases, which may have been taught or

> "What we have to do ... is find a way to celebrate our diversity and debate our differences without fracturing our communities."
>
> —Hillary Rodham Clinton
> U.S. Secretary of State

learned. If you are a person of color belonging to any one of America's minority groups, you can probably add a few examples of your own. And, if you are a part of the majority race and have had experiences with cultures outside of your own, you too may be familiar with a similar occurrence that transpired with a family member or friend.

Equally as disconcerting as the situation itself, is the fact that there will be many of the majority, however, who will immediately offer explanations and rationalizations that are designed to quickly and quietly explain away each of these situations. They refuse to acknowledge that race and gender are still dominating factors in today's society. In fact, some individuals would even go so far as to admonish me for "blowing the situation out of proportion," a comment that has been openly made on occasion by colleagues during discussions of race and gender.

I have concluded that unfortunately, some will never take the time to fully understand the hurt and longstanding pain that results from each of these situations. More optimistically however, I believe that many more persons than not would welcome open dialogue and opportunities for understanding why situations that may seem harmless to some, cause so much pain to others. I strongly feel if given the forum, many would openly and honestly address these issues. The United States Secretary of State Hillary Rodham Clinton said, *"What we have to do...is find a way to celebrate our diversity and debate our differences without fracturing our communities."* For these reasons, I believe diversity education can never simply be a request in this country. For those who will not seek to educate themselves, the educational systems of our country must do so instead. William J. Edwards an African-American educator, says it best: *Education is the source of all we have and the spring of all our future joys.*

> "Education is the source of all we have and the spring of all our future joys."
> —*William J. Edwards*
> *Educator*

My previous adversities are what makes diversity education so important to me. Those past experiences as a young adult helped to define the woman I am. I chose not to become a bitter person, making every person I encounter responsible for the past hurts inflicted by others because I too am a firm believer in education and its limitless possibilities. As an education major I earned South Carolina certifications in English, Middle School Language Arts, and Secondary Administration and Supervision. During my years as a public school educator, I made every effort to expose my students to worlds beyond their own. I worked hard to ensure my classroom practices were inclusive of all my students. There was a point in my professional career where I decided I wanted to educate more than I wanted to teach. It was at this time that I made the transition from K-12 to private higher education. I decided the time had come for me to help students in a different capacity. I knew firsthand from my undergraduate academic experience that I wanted to work in higher education and I received the opportunity to do so at Benedict College.

Historically black colleges or universities or HBCUs as they are commonly called, serve a vital role in the education of African - American students. In the Title III Higher Education Act of 1965, Congress officially defined an HBCU, among other things, as an institution whose principal mission was the education of black Americans. This mission for HBCUs still holds true today. As a graduate and current employee of an HBCU, I understand and appreciate the role that HBCUs play in the education of all students, but specifically students of color.

> "I understand the role HBCU's play in the education of all students, but specifically students of color."
> —Tondaleya Jackson

For the past decade I have had the privilege of working at an HBCU. Benedict College is a private, liberal arts, historically black college in Columbia, South Carolina. The College's mission statement says: "We will be a full opportunity college with high quality programs of teaching, research, and public service." Currently, I serve as the Director of Service-Learning and Leadership Development. In this capacity I, with the assistance of my staff, am responsible for helping to facilitate the service component of the College's mission statement. We ensure each of the College's enrolled students meets the College's requisite academic service-learning and seminar requirements and engages in leadership development opportunities. Service-learning partnerships include school districts, non-profits, and a host of agencies and organizations that work with a wide range of racially, culturally, and ethnically diverse persons. The academic-based seminars are general education courses that serve as the vehicle by which service-learning is implemented and simultaneously the platform by which opportunities for freshmen and sophomores to become acclimated to the college environment exists. Seminar topics include time management, effective test-taking strategies, and many more academically-centered topics including diversity. Each of the aforementioned provides students with access to enrichment conferences, workshops, topics, speakers, forums, and opportunities in general that will enable them to learn and grow in a globally diverse society.

Many of the African-American students I work with regularly recognize the biases placed upon them by pre-conceived societal norms; yet ironically they must be made to realize they too have placed biases, prejudices, and pre-judgments upon others. It is imperative that students of the 21st Century recognize and understand diversity extends far beyond black and white, male and female. As defined in the College's mission statement, Benedict seeks "geographic, international, and racial diversity in our student body, while continuing to facilitate the empowerment, enhancement, and full participation of African Americans in a global society." In my position, I apply for educational grants and other types of funding that help to give students opportunities they might not have otherwise. Exposing students to culturally diverse and enriching experiences removes many of the underlying misconceptions that negatively impact diversity efforts. I receive a special satisfaction anytime students openly share their previous biases and tell me how they have grown as a result of participating in some off-campus travel, conference, workshop, training, etc. that I helped to make possible. These are the moments when I know I am making a difference in someone's life. Providing students with these opportunities for growth is a large part of why I find my work at the College personally and professionally fulfilling.

> "Therefore all things whatsoever ye would that men should do to you, do ye even so to them; for this is the law and the prophets."
> [KJ version, Matthew 7:12]
> —Jesus of Nazareth speaking on ethics

Diversity is commonly defined as difference or variety. To fully realize this difference and respect the variety that diversity brings, we can begin by embracing the Golden Rule. *Matthew 7:12 says*: "Therefore all things whatsoever ye would that men should do to you, do ye even so to them: for this is the law and the prophets" *(King James Bible)*. The scriptural version is most often simply stated as treat others as you want to be treated.

While I referenced the Christian version above; the concept of the Golden Rule can be found in many of the world's religions. In the Baha'i Faith, Baha'u'llah says: "Ascribe not to any soul that which thou wouldst not have ascribed to thee, and say not that which doest not. Blessed is he who preferreth his brother before himself." Confucious says, as found in the *Analects 15:23*: "Do not do to others what you do not want them to do to you." And in Islam: "None of you believes until he wishes for his brother what he wishes for himself" *(Number 13 of Imam Al-Nawawi's Forty Hadiths)*. A number of similar comparisons can be found at the following link source: http://www.religioustolerance.org/reciproc.htm.

While it sounds pretty cliché, the fact remains that if we genuinely treat other human beings in the same manner that we would want to be treated, the world would truly be a better place. I encourage each of you to go forth and embark upon a journey that will allow you to embrace opportunities to interact with and better understand persons from diverse backgrounds. No magic wand, mysterious fairy, or secret formula will suddenly make the world a better place. While social networking sites offer us opportunities to connect when traveling is not an option, keep in mind that nothing replaces genuine interactive dialogue. Through these thoughtful exchanges, you will find your beliefs have expanded and your journey filled with knowledge, understanding, and tolerance.

> "Exposing students to culturally diverse and enriching experiences removes many of the underlying misconceptions that negatively impact diversity efforts."
> —Tondeleya Jackson
> Benedict College

Setting aside your spiritual, or lack thereof, beliefs momentarily, I dare you to consider the possibility of a higher power recording your actions on a chart in heaven. The mere thought, if embraced, no matter how loosely, might persuade you to behave differently. I encourage you to make sure you will be proud of your actions, words, and deeds, no matter how big or small, at tomorrow's meeting with 'Our Father with a chart in heaven.'

Exercise: *Your Diversity Chart*

List and discuss one project, program, or thing you have done to empower someone less powerful, less prestigious, different, or poorer than yourself. [This can be your participation in a club or group project.]

_____
_____
_____
_____
_____
_____
_____
_____

How did you feel when the project was complete? _____
_____
_____
_____

> "I have taken control of my destiny in the Spirit of Community."
> —Jesus Jaime-Diaz

Jesus Jaime-Diaz
Master's Candidate, OSU

WILL'S NOTE: Jesus is every educator's dream. He approached, no, charged me after a lecture and asked what I thought he should do with his life. So I told him. I'm not a counselor. I respect counselors deeply, I just don't have their patience.

❖ ❖ ❖

Jesus: "What should I do with my life?"

Will: "Finish your AA at Blue Mountain Community College. Come to Oregon State and get your B.A. Then we'll get you in a Master's Program and you can begin to tell your story and do what you want which is help your community. Then the Ph.D., and …

Jesus: "Whoa … Dude … Slow down."

Will: "Whoa … Dude … You Speed Up!"

Jesus: "I was in a Gang."

Will: "Are you killing anybody at the moment?"

Jesus: "No."

Will: "Good. We can work with that."

Jesus: "I'm married."
Will: "Do you love her?"

Jesus: "Yes."

Will: "Good. We can work with that."

Jesus: "You make it sound possible."

Will: "You've already done the hard stuff. You survived. You didn't give up. You didn't get bitter. You're not in jail. You're not on drugs. You are a Survivor. Now we get to the fun stuff."

Jesus: (tears)

Will: (tears)

Jesus/Will: (hug)

He's doing it! I have taken him to Dallas, TX with me, where he blew the room away. Geoffrey Canada of the Harlem Children's Zone, Ron

Clark, of the Ron Clark Academy, Dr. Debbie Silver, and Dr. Bonnie Davis, hugged him and asked for his card. He will inspire tens of thousands, maybe millions!

You are writing your own story. Let Jesus' journey inspire you to achieve your dream. It if doesn't kill us, it makes us stronger, and no one holds us down except ourselves. It is an honor to be his teacher, and his friend. Now Jesus gives us a life lesson!

THE FIGHT TO ACHIEVE FULL POTENTIAL
Jesus Jaime-Diaz

Introduction

We all have our unique stories and struggles. We correlate them with trials and tribulations in order to make sense of the lives we live and the meaning of our life in this world. I will be talking about how I am trying to achieve my full potential from a Chicano perspective. By that I don't mean a specific ethnic group, but the ideology that one is never closer to themselves then when they are connected to their community. The community I talk about is one of hopelessness, despair, anger, and self-hatred. It is where I grew up.

Family Situation

I recall as a kid how hard my mom and dad would work to make ends meet. At times they would both work two jobs to try and make ends meet to try and provide a better way of life for their kids. They for some reason believed that money would solve everything; however they were not able to see the effects of culture conflict on their children. I remember as a kid it was rare when we would see our parents; my mom was always drained of energy, she had to work full time and raise six children and my dad was always upset at the way life was. He would come back from work yelling at us for anything and everything. It felt like we were in some kind of military boot camp. My dad believed that a man had to be a strong worker with his hands. It is what was instilled in him, and what he indoctrinated into his kids. I remember as a kid he would take us to work out in the field in sub-zero weather to "learn how to be men," I remember at times I could not feel my toes or my fingers, sad to say I would even cry. I hold no negative feelings toward my father - he only tried to instill discipline in his children the only way he knew. However, when I recall those days I

> **"When one is not fulfilled in life, they are not happy. When you are not happy within yourself, how can you possibly shine happiness on someone else?"**
>
> —Jesus Jaime-Diaz

do become very sentimental. I believe that constant labor is what eventually led to the separation and eventual divorce of my parents. When one is not fulfilled in life, they are not happy. When you are not happy within yourself how can you possibly shine happiness on someone else? Their constant domestic violence had a drastic affect on their children. We were exposed to so much negativity it eventually carved a path in the lives we would live when we would start families of our own. In a way it would be a very destructive one.

The Negative Effects of Racism

The primary reason why racism is used in society is to dehumanize a person. It makes you respond with high emotions, and thus blinds you from being able to think critically. I remember as a kid I would always try to get along with people, but I always felt the indifference towards me. Kids did not want to play with me, teachers had little patience with my ability to learn. No matter how hard I tried to fit in, I was excluded. With time, this rejection turned into a destructive vehicle of self-hatred and violence. I, along with friends, began to defy racist bigotry through violence and intimidation. Many of these kids are unsung heroes, because they challenged inequality in the only way they knew how. They felt the sting of rejection and they fought it, to try and sustain a level of self-worth. However, with time, they paid a heavy price. As I fought my way through the trenches of my teenage years, I did not care for school. The treatment it seemed was always about disciplining us rebels without a cause. We were never asked as kids, "What is wrong? What is it that hurts?" It was always a "swim or sink mentality." You learn our ways or you will be a nobody in this world. The interest in school was taken away by using a war of position, with its primary weapon being racism. With time I, along with many, would be dehumanized by the racist criminal justice system and hounded by elements of law enforcement. This made me have further hate towards white people. I had only met mean-spirited Anglos that looked down upon me, my culture and way of life.

With time, the racism I endured succeeded in achieving its purpose, and that would be to put me in a subservient position of an intensive laborer. However, I would eventually escape the entanglement of modern defacto segregation. I would break out to be a voice for those deemed as the wretched in society by some.

> "In life the pain you carry can serve as a tool to motivate you."
> —Jesus Jaime-Diaz

Overcoming Barriers, the Breakout

In life the pain you carry can serve as a tool to motivate you. I remember when people would talk about school, I would feel a hurt of failure. I did not like to feel like I had not achieved anything in my life. All of my family had dropped out of school, except my youngest brother. However, one of my brothers had gotten his GED, while incarcerated. I decided that I would get my GED, to feel better about myself, but also to serve as a role model for my youngest brother in high school. A month into my GED schooling my youngest brother passed on in a house fire. I felt there was no point in living. However, he was a fan of the OSU Beavers, and before he passed on we had talked about him attending college when he finished high school. I decided to make him a promise and go on a crusade of higher learning in his memory.

Positive Influences along my Journey

I remember a wonderful lady by the name of Jeannie Lockwood at Blue Mountain Community College in Hermiston, Oregon. She was one of my GED teachers who gave me so much positive reinforcement. I remember she would say to me, "Go to school to wake up everyday in the morning loving what you do. Don't see life as a job." I remember she said I had the life experience to make a difference in many people's lives. This lady I believe was an angel. She got me through the hardest days I have had to face in life, soon after my little brother passed on. Sadly, a year after I began community college, she passed on from cancer. She worked up until almost her last day in this world teaching her students. Wherever she is, I thank her for her kindness. As I continued through community college, I worked, and I can happily say that I paid for my Associate degree. I would work on the weekends and go to school during the week. During my time in community college, there are so many people that I am thankful to for my development. I became a student ambassador, and also part of student government. The biggest contribution to my community college was in starting a MEChA (Student Movement Chicanos of Aztlan) chapter, and assisting in the development of a multi-cultural center. At the time, I knew I was on my way to OSU. But my goal was criminal justice and to eventually become a DEA agent. What a coincidence - I wanted to be apart of the same system that had oppressed me so much as a kid. That would all change on a trip I would take to San Diego California, for a student leadership conference as student government officer. At the conference, I would be introduced to Dr. Will Keim and his inspirational rhetoric. After he

> "Go to school to wake up every morning loving what you do. Don't see life as a job."
> —Jeannie Lockwood

spoke, I introduced myself to him and told him I was from Northeastern Oregon. He told me he was from Corvallis, Oregon. What a miracle that we crossed paths. He told me I could make a difference, but that I would have to tell my story, in order to inspire other people. I agreed and prepared to enter the university and accomplish my promise and purpose in life. There have been so many people that have given me encouragement, and I am sorry that I cannot name you all at the moment. I want to thank my wife for standing by me through the worst of times, I hope at the end of it all you know it was worth it.

Educational Accomplishments

In June of 2002, I received my GED through Blue Mountain Community College, In June of 2005, I received my Associate of Arts Oregon Transfer Degree (AAOT), in June of 2009, I graduated from Oregon State University (OSU), with a double major in Ethnic Studies with an emphasis in Chicana/o Studies and Speech Communication. I am currently a graduate student at OSU pursuing my Master of Arts in Interdisciplinary Studies, with an emphasis in Adult Education, Speech Communication & Ethnic Studies. I hope to eventually pursue my doctorate in Adult Education with an emphasis in community college leadership. I don't write down my accomplishments to brag. I write them to reinforce my self-determination, and how I have taken control of my destiny in the spirit of community. We can stand by and let racism dominate us, or we can become a spiritual guerilla fighters and redefine our self worth as human beings. **It is your life. Live it fully!**

> "You can become a spiritual guerilla fighter and redefine your self worth as a human being."
> —Jesus Jaime-Diaz

"They said that the wretched had no hope. It has been proven wrong."

Jesus Jaime-Diaz

Stage Three: Thrive ... Diversity

Exercise: *"Like A Phoenix"*

List three experiences that at the time seemed discouraging, degrading, or devastating. Then, describe the life lesson that you learned, either immediately or later, from that event.

Experience	Life Lesson
(Will) My Dad died earlier than I expected	(Will) I will never take life for granted
(Jesus) No one would let me play four square	(Jesus) I will try hard to make everyone feel included
YOU	**LESSON**

1. _____

2. _____

3. _____

> **"No one can make you feel inferior without your consent."**
>
> —*Indira Gandhi*
> *1917-1984*
> *Prime Minister of India*

> "The great human drama is that our hopes are held hostage by our fears."
> —Tray Robinson

Tray Robinson
Students Affairs Administrator, CSUC

WILL'S NOTE: I met Tray on a retreat I facilitated for Chico State University. We hit it off right away because "we think we're funny." Sharing a laugh led us to a conversation about education, today's students, and world events.

His personal story inspired me to ask him to share it with you. He is a strong advocate for all students everywhere, and I know he would respond if you contacted him. He is a firm believer in individual response ability and he advocates each person's inalienable right, and responsibility, to life, liberty, and the pursuit of happiness.

"If you keep living you will learn" and other gems will inspire you to find your place in the academic community. It is up to me, and you, to be as Gandhi urged, 'The Change we hope to see in The World.'

❖ ❖ ❖

IT'S UP TO YOU!!
Tray Robinson

College is great because of the living-learning environment that it cultivates. Most of you will make great strides in self-discovery and may meet your future work colleagues, bosses, or employees during these years. A few of you will even meet your future spouses (like I did…don't get nervous!). The campus of life, just like your college or work environment, is a blend of diverse people from all walks, persuasions, and classes. They will have diverse experiences, opinions, and points of view. More importantly, your educational experiences are a prelude to the world you will see when you leave, and be in, for more than just the relatively brief time in which you go to school. What may be a bit more obvious during the "student years" is really what is true for all of us: we are supposed to push ourselves to learn as much as possible, and that process never ends.

If you keep living, YOU WILL LEARN. Because you have a positive self-image (step one), and you can listen to others objectively. Because different styles, viewpoints, or perspectives do not make you insecure (step two), you will seek dialogue (here and elsewhere-step three) with those that you do not have dialogue with yet. If you start with this now, college (outside the classroom as much as inside) can be preparation for life.

The great human drama is that our hopes are held hostage by our fears. To get at something we want, we have to face something we're scared of. (If you want to learn how to swim, you can't do it without the water). As a society, we have to face the still very real fear that we feel, both of being different and of seeing differences. We should always be reminded that diversity is strength. Make a choice to be a conduit for understanding, for peace, and for progress. Your college years are a dress rehearsal for life. In this dress rehearsal, remember your peers are your audience, now and forever. And if you remember the strength that is rooted in our diversity, you will do fine with your audience, winning them over with your objectivity, your hard work, and team spirit. And YOU WILL WIN!!

> "To get something we want, we have to face something we fear. If you want to learn to swim, you can't do it without the water."
> —Tray Robinson

My friend and brother Dr. Will Keim asked me to respond to five questions. I have been very honest in hopes my responses will help you arrive, survive, thrive, and aspire higher in college.

What have been your greatest challenges personally and professionally?

Growing up in Compton, California and moving approximately 500 miles north to attend Chico State University was one of the most challenging experiences of my life. I was moving from a familiar environment that was predominately African American and Latino (Latino population mostly Mexican) to rural Chico, California, a predominately white environment. I can recall my first trip to Chico on the Greyhound Bus which took us through farming communities smaller than any city I had ever seen. We passed many almond trees, rice farms, Holstein cows, and large trucks; I thought to myself, "What and the hell am I getting myself into." As we arrived in Chico, I was intrigued by the beauty of the campus community, which consisted of beautiful large trees, creeks and amazing architecture. I was reminded of an oasis. This would be my new home for the next several years, and I would do everything in my power to embrace it, regardless of the fear which existed within me. God would never give us more than we could bear.

Before attending Chico State, I only had one white classmate - that was during my junior year in high school and he was the football coach's son. It was a new experience for both myself, my white friend Bobby, and my fellow classmates as we all dealt with perceptions and stereotypes that existed among both races.

My formal K-12 education did not prepare me for what I was to experience at Chico State, both educationally and culturally. I was

> "Bouts of depression, anxiety attacks, and being fed up with lying to my friends and loved ones forced me to come out of the closet in 1995 and I felt liberated. Those were some of the most trying times of my life, but my faith, friends, and love for humanity allowed me to prevail."
>
> —Tray Robinson

surrounded by cultures that were unfamiliar to me as I attempted to navigate my way through college. I was also trying to deal with issues of remediation, as my college entry exams did not produce the necessary scores to place me in the appropriate math and English classes that would count towards my degree. Not having access to the cultural resources that I was accustomed to back in Compton also wore on me. There were no barbershops, limited cultural restaurants, no true hip hop radio station, and very few students, faculty, and staff who looked like me. In addition to dealing with educational and cultural issues, I was also trying to deal with my sexuality. Growing up in an environment that was consumed with gangs, drugs, prostitution and killings did not allow me to deal with being gay, so I thought Chico would provide me with a new start in doing so. Bouts of depression, anxiety attacks and being fed up with lying to my friends and loved ones forced me to finally come out of the closet in 1995, and I felt liberated. Those were some of the most trying times of my life. But my faith, friends and love for humanity allowed me to prevail. My motivation to complete my undergraduate degree was to prove my eleventh grade high school English teacher wrong, who laughed at me when I told her I wanted to go to college. I also wanted to be the first person in my immediate family to graduate from college. As I walked across the stage to receive my diploma, it was in honor of my father who passed away a few months prior. Though he was not sitting in the audience with my friends and family members, his spirit surrounded me.

Being one of the few black employees on the college campus in which I am employed can be stressful at times. There is always a constant pressure to be a positive representative of my black community, primarily due to negative perceptions and stereotypes that plague us. I am often the only black voice in meetings, with an expectation (whether that perception is my own or by others in the meeting) to represent the entire black community. Before coming out of the closet, I was often subjected to gay jokes by my colleagues who did not know I was Gay at the time, and every now and then a derogatory Aids joke by people who did not know that my oldest brother died of Aids in 2000. These experiences provided me with a voice to now speak on behalf of others who are dealing with similar issues. God continues to use me as a vehicle to fight for equality through love, patience and kindness.

Are we making progress?

Being a witness to the election of our first black (though he is truly biracial) president has provided me with a sense of hope. Seeing our students show up to the polls in massive numbers was a testament to the ability of change, yes progress is being made. Having said that, we still exist in a very racist society as we continue to deal with equality issues on sexuality, socio economics, immigration, religion gender, age and ability.

What incident was the most heartbreaking?

Having witnessed the election of our first black president, I was full of excitement and joy; I was overwhelmed with emotions as I thought I would never see this day in my lifetime. Tears ran down my face as my fraternity brother, sister in-law, and I listened to President Obama address the crowd in Chicago, as he was voted in by the people, as the 44th President of the United States of America. The passing of Prop 8 would turn these feelings of hope into anger, frustration and disappointment in my fellow Americans, as I was once again being denied the same equal rights that every heterosexual couple was granted. My partner and I have been together for 14 years and should be able to marry if we choose to. I was depressed and mentally drained. "Why was God not supporting his Gay Children? I know he loves us as he loves all others," I asked myself. I do believe the inequalities we are facing as gay people will someday subside and my American brothers and sister will look back on history and feel ashamed as they have done in regards to the treatment Native Americans, Blacks, Latinos, Asian, Women etc. As Frederick Douglas said, "Without struggle there is no progress."

> "Without struggle there is no progress."
> —Frederick Douglas

What incident gave you the most hope?

Receiving my Bachelors of Arts degree in Liberal Studies Bilingual, I was the first person in my immediate family to both attend college and graduate which provided me with both a sense of hope and accomplishment. I can achieve anything I set my mind to. I felt like "the rose that grew from the concrete." (2 Pac Shakur). There are so many young talented men and women from communities similar to mine who are just as intelligent and ambitious, but are in need of someone who believes in them and is willing to give them an opportunity.

What can students do on their campuses to create a hate-free community that tolerates and affirms diversity as well as creates opportunities for growth for those unsure about how they feel about the issue of diversity?

When focusing on issues of diversity, I strongly believe in starting with ourselves as we attempt to create welcoming communities on our campuses. It is important that we learn about our own identity and first become comfortable in our own skin. It is also important that we recognize and confront false perceptions and stereotypes that we have of others: research what is true and move forward.

We must look at diversity as a global concept and not only focus our energies on race and ethnicity (which are incredibly important), but also deal with issues of sexuality, socio economics, faith, gender, ability, and privilege. We should be advocates and champions for all people, and not feel like we are better than others as we all are human beings, we are brothers and sisters. It is impossible for us to understand everything about everyone; that is the beauty of diversity. But we can learn and respect one another. It is important that we facilitate and participate in diversity trainings as an opportunity to educate ourselves and others about issues surrounding diversity. We have to hire faculty and staff who are committed to fostering diversity on our respective campuses. Diversity has not only to be a documented core value, mission or vision statement at our institutions, but a daily practice that facilitates the way in which they operate and function. It is important that campus leadership (The President and his/her cabinet) challenges the campus to do everything possible to support outreach and retention efforts centered around issues of diversity. Regardless of our role on campus, we should be involved in the process of creating environments that are safe, inclusive and welcoming for all students, faculty, and staff, no matter who they are and where they come from.

> "We should be advocates and champions for all people. We are all human beings. We are brothers and sisters."
> —Tray Robinson

Can you give them the names of five books or resources that might help students learn?

1. Chronicle of Higher Education *Catering to a Diverse Crowd* by Piper Fogg

2. *Ethnicity and Family Therapy*, Third Edition
   Edited by Monica Mc Goldrick, Joe Giordano and Nydia Garcia-Preto

3. *Pedagogy of the Oppressed* by Paulo Freire

4. *A lifetime of Observations and Reflections on and off the Court* by Coach John Wooden with Steve Jamison

5. *Ordinary Men, Reserve Police Battalion 101 and the Final Solution in Poland* by Christopher R. Browning

"My best wishes and God's blessings to you on your journey."
Tray Robinson

Exercise: *You Are What You Read*

List five books that you have read that you believe have helped you and would help others understand you, your ethnic group, or something you are interested in or believe in.

BOOK	AUTHOR
1.	
2.	
3.	
4.	
5.	

Favorite Book of All Time/Author _____

_____.

John Graham
The Power of One

> "Our Strategy is simple: Others see or hear the stories of these remarkable people (Giraffe Heroes) and are moved to stick their own necks out to help solve the public problems they care about."
>
> —John Graham
> Giraffe Heroes
> www.giraffe.org

WILL'S NOTE: John and I became friends at the United States Air Force Academy National Symposium on Character and Leadership when we presented there. His personal story is amazing. (Check out the website)

He affirms "The Power of One" to making a difference. He identifies people willing to stick their necks out to help others, ergo, The Giraffes Project. John believes that a sense of personal satisfaction can come most directly from the joy of serving others, from making life better for them.

He has wandered jungles, rain forests, and the world and has seen things most of us turn our eyes away from. Let him empower you to act with "The Power of One" to change the world one relationship at a time.

❖ ❖ ❖

THE POWER OF ONE
John Graham

As President of the Giraffe Heroes Project, I work every day with "Giraffe Heroes"—people "sticking their necks out" for the common good. These heroes are young and they are old. They are women and they are men. They are every color in the rainbow. They are involved in just about any issue you can think of. Giraffe Heroes are people like:

- Casey Ruud, a safety inspector who put his job on the line when he refused to ignore dangerous safety violations at the Hanford Nuclear plant in Washington State;
- Mimi Silbert, who has devoted her life to "Delancey Street," a program that takes in former prison inmates and turns out hard-working, responsible citizens, who do not return to jail; and
- Neto Villareal, a high school football player who risked losing his college football scholarship when he took a stand against fans' racist insults leveled at him and other Latino players on his team.

The Project acts as a kind of PR agent for Giraffe Heroes. We find them and then tell their stories in books, articles and blogs, on our website, in schools and in the media. We've told the stories of over 1,100 Giraffe Heroes over the last quarter-century. Our strategy is simple: others see or hear the stories of these remarkable people and are moved to stick their own necks out to help solve the public problems *they* care about. Giraffe Heroes are models and catalysts for the rest of us.

> "What drives the heroes to take risks and to work as hard as they do? There was a problem and nobody was doing anything about it, so they had to act."
>
> —*John Graham*
> *Giraffe Project*

What drives these heroes to take the risks and to work as hard as they do, often to no acclaim or reward? When we ask them, often their first response is surprise. What were they supposed to do, they ask? There was a problem and nobody else was doing anything about it, so they had to act.

But the deeper you dig into their motivations, the clearer it gets that Giraffe Heroes do what they do not just because the problems they see are large and urgent. *They act because what they are doing is meaningful to them*—that is, that it satisfies a deep sense of purpose at the core of their beings. Then they let this deep conviction drive them forward.

And when you ask Giraffe Heroes where this sense of meaning, this personal sense of purpose comes from, they'll tell you that it comes from service—from helping solve public problems, from making life better for other people.

Bottom line: It's the personal meaning they find in service that moves Giraffes Heroes to take the risks they do. It's also a major source of their power and charisma. It's what helps make them so inspiring to people who hear their stories and so effective in answering the call from their communities, their nation and sometimes from the world.

This path is not reserved just for Giraffe Heroes. It is open to all of us.

John Graham www.giraffe.org graham@giraffe.org

Exercise: *The Power of One*

1. Identify one person who has positively impacted or changed your life. What did he or she do?

   _____
   _____
   _____
   _____

2. Choose one person you would like to help. What specifically will you to do mentor, advise, or help them?

   _____
   _____
   _____
   _____

3. Visit www.giraffe.com and read an inspiring story of someone sticking their neck out for someone or something else. Read and Reflect. Whom did you read about? What did they do?

   _____
   _____
   _____
   _____
   _____
   _____

> "The wave of the future is not the conquest of the world by a single dogmatic creed, but the liberation of the diverse energies for free nations and free men."
>
> —*John F. Kennedy*
> *1917-1963*
> *35th President of the United States*

Valeria G. Beasley-Ross,
Director of Multicultural Affairs, and
Dr. Charles Ross,
Professor, University of Mississippi

Charles is a native of Columbus, Ohio. Chuck comes from a two parent home. My parents divorced before I finished Junior High School. My mother was one of the first secondary education school teachers to integrate a small country school system in Mississippi where I grew up. Charles' father was a Professor at the Ohio State University and his mother a lawyer. Big city man, small town woman. The fact that we are from different geographic regions has played a major role in our lives. We are both higher education professionals. We are an African American couple. We work on a predominantly white campus, the University of Mississippi that has demonstrated commitment to addressing it's often discussed past.

❖ ❖ ❖

ROSS AND ROSS: AN AFRICAN AMERICAN COUPLE
Charles K. Ross, Ph.D. & Valeria Beasley-Ross, M.S.

Several years ago the 'Ross and Ross' Couple met at a campus program entitled "The Minority Perspective". More than a decade later, we both often wonder ask each other if there was any indication at that time that the two of us would end up married and both still employed by The University of Mississippi?" Our answer … neither of us had a clue. However, we both feel that the way it worked out is "SWEET".

We are Charles "Chuck" Kenyatta and Valeria Lynn Beasley-Ross. We are both African American. We will celebrate our tenth wedding anniversary this upcoming May. Our relationship has been a mixture of fun, rewarding, challenging, and stress-ridden. On most days we would not dare consider changing a single occurrence that facilitated both of us being exactly the couple we are – where we are today.

We are both higher education professionals. We work on a predominantly white campus, The University of Mississippi. Yes, this is the University that many reference when they mention campuses with difficult racial histories. However, The University of Mississippi is also an institution that has also demonstrated commitment to addressing its often discussed past. The two of us have been a part of many positive historical moments on the campus, and we have grown

> "The University of Mississippi is also an institution that has demonstrated commitment to addressing it's often discussed past."
> —*Valeria Beasley-Ross*

to respect greatly and admire the institution where we currently reside as employees.

We have very different backgrounds, but these different backgrounds are probably what have helped us remain not only successful in this marriage but perhaps more importantly "sane." Chuck comes from a two-parent home. Both of his parents are professionals. His father was a professor at The Ohio State University and his mother was an attorney. My parents divorced before I finished junior high school. My mother was one of the first secondary education school teachers to integrate a small county school system in Mississippi. Chuck had a very urban experience growing up. His secondary education experience was in a school where the majority of the students and teaching staff were African American My secondary education experience was spent at a small, rural, predominantly white institution.

> "The fact that we are from different geographic regions has played a major role in our lives. In the beginning it was the source of many disagreements."
> —Valeria Beasley-Ross

I call Chuck "Mufasa" - you know the king of the lions on *The Lion King*. Because he is a very strong, assertive, amazingly intelligent man. (My, does it sound like I am a little biased regarding his greatness). He is a native of Columbus, Ohio. He was born in Gary, Indiana but lived the majority of his life with his parents in Columbus, Ohio. His current position is Director of African American Studies and Associate Professor of History and African American Studies. I am a true Mississippian. I was born in Indianapolis, Indiana but only lived there for the first two months of my life. The remainders of my years have all been lived in the wonderful State of Mississippi and always in very small towns.

The fact that we are from different geographic regions has played a major role in our lives. In the beginning it was the source of many disagreements. I had an idea of what life in the South was, and I felt the need to protect Chuck from himself. When I think about the fact that this is what I thought, I laugh and cry at myself. Chuck comes from a family where his parents were extremely active during the civil rights movement and also various political accomplishments for African American. So, of course, being a quiet soul during difficult situations that stem from race has never been one of his strengths.

I recall an incident Chuck and I experienced while we were dating. We had driven to Vicksburg, Mississippi for Chuck to speak during Black History Month. We decided after Chuck's presentation to tour

Stage Three: Thrive ... Diversity

the city and the end of the tour landed us at Huddle House for a late dinner before heading back to Oxford. We were seated in a booth, and in the booth behind us was a group of young adults (who appeared to be college student age). They were all white, and it sounded as if they had probably had a few drinks. One of the males in the group began to cause a commotion after we sat in our booth and he stated to his friends, "I am not sitting by a nigger woman." I looked up, Chuck was already irate. I, on the other hand had already started to question myself about first whether I had heard him correctly (because I had never been called that word before), and secondly to apologize for the young male because I was absolutely sure he did not realize what he had said. Totally opposite to my behavior Chuck was out of his seat already and asking the person what was his problem and insisting that the person apologize to me. I was petrified. All I could think about was how important Chuck's job at The University of Mississippi was and that he did not need to be in any type of altercation with a white male. This, of course was the furthest thing (based on how Chuck was approaching the person) from my fiancé's thoughts. The situation ended with a security guard in the restaurant throwing the entire group of young people out because they had been bothering other restaurant customers before we arrived. I remember the incident causing us to argue all the way home from Vicksburg.

> "One of the males in the group began to cause a commotion after we sat in our booth and he stated to his friends, 'I am not sitting by a nigger woman.' Chuck was already irate."
>
> —Valeria Beasley-Ross

The argument was a result of what Chuck and I call "blackcoupleitis." Blackcoupleitis causes a myriad of results and requires those who are inflicted to use numerous strategies when faced with racial challenges. One major symptom that those who have blackcoupleitis have to deal with is stress from unique situations that may occur because they are a Black couple. It can additionally have many side effects. The argument that resulted from the incident in Vicksburg was a side effect. I felt we could not react to the name calling by the individual because it could result in a negative repercussion for Chuck. I did not think about the fact that "MY MAN" had the right to stand up for me. Not only did he have the right, I should have expected him to stand up for me, and I should feel that I was worthy of some reaction to the individual's racial slur. Most importantly I should have felt a sense of pride over my man coming to rescue me and I should have felt comfortable supporting my man's strong stance.

After marriage, I am finding that we are oftentimes still the only black couple in the room. It is not longer as uncomfortable–at least not as uncomfortable as it was. Our friends and colleagues must be given credit for this. Sometimes we do have to serve as the Black voice, but most times it is in the presence of people who are respectful of our voices. There are still those challenging moments when during social outings we are the only people of color in the establishment or at another couples home. However, again, we have good friends and this accounts for how well these times work for us.

> "Sometimes we do have to serve as the Black Voice, but most times it is in the presence of people who are respectful of our voices."
> —Valeria Beasley-Ross

Another result of blackcoupleitis is, as a couple, we are often on committees or asked questions because it is believed we represent the voice for the people of color. So, in addition to our on-paper job responsibilities, we have the responsibilities that accompany blackcoupleitis. We have served on the black history month committee together virtually since we have been together. We have been involved in the black faculty and staff committee during this same period of time and we are often expected to help coordinate many of the organization's formal and informal activities. We have been involved in many incidents involving African American students, faculty, and staff that cover a wide range of topics from problems students experience in and outside the classroom, black student organizations and their activities, involvement in athletic recruiting and retention of black student athletes, the recruitment of black faculty, and acting as liaisons to the administration when issues of race impact the larger campus. Few, if any of these involvements, are listed in our job descriptions. However, we believe they are expected, and more importantly, are looked upon as a responsibility of us as a black couple.

We have grown to appreciate each other's perspectives and to use those perspectives when we address issues related to race. As an African American couple on a predominantly working on a predominantly white campus of course there have been challenges. However, I imagine all couples where both people work on the same campus face challenges. One major challenge is you never get away from your spouse; neither can your spouse get away from you. Work becomes merely an extension of your personal home address.

Our relationship requires work, all the time. If we argue during breakfast and the two of us have a meeting together-what do we do? Let me tell you –that situation has happened several times and it is not an easy one to work through. We cannot have a real "I am mad at you moment" because before the end of the day we have to develop some way to be civil with each other or risk everyone knowing we disagree – you know like normal couples do.

In addition to our on the job pressures, we have children, whom we have to remember are our blood kin. We run across many needy people of color. Students who are African American are struggling to fit in. So they visit our offices daily. Sometimes they actually need something; however, the majority of the time they merely want us to do a patch-up job of their emotional and personal needs. Chuck and I love this part of our jobs and we take it very seriously because we never want any students to not thrive in the university's environment merely because his or her skin color has made them feel like they do not belong. The problem here is that we have to remember that we have two college students who are our blood relatives–our daughters (Courtney and Tonell). They must come first. So, we oftentimes have to remind ourselves that our family takes precedence to the situations that blackcoupleitis is facilitating.

We have shared a lot of why it is difficult, and all of the things we shared were true and important. However, the most important part of our story, we feel, is the story of the joys we experience from being a couple that has made it through the challenges. Yes, we have to work on balancing work, family time, personal time, and husband-wife time. We have definitely not mastered these four paradigms, but we do believe we have developed a pretty effective strategic approach. Communication is a major part of this strategy. We talk . . . A LOT! Sometimes about work, children, our parents, and financial matters- but often times-we just talk to each other.

A constant in our relationship has been our early, mid-morning conversations. These conversations consist of one of us waking up (somewhere between 2 am-4 am) and deciding that we just want to have a conversation. Those before-day conversations (we believe) give us balance. Another major part of our balancing strategy is our purposeful planning of time for ourselves. A year ago we spent a week in New York in January. It was one of the happiest and most fulfilling experiences of our life. We recognized after that trip that we must make time to give each other and our marriage our undivided time and attention.

Another key to our happiness, we believe, is our friendship circle. It is one of our most cherished possessions. Our friendship group is

> "We have two college students who we are blood relatives - our daughters Courtney and Tonell. They come first! So we often times have to remind ourselves that our family takes precedence to the situations that 'blackcoupleitis' is facilitating."
>
> —Valeria Beasley-Ross & Dr. Charles Ross
> The University of Mississippi

> "Another key to happiness, we believe, is our Friendship Circle."
> —Valeria & Chuck

diverse. We are fortunate and blessed to have friends from numerous countries and ethnicities, white friends, gay friends, senior citizen friends, young friends, and friends that span all of the recognized class groups in America. Our lives are enriched by this beautiful tapestry of individuals. We share with them when we need professional support or personal support, and we share our sad times and our best times with our friends-our extended family.

Last, and extremely important, is that first and foremost the two of us see each other as friends. We often tell people who ask us about our story that we were best friend's way before we were girlfriend and boyfriend. We knew each other's backgrounds. We both knew the good and the bad on each other, and we grew an unconditional love for each other because we nurtured a friendship into a committed relationship. This nurtured relationship has produced a similar set of values, ethics and goals, so much so, that we often can predict what the other is thinking or what action one is going to take.

Take life one day at a time. Embrace your imperfections and build on your strengths. Challenge yourself to sincerely get to know people-all people. Through explorations with others you will become a better you.

We hope what we have shared will somehow enrich your life.

❖ ❖ ❖

WILL'S NOTE: "I met Val Ross on my first visit to The University of Mississsppi. She works in the Division of Student Affairs and has a keen eye and care for the well-being of all students. We have become good friends. On my second visit to Oxford, she introduced me to her husband Dr. Charles Ross who is a Professor at Ole Miss. They balance their professional lives, their family responsibilities, and their love for one another in an amazing way. They have helped the University of Mississippi, in my opinion, make great strides towards their goal of "Open Doors" and nothing epitomizes this better than the beautiful statue of James Meredith on campus. Val and Charles Ross are helping the University of Mississippi create a bright future plan while being open and honest about the past. P.S. A second great indicator of Mississippi's commitment to the future is the stained glass window in the University Church which weaves together the Christian Cross and The Star of David. A picture of the window hangs in my home in Oregon."

> "Val and Charles are black. Donna and I are white. If you put that aside for a minute ...
> We all work hard to keep our marriages together.
> We have have advanced academic degrees.
> We all worry about and love our children.
> We all care for our aging parents and in-laws.
> We are all teachers.
> We are all believers.
> We are want to be loved and valued, housed, fed, and clothed.
> We have much more in common than we do apart."
> —Dr. Will Keim

Conclusion

It should be clear by now that we believe one person can make a difference and further, that person is you.

- **Right Here**
- **Right Now**

> "We are different, but we have more in common than we do apart."
> —Dr. Walter Kimbrough
> President, Philander Smith College

This is your time to discern your vocational calling, develop self-worth, and value difference or diversity as a great strength. Several of my friends have shared with you their struggles and the things they have overcome. Now it is your turn. All of the perspectives involved someone helping the writers to see into themselves and out into the world.

It is time for you to write your story. A group of high school freshman were asked to write an "All Hands On" poem after my talk with them at 7:40 in the morning! Each student contributed one line. They wrote their story. Read their poem and hear their joys, sorrows, and concerns.

It humbled me to realize that people are listening to what we say and watching what we do. The "All Hands On" poem written by the Crescent Valley High School Freshman Orientation class should convince you that you do matter and you can make a difference.

- **Right Here**
- **Right Now**

An All Hands-On
Poem About Life Inspired by Will Keim, Ph.D.

My life is valuable, so I want to live it up to its fullest.
My life is full of thrilling activities.
My life is short and I want to make the most of it.
My life has changed because of you coming.
My life is not a lot easier to understand.
My life is fun and I need to live the rest of my 20,000 days the same way.
My life is too short to let others live it for me.
My life is full of fun ... I need to live it not take it for granted.
My life is short and I want to make the best of what God has given me to share with others.
My life is full of athletics and academics, but I still have time for family.
My life is only the beginning of masterpiece because what I do will affect my world forever.
My life is going to change because I am going to change from now on.
My life is full of humor; I want to live it the best way I can.
My life is something abstract and random.
My life is exciting.
My life is very interesting, sometimes disturbing, but mostly fun.
My life is my own and I want to live it the best way I can.
My life is good and I hope to keep it that way.
My life is full of hope and positivity.
My life is fun and full of hope.
My life is important to me, so I want to make peace.
My life is full of the opportunity to make the best of what I still have left.
My life matters to me.
My life is full of opportunities to make peace and serve the community.
My life is full of opportunities and I have the change to succeed as much as possible.
My life is going to be better.
My life is made the way I want to live it.
My life is 25,000 days long, live everyday to the fullest.
My life is who I am.
My life is full of opportunities.
My life is peaceful and happy.
My life was a mess, but it's now organized.

Written by B Block Freshmen in Room C4 at Crescent Vally High School

Stage Three: Thrive ... Diversity

Isn't that amazing? They were listening, thinking, and reflecting! Are you? I hope so. Everything is riding on your decision to take yourself seriously and invent your life story, your poem, And then live it into existence.

"I AM" Exercise:

Take a few minutes to write an "I AM" Declaration. It goes like this (using my life as an example):

> "Moses said to God, 'Whom shall I say sent me when I get to Egypt?' And God replied, 'Tell them I Am that I Am sent you.'"
>
> —Old Testament
> *The Bible*

This is the beginning of my Story...

Will

I am a man
I am a husband
I am a father
I am an educator
I am a friend
I am a caucasian
I am _____

*Your Assignment is to do as many "I AM" statements as you can in 10 minutes.

YOUR   STORY   HERE

_____   _____   _____

_____   _____   _____

_____   _____   _____

_____   _____   _____

_____   _____   _____

_____   _____   _____

_____   _____   _____

10 minutes: Keep Going!

> "Knowledge of others is information. Knowledge of self is true power."
>
> —*The Tao Te Ching*
> *Sixth Century B.C.*

When you are finished, after 10 minutes, and if you are honest, you will have a good start on identifying how you see yourself.

Treating others as we would like to be treated and valuing others' experience as we would like to be valued is a powerful first step toward true friendship and understanding.

The appreciation of diversity helps us understand ourselves and the rich tapestry that is our nation. The beauty is to be seen in all the manifestations of the human spirit. Indira Gandhi said: ***"No one can make you feel inferior without your consent."***

AN AFFINITY FOR DIVERSITY

Do you think it is just your professors who are concerned with diversity? Think again! The CEO of Caterpillar, Inc. says: "Certainly it's important that we're diverse in how we look as a company, especially as we work to attract the best talent around the world to serve our customers. But it's even more important that we're diverse in how we think."

Caterpillar's Global Diversity Officers encourage eight "Affinity Groups" to address diversity and thinking in new ways. They are:

- Caterpillar African American Network (CAAN)
- Caterpillar Armed Forces Support Network (CAFSN)
- Caterpillar Asian Indian Community (CAIC)
- Caterpillar Chinese Affinity Group (CCAG)
- Caterpillar Experienced Professional Direct Higher Affinity Group (EPDH)
- Caterpillar LAMBDA Network (CLN)
- Caterpillar Latino Connection (CLC)
- Women's Initiatives Network (WIN)

This is a company committed to "creating a positive culture in which safety, diversity, integrity and performance are highly valued by all" (Peoria Magazine). It would appear that an "Affinity for Diversity" is an emerging corporate value as well as a campus concern.

Dr. Will Keim

Service 13

> **"You can't live a perfect day without doing something for someone who will never be able to repay you."**
>
> —*John Wooden*
> *1910-2010*
> *College basketball coach*

Mentoring others

A bus pulled up in front of the Boys and Girls Club in Camas, Washington. As the children happily lined up to board the bus, an interested passerby asked, "Where are you going?" One little girl giggled excitedly and said, "We're going with the DU guys. They're fun." The Boys and Girls Club director, seeing the quizzical look on the man's face, explained: "We're headed to the Delta Upsilon fraternity leadership Institute in Portland. Everyone had so much fun last week, we're doing it again!" They played ball and tag, juggled, threw footballs, and played pool. A three-hour community-service project had resulted in new friendships. Three hours, and everyone wanted to do it again. Three hours, and a group of children now had a group of young men to look up to—mentors. Every time you serve someone else, somehow your own problems are put in perspective. The small bathroom shared with two roommates is no big deal compared to the beat-up station wagon the kid at the club calls home. The cafeteria chicken is delicious when compared to the peanut-butter sandwich the child will eat today at the club—his only meal of the day. We should all count our blessings, and share them with others.

> **"No one has ever become poor by giving."**
>
> —*Anne Frank*
> *1929-1945*
> *Writer, Holocaust victim*

> "Life is a lot like tennis... How well you do depends largely on how well you serve."

Will speaks:

I am often asked about today's generation of students. Are they selfish? Are they Generation X, Generation Y, The Millenials? Are they Me-Now? I am always amazed with these type of questions because they underscore a real lack of knowledge about young people. No generation to date has given more hours to community service. No group of young people has been more concerned with being "green" and caring for the environment. I have met a student from the University of Mississippi who started a school in Africa on his own after a visit there. A young man from Wake Forest University collected shoes from student athletes and took them to the Dominican Republic to give children a chance to play sports safely. Selfish? Self-centered? Guess again. This generation, in the words of my fraternity brother Kurt Vonnegut, "are as much Generation A as Adam and Eve were." I believe if we as older adults would follow their lead, then the world would be a much better place.

—Dr. Will Keim

Time Out.

Before you decide to volunteer, join a club, become a reporter, go Greek, try out for a team, become a resident assistant, take 19 credit hours, or work 30 hours while you take a full course load, let's call "TIME OUT" and assess your strengths and weaknesses.

1. On your mark.
Choose a good attitude.
Show up.
Be on time.
Be prepared.
Work hard.

2. Get set.
Analyze your strengths.
Identify your weaknesses.
Be honest and kind with yourself.

3. Go.
To breakfast.
To class.
To practice.
To the library.
To the career center.
To a spiritual place.
To campus programs.
TO BED
(6-8 hours of sleep per night).

Your schedule makes us tired! Get some rest.

> "Seventy percent of success in life is showing up."
>
> —Woody Allen
> *Film director, comedian and actor*

Stage Three: Thrive ... Service

Who are you?
How well do you know yourself?
Do your friends know you?
Let's take an inventory.

Four words I use to describe me:

_____   _____

_____   _____

> "Loneliness is the human condition. No one is ever going to fill that space. The best thing you can do is to know yourself ... know what you want."
>
> —Janet Fitch
> Author, White Oleander

Four words my friends use to describe me:

_____   _____

_____   _____

Do the lists match? If not, why?

My top three strengths:

_____

_____

_____

Three weaknesses I have:

_____

_____

_____

If I could change one thing about myself, it would be:

_____

_____

_____

Three of my talents or skills that could be useful to others:

_____

_____

_____

> **WHAT MAKES PEOPLE HAPPY?**
>
> "Consider the incredible generosity of the Bill and Melinda Gates Foundation and Warren Buffet. Mr. Buffet gave 18 billion dollars to the Gates Foundation because, 'I knew they could give it away better than me.' Tackling poverty, hunger disease, infant mortality, and education, it would seem that giving and serving, not taking or being served, brings true happiness."
>
> —Dr. Will Keim

Time In.

> "Will Keim is committed to excellence and someone you can trust, who really cares about you. When he speaks, we all should listen."
>
> —Lou Holtz
> College football coach
> ESPN Commentator

Will speaks:

"I was thrilled to see Lou Holtz, one of the winningest coaches in college football, in the Crown Room at Delta Air Lines in Atlanta. I said, 'Hello coach, I don't want to bother you, but we are both in the same fraternity.' He said hello and shook my hand. I continued, 'I'm at a point in my career where I need someone famous to say something nice about me.' He said, 'Mail me a tape. I'd love to help you.' A week later he sent a wonderful quote that opened many doors for me (and we used it on this page). He mentored me. He didn't have to. He's just that kind of man…a mentor and a friend. I am honored to call him my brother. I hope you have a mentor."

Find a Mentor.

—Will Keim

Wisdom on finding a mentor

Warren G. Bennis is a Distinguished Professor of Business Administration at the University of Southern California. He also serves as the Thomas S. Murphy Distinguished Research Scholar at Harvard Business School. He has written twenty-five books on leadership and change. Here is some of his advice:

> "While the popular view of mentors is that they seek out younger people to encourage and champion, in fact the reverse is true. The best mentors are usually recruited, and one mark of a future leader is the ability to identify, woo, and win the mentors who will change his or her life."

You would be wise to heed his wisdom and recruit a mentor. No one is an island and the "self-made man or woman" is a myth. Seek a mentor to guide and encourage your journey.

> "We ourselves feel that what we are doing is a drop in the ocean. But the ocean would be less because of that missing drop."
>
> —Mother Teresa
> 1910-1997
> Catholic nun and humanitarian

A Formula For Success

$$i + w^2 \text{ (mentor)} = \text{change your life}$$

("identify, woo, and win a mentor" Warren G. Bennis)

New Students and Sophomores

Identify someone who is older, or perhaps wiser, who might serve as a mentor to you. Don't be afraid to ask—be assertive, direct and honest.

Juniors and Seniors

Choose an underclass student whom you will make an effort to mentor as a protege. Be honored if someone asks you to be a mentor.

> "We can do no great things. Only small things with great love."
> —Mother Teresa
> 1910 – 1997
> Catholic nun and humanitarian

Commit yourself to one hour a week to talk, e-mail, visit, or hang out with each other.

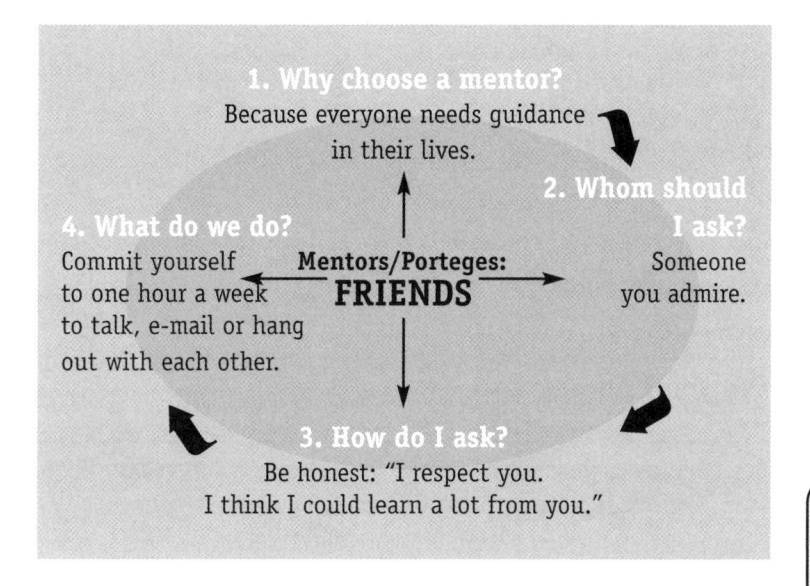

1. Why choose a mentor? Because everyone needs guidance in their lives.

2. Whom should I ask? Someone you admire.

3. How do I ask? Be honest: "I respect you. I think I could learn a lot from you."

4. What do we do? Commit yourself to one hour a week to talk, e-mail or hang out with each other.

Mentors/Porteges: **FRIENDS**

The act of giving

By now it should be obvious to you that we believe good character includes service, and that great learning takes place in the act of giving assistance to others. Mentoring is just one way to be of service.

As Mother Teresa said, we can do "small things with great love" and inspire others to join us in the effort. Nothing puts your problems in perspective better than helping others in their time of need. It is always wise to follow the Golden Rule, because what you "do unto others" may eventually "be done unto you."

Actor Gerard Butler on his work with Kids Kicking Cancer and Haiti Relief Efforts

> "For a good part of my life, I've been a bit of a rogue - not always living the best, healthiest, most respectable life. But I feel like I've turned myself around, gotten my personal life and career together, and I love what I do. Along with this contentment has come an increasing desire to give back to others."

Looking for a way to serve?

> "I have had students serve in the five programs listed below. Their experience, in their own words, was life changing. There are also great local service opportunities on or near every campus."
>
> — *Dr. Will Keim*

- Peace Corps
  www.peacecorps.gov/
- AmeriCorps VISTA
  www.americorps.gov/a
- Habitat for Humanity
  www.habitat.org/
- St. Jude Children's Research Hospital
  www.stjude.org/stjude/
- Children's Miracle Network
  www.childrensmiraclenetwork.org/

Did You Know ...

> Rotary International is the world's first service club organization, with more than 1.2 million members in 33,000 clubs worldwide.
> Their motto is **"Service Above Self."**
>
> *(source: www.rotary.org/)*

Find your place to serve!

Spirituality   14

> **"One truth stands firm. All that happens in world history rests on something spiritual. If the spirit is strong, it creates world history. If it is weak, it suffers world history."**
>
> —Albert Schweitzer
> 1875 – 1965
> Doctor and humanitarian

The Meaning of Spiritual Tolerance

Dr. Marcus Borg was hosting an internationally broadcast conference entitled, "God At 2000" to offer insights into spirituality in the new 21st Century and had gathered many great minds from several religious traditons at Oregon State University. Dr. Borg served on my dissertation committee and is one of the best teachers in the world. He is unique in that he does compelling research, publishes best-selling books, holds a class with the power of his spoken word, and makes time for students as well.

The panel consisted that day of Professors Eck, Armstrong, and Nasr, and Rabbi Lawrence Kushner. On the stage that day was Archbishop Tutu and a wonderful Lutheran minister who was moderating the panel discussion about how spirituality and religious tolerance and intolerance might play out in the lives of individuals and nations. The panel represented Christian, Jewish, and Muslim points of view, as well as insights into Buddhist and Taoist spirituality.

Suddenly the discussion was interrupted by a man who charged into the auditorium from outside, in his own mind, a devout Christian, who resented the discussion of any point of view but his own. He shouted at the top of his lungs, "You are all going to burn in hell. Jesus Christ is the way, the truth, and the life, and nobody gets to the Father except through the Son. You will all burn in hell for eternity." They let him rant for about five minutes, and when he began to get repetitive, he was escorted out. 1200 people sat in total silence, and I can only imagine what the international audience was thinking.

A peaceful, multi-religious discussion about tolerance and love, and respect and listening had been violated by a man whose own opinion, in his mind, was the only one worth hearing.

I was at first in shock that anyone would condemn Archbishop Tutu, winner of a Nobel Prize in Peace, to hell. And for that matter, the other great religious thinkers on the panel. Then I got mad, and as a Christian, wondered what people who think this man represents all of us were thinking of me. That man had a right to his opinion, but it clearly did not represent any version of love that my church had taught me.

Finally, Rabbi Kushner asked, "May I say something?" The Moderator answered quickly, "Please!" The audience laughed a nervous chuckle. The Rabbi said, "I have always found one's tolerance of another's spirituality to be a direct barometer of that person's own spiritual security." In one sentence, the tension was gone and wild applause broke the sad silence. The Rabbi continued, "I have always throught of the spiritual quest as being toward the top of a mountain where Truth lives. Some people start from a base which is quite warm and they are dressed for warm weather. Others start from cold bases and have many layers and jackets on. The thing is that by the time they reach mid-mountain, they are usually dressed the same. Some have taken clothing off; some have put it on. The important thing to remember is that they are all seeking the truth and the top of the mountain."

> "I have always found one's tolerance of another's spirituality to be a direct barometer of that person's own spiritual security."
> —Rabbi Lawrence Kushner

This moment is what I think about when I think about spirituality. It is about finding common ground. Much killing and horror have been committed in the name of religion. Seek to find your own spirituality and be secure in it. If you are, then you will find within yourself a tolerance that allows the next person to find their way. James Marcia called this "Commitment in Relativism"; that is, you acknowledge many ways to believe and think, and in the midst of them all, you choose your way and trust the Higher Power. Whether you call on God, Yahweh, Allah, Buddha, Higher Power, or Wakantanka, that is your business. Freedom of religion is one of the greatest choices and rights we have, and it is shared by all those who seek the spiritual path. It also guarantees people who choose not to believe their own place in the discussion.

Stage Three: Thrive ... Spirituality

> **Something To Think About**
>
> "The loneliness of poor people in this country is so stark because of the absence of family and support networks. There is a total abondonment of the elderly and the homeless, in many cases, even children. And it's incredible. I think in many parts of this country we're pioneering new levels of inhumanity."
>
> *Jerry Brown, Former Governor of California*

Discovering your spirituality

Spirituality is about things unseen, but felt most profoundly. It is called by many names, but it all has to do with our search for meaning, the Higher Self, the Creator, the Source of All That Is.

We are not preaching religion. We are talking about spirituality, about knowing a presence in life that transcends what we can feel, touch, smell, taste, or eat. Collegiate life is a wonderful time to discover or rediscover your own personal spirituality. Especially around midterms—there are a lot of people praying about those.

Billy Mills, the Native American Olympic gold medalist, tells about a Lakota tradition of holding a child up facing the heavens and saying to the little one, "Behold the only thing greater than yourself."

Professor Diana Eck of Harvard University defines "spirituality" as "real religion that touches the heart." The religious writer Rabbi Kushner adds, "Our tolerance of others' spirituality is a direct barometer of our own spiritual security."

Some define their spirituality as a belief in God. Some use different words. Twelve Step programs say "Higher Power." Lakotas say "Wakantanka." Others say "Allah," "Ishvara," "Tao," or "Jehovah." The choice is yours.

When we talk of spirituality, we are talking about solid values and beliefs that will help every student grow and achieve his or her own peace. We are talking about:

- Compassion
- Love
- Tolerance
- Patience
- Kindness

> "Always do right. This will gratify some people and astonish the rest."
>
> —*Mark Twain*
> *1835 – 1910*
> *Author and humorist*

> **One More Thought:**
> "If you want to solve the world's problems, you have to put your own household, your own individual life, in order first."
>
> *Chogyam Trungpa*
> *1939-1987*
> *Buddhist Meditation Master*

> "Religion is for people who don't want to go to hell. Spirituality is for people who have already been through it."
>
> —*Sister Joan Chittister*
> *Benedictine nun,*
> *author and lecturer*

Write down three of your "I believe" statements:

1 I believe:
_____
_____
_____

2 I believe:
_____
_____
_____

3 I believe:
_____
_____
_____

Take an hour of power each day.

Every day, try to reserve thirty minutes for exercise followed by thirty minutes for prayer, reflection, meditation, or contemplation. This hour a day will:

- Reenergize you.
- Recreate you.
- Revitalize you.

You say, "I don't have an hour each day."
We say, "Then stress out."

MAKE TIME FOR REFLECTION

Stage Three: Thrive ... Spirituality

Myth: "I don't have time. Other people have more time than I do."
Fact: Everybody gets twenty-four hours a day, seven days a week. Everybody.

What do you do with your 24 hours?

Okay, let's keep this real. You say you don't have time to take an hour out for exercise and contemplation? Take our "Keep it Real Challenge." Using the chart below, keep track of one day in your life and see where your time goes. Be honest. Be real.

> "The best thing about the future is that it comes one day at a time."
> —Abraham Lincoln
> 1809 – 1865
> 16th President of the United States

Morning
5 – 6: _____
6 – 7: _____
7 – 8: _____
8 – 9: _____
9 – 10: _____
10 – 11: _____
11 – 12: _____

Noon
12 – 1: _____
1 – 2: _____
2 – 3: _____
3 – 4: _____
4 – 5: _____
5 – 6: _____
6 – 7: _____
7 – 8: _____
8 – 9: _____
9 – 10: _____
10 – 11: _____
11 – 12: _____

Midnight
12 – 1: _____
1 – 2: _____
2 – 3: _____
3 – 4: _____
4 – 5: _____

**Step 1 to good time management
is knowing how you spend your time.**

Sum it up.

Review your "Keep it Real" chart and total the number of hours you spend on each activity:

Class: _____
Lab: _____
Study: _____
Eating: _____
Athletics: _____
Meetings: _____
Meditation: _____
Prayer: _____
Sleep: _____
Work: _____
Goofin' around: _____
Other:
_____: _____
_____: _____

TOTAL: _____

(Must equal 24 hours!)

Make some changes.

Just because you've always done it one way, does not mean you can't change. Step out of old habits. Step out of the shadow of your parents, big sister or brother, past achievements, and even defeats and self-doubts. Step into the light that is your life. Your moment. Your collegiate experience.

Now is a great opportunity to identify and develop greater meaning and purpose in your life.

> "Nothing endures but change."
> —Heraclitus
> 540 – 480 BC
> Greek philosopher

List some changes that you'd like to consider:

_____
_____
_____
_____
_____
_____
_____

Financial Literacy 15

> **"Success means accomplishments as the result of our own efforts and abilities. Proper preparation is the key to our success. Our acts can be no wiser than our thoughts. Our thinking can be no wiser than our understanding."**
>
> — *George S. Clason*
> Author of *The Richest Man in Babylon*
> (First published in 1926 and one of my
> favorite books on the subject of personal finance.
> To date the book has sold more copies than any other title of its kind.)

Choices Matter: Secrets to Financial Success
By Sheryl Garrett, CFP®

Effective money management is all about making healthy choices about spending and avoiding making too many financial blunders. Be thoughtful about your spending.

You've probably heard the sage financial wisdom, *"Live within your means"*. Unfortunately that phrase is misinterpreted. If you literally live "within" your means you're living paycheck to paycheck. That's better than spending more than you bring in; however, that's not what is actually meant by this sage advice.

We need to live *"beneath"* our means. A portion of every dollar that is earned should be set aside to help care for you in the case of emergencies and opportunities. See Rule #2 Control thy expenses, which in turn helps you fulfill Rules #1 and #3.

> "Lo, money is plentiful for those who understand the simple rules of its acquisition:
>
> 1. Start thy purse to fattening
> 2. Control thy expenditures
> 3. Make thy gold multiply
> 4. Guard thy treasures from loss
> 5. Make of thy dwelling a profitable investment
> 6. Insure a future income
> 7. Increase thy ability to earn
>
> Excerpted from *The Richest Man in Babylon*. The ancient rules are just as sound and complete as they were 5,000 years ago.

> **Sheryl Speaks:**
> "The subject of personal money management is not complicated, however, the wisdom and discipline required to do what is in your best interest, is not necessarily easy.
>
> Focus on the things that you can control and on the things that matter. No one will take better care of your money than you will. **Rule of the road – presume everybody wants your money.**"

> *"We need to live 'beneath' our means."*
> —Sheryl Garrett, CFP

It takes discipline and patience. However, there is no sure fire alternative to achieving financial success in your life without controlling expenses. No matter how much income you have, it seems to be the American way to spend all that we bring in. Most people are struggling financially. Most Americans cannot and will not be able to maintain their standard of living in retirement. Some can't even afford to think about retirement. But you don't have to end up another negative statistic. **Take charge! Begin now!**

If you have credit card debt and/or little or no cash reserves – you are or have been spending *beyond* your means. Sometimes life happens and you have no better alternative than to use your credit cards to remedy the situation. But those situations better be *real* emergencies, because if they're not, you won't have any line of credit left when a *"real"* emergency occurs – and they do.

EXERCISE: *Taking Stock*

- **LIST ALL CREDIT CARD DEBT**

CARD	TOTAL DEBT	MONTHLY PAYMENT

Stage Three: Thrive ... Financial Literacy

What kind of reserves do you have? If your transmission in your car goes out, or you have your front tooth knocked out playing touch football, where are you going to get the $1,000 to $3,000 dollars to take care of these unplanned expenses? Do you have plenty of money in your emergency fund? Could you ask for help from your parents or family? How would asking for financial help go over in your family? How would you feel about asking for money, especially if you had to explain in detail why you're in the position you're in? Would you charge the expense on a credit card, if you could? What effect would that have on your available credit or your credit score? These issues matter! See Rule #1: Fatten thy purse. I guess you could just ignore these problems and hope your transmission and tooth heal themselves.

- **LIST YOUR CASH RESERVES** _____
_____
_____
_____

> "Your most significant asset is your ability to make money."
>
> —Sheryl Garrett
> CFP, The Garrett Planning Network

How much should you have in cash reserves? As much as you can get - as fast as you can get it! Financial experts commonly recommend that we keep at least three months' worth of required living expenses set aside in a cash reserves/emergency fund, such as a bank savings account, a money market mutual fund, or very conservative investment account. Three months should be your minimum. Six months is ever better.

Your most significant asset is your ability to make money. Believe it or not, you are a money making machine. Invest properly and maintain your investment in your *"human capital"* and you'll reap the financial rewards all of your life. See Rule #7.

- **WHAT ARE THREE JOBS YOU HAVE HELD TO THIS POINT TO MAKE MONEY?** _____
_____
_____
_____

Education is one of the strongest influencers on income. The tables below illustrate the difference in income per year based on education level. Now, parlay that income differential over an entire career. Your most significant asset is your ability to make money. Nurture and protect that asset. See Rule #7 and #6.

Demographic		High school graduate		Some college		Bachelor's degree or higher		Bachelor's degree		Master's degree		Professional degree		Doctorate degree	
		Median	% +/- national median	Median	% +/- national median	Median	% +/- national median	Median	% +/- national median	Median	% +/- national median	Median	% +/- national median	Median	% +/- national median
Persons, age 25+ w/ earnings (2005)	Both sexes	$26,505	-17.5%	$31,054	-3.5%	$49,303	+53.4%	$43,143	+34.2%	$52,390	+63.0%	$82,473	+156.6%	$70,853	+120.4%
	Males	$32,085	-18.6%	$39,150	-0.6%	$60,493	+53.5%	$52,265	+32.6%	$67,123	+70.3%	$100,000	+153.8%	$78,324	+98.8%
	Females	$21,117	-20.3%	$25,185	-5.0%	$40,483	+52.7%	$36,532	+37.82%	$45,730	+72.5%	$66,055	+149.2%	$54,666	+106.2%
	Both sexes employed full-time	$31,539	-19.8%	$37,135	-5.6%	$56,078	+42.5%	$50,944	+29.5%	$61,273	+55.8%	$100,000	+154.2%	$79,401	+101.8%
Households (2003)		$36,835	-20.5%	$45,854	=0.8%	$73,446	+58.8%	$68,728	+48.6%	$78,541	+69.9%	$100,000	+116.2%	$96,830	+109.4%

SOURCE: US Census Bureau, 2004/06

Stage Three: Thrive ... Financial Literacy

The choices you make about your vocation and how far you want to pursue your chosen vocation have a great impact on your financial life. But money does not buy happiness. Select your vocation based on your passion and calling in life, not just because of financial rewards.

Albert Einstein, German born Nobel Prize winning physicist who developed the special and general theories of relativity, said that **"The most powerful force in the universe is compound interest."** If a smart guy like Einstein thinks compound interest is pretty significant - I think we ought to consider it important too.

> **"Money does not buy happiness."**
>
> —Sheryl Garrett, CFP
> *The Garrett Planning Network*

So what is compound interest? According to *Wikipedia*, it is a very complex mathematical equation that results in more interest accumulating to you over time, or being charged to you if you're the borrower, then you would be charged if simple interest applied.

Bottom line - the long term power of compounding over time is dramatic. Take a look at the example below, reprinted with permission by Roger C. Gibson, CFP®. The table on the next page demonstrates the phenomenal power of positive compound interest through time and the benefit of early savings.

Sheryl speaks:

In over twenty years providing financial advice, I have frequently asked, "what is the one thing you wished you had done differently in your financial life?" Almost universally they replied, "I wish I would have started saving earlier." No matter their age, 27 or 77, the universal reply was, "I wish I would have started saving earlier". Learn from their wisdom. Let the power of compound interest through time work for you and begin saving now, or increase your saving if you're not saving at least 10% of all the money you bring in. See Rule #3.

	Bill		Phil	
Age	Contribution	Year-end Value	Contribution	Year-end Value
19	$2,000	$2,200	$0	$0
20	$2,000	$4,620	$0	$0
21	$2,000	$7,282	$0	$0
22	$2,000	$10,210	$0	$0
23	$2,000	$13,431	$0	$0
24	$2,000	$16,974	$0	$0
25	$2,000	$20,872	$0	$0
26	$2,000	$25,159	$0	$0
27	$0	$27,675	$2,000	$2,200
28	$0	$30,442	$2,000	$4,620
29	$0	$33,487	$2,000	$7,282
30	$0	$36,835	$2,000	$10,210
31	$0	$40,519	$2,000	$13,431
32	$0	$44,571	$2,000	$16,974
33	$0	$49,028	$2,000	$20,872
34	$0	$53,930	$2,000	$25,159
35	$0	$59,323	$2,000	$29,875
36	$0	$65,256	$2,000	$35,062
37	$0	$71,781	$2,000	$40,769
38	$0	$78,960	$2,000	$47,045
39	$0	$86,856	$2,000	$53,950
40	$0	$95,541	$2,000	$61,545
41	$0	$105,095	$2,000	$69,899
42	$0	$115,605	$2,000	$79,089
43	$0	$127,165	$2,000	$89,198
44	$0	$139,882	$2,000	$100,318
45	$0	$153,870	$2,000	$112,550
46	$0	$169,257	$2,000	$126,005
47	$0	$186,183	$2,000	$140,805
48	$0	$204,801	$2,000	$157,086
49	$0	$225,281	$2,000	$174,995
50	$0	$247,809	$2,000	$194,694
51	$0	$272,590	$2,000	$216,364
52	$0	$299,849	$2,000	$240,200
53	$0	$329,834	$2,000	$266,420
54	$0	$362,817	$2,000	$295,262
55	$0	$399,099	$2,000	$326,988
56	$0	$439,009	$2,000	$361,887
57	$0	$482,910	$2,000	$400,276
58	$0	$531,201	$2,000	$442,503
59	$0	$584,321	$2,000	$488,953
60	$0	$642,753	$2,000	$540,049
61	$0	$707,028	$2,000	$596,254
62	$0	$777,731	$2,000	$658,079
63	$0	$855,504	$2,000	$726,087
64	$0	$941,054	$2,000	$800,896
65	$0	**$1,035,160**	$2,000	**$883,185**
Total Invested	**$16,000**		**$78,000**	

Were you amazed at this table?

❏ YES

❏ NO

❏ TOTALLY

Graphic assumes a 10% gross return on investments.

Stage Three: Thrive ... Financial Literacy

Notice in the end, Bill only invested $16,000 toward his retirement, yet Phil saved $78,000 and never caught up with Bill. Start or increase your savings now. Let the miracle of compound interest through time let you reach financial security the easiest way possible.

The following table illustrates how much you would need to save each month to provide you with $1,000 per month in retirement income beginning at age 65 and continuing for the rest of your life. Notice the relatively small percentage of your income that you need to save to fund your retirement by age 65 if you start at an early age. And notice how quickly saving for retirement becomes a very difficult objective. **Time is on your side now!**

Current Age	Savings / Month	Savings % of Income
18	$48	5%
25	$86	9%
30	$131	13%
35	$201	20%
40	$315	32%
45	$509	51%
50	$867	87%
55	$1,640	Can't compute
60	$4,083	Can't compute

Just in case you weren't convinced by the last table, the table below illustrates just how much it will cost you in compound interest through time if you wait. If you start saving for retirement at age 25 verses waiting until you're 35 years old, you'll have almost $500,000 more by age 65.

Presuming an Investment of $250/month @ 8% return

Age Started	Value at Age 65	Cost of Waiting
25	$872,000	
35	$372,590	$499,410
45	$147,255	$724,745
55	$45,736	$826,264

You may be thinking… I can't save $250 each and every month. Well, at some point in the very near future, if not now, you definitely can be saving at least $250 per month. The chart above shows you how time is your strongest ally in the quest for financial independence. It's not about how much money you earn – it's how much of what you earn you end up saving.

Let me illustrate a couple of strategies you can employ, which are easy and very practical ways to save yourself at least $250 per month. The table below illustrates the short-term and long-term costs of owning a car. Take for example that you need a car, have no trade-in and have $1,000 to spend for your down-payment. You'd also like to keep your monthly car payments under $500. Given this information, you could purchase a new car or a used car… presuming your credit isn't awful. At the outset it doesn't look like a huge difference. The monthly payments are very similar and the purchase prices aren't all that different. So, what's the big deal? The biggest factors affecting your long-term cost of driving is which car you buy and how long you continue to drive the car before replacing it.

> "It's not about how much money you earn - it's how much of what you earn you end up saving."
> —Sheryl Garrett, CFP
> The Garrett Planning Network

Major Purchase Comparison	New Car	Gently Used Car
Total Price	$26,790	$20,370
Down Payment	$1,000	$1,000
Total Financed	$25,790	$19,370
Monthly Payment	$493	$460
Number of Months	60	48
Trade in Value	$15,500	$7,400
Age at Trade In	2 years old	7 years old
Loan Balance	$16,300	$0
Depreciation	$11,290	$12,970
Interest	@ 5.5%	@6.0%
Lost Value during Ownership	$14,440	$14,440

In the above example, if you purchased the new car and drove it for two years and then traded it in on another new car, like many people do, you'd end up losing over $14,000 during that time period, primarily due to the heavy depreciation on new cars in the first couple of years. On the other hand, if you purchased that same car when it is two years old and continue to drive it for five years, your additional cost of ownership is only about $1,000, above and beyond your monthly car payments. Also notice that you only had to make payments on the used car for 48 months. This comparison assumes that you'll continue to set aside the $460 per month that you were paying toward your car loan during year number five.

So, what have you given up? The new car smell! By simply choosing to buy gently used cars and driving them for five years the positive impact on your wallet is actually much greater than it appears. With the new car you would go through this routine 2 ½ times (every two years verses every five years) as compared with the lost value on the used car. Projecting this cost out over your driving lifetime can result in a total cost of $300,000 to $500,000. Are you absolutely certain that driving fresh new cars is worth this much to you? That money could have been used to buy a nice house or would make a significant investment portfolio. It's ALL about choices. *Your choices matter!*

> "It's all about choices. Your choices matter."
>
> —Sheryl Garrett, CFP
> The Garrett Planning Network

CHOICES MATTER

The choices you make about big purchases, like cars, certainly have a dramatic effect on your financial future. However, let's not dismiss the little things. We need to be thoughtful about all of our expenditures.

Take for example the following items. The list of full cost items can easily add up to $250 per person per month.

FULL COST	LOW COST
Dining Out	Cooking
Purchasing Prepared Meals	Gardening
Fast Food / Drive Through	Making Sandwiches/Lunches at Home
Cable / Pay Per View	Free TV
Movies, Theatres, Bookstores	Parks, Libraries, Museums
Going "Out" with Friends	Entertaining Friends at Home
Financing Purchases	Paying Cash

How many of your friends have an unlimited supply of money – excluding anything from their parents? Likely none! College students need to be frugal. Dining out is a luxury to be enjoyed only on special occasions. And on those special occasions, skip the drink and desert and you can lower your dinner bill by several dollars, but still be able to enjoy dinning out with friends or a date. Preparing the same type of meal at home typically cost about 25 to 30% of what it would cost you in the restaurant. And think about how impressed your friends or date will be if you actually cook for them – what a concept – smart with money and can cook!

Entertaining at home, or at someone else's home, is a much less expensive alternative than going out to a bar or a nightclub. Booze costs about ten times more when a bartender pours it for you. Renting or watching a movie with friends or a date might cost a total of $4.00. Going out to the movies – you could easily drop $15.00 per person. Instead of going out, have friends bring over their favorite munchies and drinks to share and you get the movie. Everybody has a good time and everybody saves money. Start a trend – have fun without spending much or any money!

> "Start a trend - have fun without spending much or any money."
> —Sheryl Garrett, CFP
> The Garrett Planning Network

EXERCISE: *Small Steps*
What small steps could you take right now that would deliver big financial rewards later?

_____

_____

_____

When was the last time you went to the park, a museum, the zoo, hiking in the woods, camping, canoeing or bicycling? All of these activities can be enjoyed at little or no cost. You might have to get a little creative, but you'll be living "beneath" your means. And that is key to financial success.

Credit card debt, student loans, car loans, and mortgages are all based on the principles of compound interest, too – the bad kind. In fact, the compounding of interest on loans was once considered so awful that centuries ago it was outlawed in many countries.

If you've got consumer debt of any kind I encourage you to attack your debt head-on! There is a great free debt repayment calculator at http://www.vertex42.com/Calculators/debt-reduction-calculator.html. The two most common and successful strategies of debt reduction are illustrated right before your eyes, so you know the best way to attack your debt and when you'll be debt free… at least consumer debt, aka dumb debt. There's probably no reason for it other than you didn't have an adequate emergency funds and/or you spend too much. Refer back to Rule #2.

Stage Three: Thrive ... Financial Literacy

Shame and blame won't get you to where you need to be. You're just starting out in your adult life. If you avoid making too many financial mistakes you'll be good. And if you do waiver in your tenacity to be smart about money, immediate and swift action will reverse the damage and time will heal.

> **PRESS ON**
> - Nothing in the world can take the place of persistence.
> - Talent will not; nothing is more common than unsuccessful men with talent
> - Genius will not; unrewarded genius is almost a proverb
> - Education alone will not; The world is full of educated derelicts.
> - Persistence and determination alone are omnipotent.
>
> *Calvin Coolidge*
> *30th President of the United States*

> "Living beneath your means is the key to financial success."
>
> —*Sheryl Garrett, CFP*
> *The Garrett Planning Network*

Exercise: *Reducing your monthly expenses.*

List five ways that you can reduce your monthly expenses and amounts for each:

_____
_____
_____
_____
_____

> "People do not Plan to Fail. Rather they Fail to Plan."

Exercise: *The Big Picture*

What is the single most important concept you have learned in this chapter and describe what course of action you plan to take about it.

_____
_____
_____
_____
_____
_____
_____
_____
_____
_____

❖ ❖ ❖

ABOUT THE AUTHOR: Sheryl Garrett CFP®, AIF® is the founder of The Garrett Planning Network, Inc. She has been dubbed "The All-American Planner," possibly because of her zealous mission to "help make competent, objective financial advice accessible to all people." Sheryl's fresh approach as a financial advisor working with clients on an hourly, as-needed, fee-only basis has evolved into an international network of like-minded financial advisors, the Garrett Planning Network.

Sheryl has also been honored to work with the House Subcommittee on Financial Services regarding predatory lending regulation, financial literacy and Social Security reform. She also works as a consultant and expert witness in lawsuits against financial advisors who rendered questionable or inappropriate financial advice.

She has authored, coauthored, or served as a technical editor on over a dozen books and several magazine columns. These books include: *Garrett's Guide to Financial Planning* (National Underwriter 2002, 2007), *Just Give Me the Answer$* (Dearborn Trade 2004), *Money Without Matrimony* (Dearborn Trade 2006), *Personal Finance Workbook For Dummies®* (Wiley 2007), *A Family's Guide to the Military For Dummies®* (Wiley 2008), and *Investing in an Uncertain Economy For Dummies®* (Wiley 2008).

As vocal advocate for financial education, Sheryl is a frequent public speaker and has been frequently interviewed on CNNfn, Bloomberg, ABC World News Now, Fox-TV; NPR's *All Things Considered* and *Marketplace;* and in *Business Week, Newsweek, Time, Forbes, Kiplinger Personal Finance, Money, Smart Money, MarketWatch, U.S. News & World Report, Glamour, Parade, Better Homes and Gardens,* the *New York Times, USA Today* and the *Wall Street Journal.* Sheryl has been recognized five times by *Investment Advisor* magazine as "One of the Most Influential People in Financial Planning."

WILL'S NOTE: Sitting next to Sheryl at a meeting in Indianapolis, I said, "I could sure use your help." She said, "I am sorry. I am so overcommited right now." I countered, "I will trade you a day of lecturing for a chapter on financial literacy for students." She said, "Deal." What a great woman she is and this chapter rocks! It could change your life for a long time if you read it and act on it. Sheryl is a caring person who knows that money is not the meaning of life, but being literate when it comes to finances can reduce stress and enhance the important things like family, faith, and friends.

STAGE FOUR
Aspire Higher

*"Two roads diverged in a wood and I - I took the one less traveled by,
And that has made all the difference."*
Robert Frost, *"The Road Not Taken"*

---

*Leadership ❖ Citizenship ❖ Sportsmanship ❖
Trees of Self-Realization and Self-Defeat ❖
The Secret ❖ 25,000 Days*

STAGE FOUR: ASPIRE HIGHER "CHAPTER SUMMARY"
Leadership ❖ Citizenship ❖ Sportsmanship ❖ Trees of Self-Realization and Self-Defeat ❖ The Secret ❖ 25,000 Days

16. LEADERSHIP

"Leadership is the process of persuasion and example by which an individual or leadership team induces a group to take action that is in accord with the leader's purposes or the shared purposes of all."
Dr. John Gardner

"Becoming an ethical leader involves making character-driven decisions about good and bad, and right and wrong. Leadership involves listening to your constituency, having empathy for those around you, and having a plan for action. Good leaders know how to delegate and create a sense of enthusiasm. They take time to reflect and recognize themselves as good stewards of their organizations. A sense of humor is essential to leadership, as is integrity and the ability to create passion for an idea, product, or concept."

❖ ❖ ❖

17. CITIZENSHIP with Michael Dunham

"We give every appearance of sleepwalking through a dangerous passage of history. We see life-threatening problems, but we do not react. We are anxious, but immobilized. I do not find the problems themselves as frightening as the questions they raise concerning our capacity to gather our forces and act…Suppose that we have lost the capacity to motivate ourselves for arduous exertions on behalf of the group?"
Dr. John Gardner,
"On Leadership", 1990

"Being a citizen to us means more than nationality. It means understanding the interdependent nature of the world and the impact each nation has on all the others. It is a positive value to be proud of one's nation and culture. At the same time, we are living together in a world that is changing and becoming more interdependent and communicative. This is truly an amazing and challenging time to be a citizen of the world community. Can we face the life-threatening problems we see together and mobilize our resources for the good of humankind?"

❖ ❖ ❖

18. SPORTSMANSHIP

"What's become acceptable is to do your best to create an intimidating home field atmosphere. And that has taken a toll on sportsmanship."
Associate Commissioner,
Southeastern Conference

"There is nothing wrong with school pride and creating a fun atmosphere and home field advantage. Yet, in intercollegiate athletics, intramurals, recreational sports, and club sports, the burning desire to win has been replaced with the desire to burn. Verbal abuse, shoving, yelling, fist-fights, and brawls have spread an air of hooliganism across the nation and frankly have made attendance at many events less than desirable. The coaches and officials are human beings, and the players are someone's son or daughter, pride and joy. We must rekindle the value of sportsmanship, a sense of 'Fan Etiquette' before the very existence of these sporting events is called into question by the Academic community as a whole."

❖ ❖ ❖

19. TREES with Professor John Argeropoulos, Northern Michigan University, Emeritus

"It is tempting in stressful times to seek relief by simply invoking positive affirmations, but positive thinking, magical mantras, or moralizing alone will rarely prove sufficient. The purpose of The Tree of Self-Realization is to serve as a roadmap that reminds us of what is possible and to serve as a symbol that encourages us to strive for its achievement."
Professor John Argeropoulos

"The model of a Tree of Self-Realization and a Tree of Self-Defeat represents an evolutionary growth in consciousness which has been calibrated in the range of 480-500 by Dr. David Hawkins on his map of Consciousness. Work by Dr. Hawkins at the Institute for Advanced Spiritual Research has revealed the existence of subtle energy forces that reflect the level of consciousness of individuals as well as societies. When people are caught up in the self-limiting beliefs of the ego or false-self, which are fear based, they exhibit lower levels of consciousness (below 200) and tend to behave as if they are victims, with little hope of escaping a life of misery and conflict. Individuals who are operating from a higher level of consciousness are more concerned with the welfare of others and exhibit greater compassion and unconditional love which serve as attractor forces that are capable of generating growth opportunities which positively impact their lives and the lives of others. It should come as no surprise that these individuals, as a group, enjoy better health, as well as greater success and happiness as a consequence of this enlightened status."

❖ ❖ ❖

20. THE SECRET

"To love what you do and feel that it matters—how could anything be more fun?"
Katherine Graham

"Many people believe that the secret to life is money, riches, and wealth. Honestly, if we had to choose between poor and happy or rich and happy, we would choose the latter. But be clear: Money does not make people happy. If it did, then the United States would be the happiest place on Earth. Yet we spend $150 billion a year on alcohol and import 150 metric tons of cocaine. If life is so good here, why do so many people live it sedated? Is there a better way? We have learned the secret of life, and we believe it can lead you to happiness and satisfaction with your college experience, and beyond.

Find Something You Love To Do And Learn To Do It Well Enough That Someone Will Pay You To Do It!"

❖ ❖ ❖

21. 25,000 DAYS

"When you were born, you cried and the world rejoiced. Live your life so that when you die, the world cries and you rejoice."
Native American saying

Did you know that 25,000 grains of sand would fit into your two hands? That's not a lot. 25,000 days—that's a full life. That's if you live a full life. If you have prostrate cancer, heart disease, or breast cancer in your family, you might get less that 25,000 days. A drunk driver could shorten your life without your consent. Singer Selena got 8,744 days. Distance runner Steve Prefontaine received 8,885. Ryan White, a victim of an HIV/AIDS tainted blood transfusion, lived 6,693 days. An 18 year old student has already lived 6,500 of his or her 25,000 days getting to college. How will you spend the days of your life to create your masterpeace? Helen Keller said, *"Life is either a great adventure or it is nothing."* Life is a one-ticket ride. Life is not a dress rehearsal. The university or college will provide academic services, counseling services, student services, health services, recreation, intramurals, intercollegiate athletics, student activities, food services, student involvement centers, campus ministries, club sports…it's all there.

Make sure the only thing missing is not you! Show up for your life. Live it fully.

Leadership 16

> **"Leadership is the process of persuasion and example by which an individual or leadership team induces a group to take action that is in accord with the leader's purposes or the shared purposes of all."**
>
> —Dr. John W. Gardner
> *1912 – 2002*
> *Educator, Leader, Activist*

On Becoming an Ethical Leader

"We give every appearance of sleepwalking through a dangerous passage of history. We see life-threatening problems, but we do not react. We are anxious, but immobilized.

I do not find the problems themselves as frightening as the questions they raise concerning our capacity to gather our forces and act . . . Suppose that we have lost the capacity to motivate ourselves for arduous exertions on behalf of the group?"

In 1990, Dr. John W. Gardner, noted author, psychologist, veteran, and former Secretary of Health, Education, and Welfare wrote the above prophetic and cautionary introduction to the book, *On Leadership*. Clearly these are questions we would ask even under normal circumstances. We must all stand before the mirror of self-examination, search our deepest souls, and ask:

- *Can I motivate myself to act on behalf of the larger good?*
- *What am I willing to sacrifice myself for?*
- *What can I do?*
- *Does one person really make a difference?*
- *How does one person become an ethical leader in today's complex world?*

During our time together in this chapter, I will provide support for the following answers to the questions above:

- Yes...the time is now...this is the moment!
- Your deepest-held beliefs, values, and principles!
- Anything you commit yourself to do!
- A world of difference!
- Let me show you...

> "While we are free to choose our actions, we are not free to choose the consequences of our actions."
> —Dr. Stephen R. Covey
> Author, co-founder of Franklin-Covey organization

This chapter is devoted to helping you learn to actualize your full potential for leadership; it concerns the development of your character; and it teaches you a four-step ethical model for decision-making that leaders can use in any situation to resolve intra-personal, interpersonal and group conflict situations in a community-building and enhancing manner.

There are some basic assumptions I would like you to consider before we move on. These are:

- **Leadership without ethics is despotism.**
- **Ethical leadership without character is like a home built on sand; it will not stand the test of time.**
- **Leadership, ethics, and character without community, exist only in the person and are therefore isolated concepts rather than lived realities.**

As an educator, I want to teach you to become an ethical leader who participates in the creation of genuine human community, where individuals can become women and men of character. This is my purpose in this chapter and in my life as an educator. I am not talking about a quick fix. Rather, I offer you tools that you may use first to become a contributor to the common good and then to emerge as a leader who inspires others to make a difference.

When will this process be completed? When you take your last breath! I am proposing a lifetime of learning, a journey toward a world lived in community with others. If this seems idealistic or unattainable, consider the alternative to genuine human community: isolation, fear, and hopelessness. Can one live like that? Consider the words of Laura Pappano in her book, *The Connection Gap:*

Stage Four: Aspire Higher ... Leadership

"We end up belonging to and identifying with a mass market, a faceless public. We bond in our minds through orchestrated public experiences that we consume privately. We feel familiar, even intimate, with people who arrive every evening on our television screens, who speak with us every morning via radio as we shower or commute, who are faithfully online, who come alive on the big screen and whom we fret over and identify with through the pages of celebrity magazines. We love Oprah (some even expect her to handle our bills.) Prepubescent girls are crazy for Leo. We rely on Don Imus to grouse and Dr. Laura to set us straight. These—and many others—are important voices in national life. But even as we identify with particular public figures, we remain alone. We may write, call in, appear in the studio audience, but it remains a one-way relationship that cannot replace local ties. And yet it seems easier to engage as part of this super-public than as part of a real community ..."

> "Ethics is the discipline dealing with what is good and bad, and with moral duty and obligation."
> —Webster's Dictionary

Leaders must engage in the community; ethical leaders engage in character-driven decision making. But how? When? With whom? We will tackle these questions together on the path to becoming ethical leaders. But first we must ask Why?

- *Why be concerned with the character issue?*
- *Why engage ethically with others in genuine community?*
- *Why connect at all, when it is easier not to?*

Ethics concerns a set of moral principles or values. Ethics are principles of conduct governing individuals or groups. As leaders of industry, emerging student leaders, organizational leaders, and leaders of our own lives, we must ask the fundamental questions, "Why engage ethically?" It is my belief that the answer is straightforward. To not do so results in anarchy, with and between persons. Chaos is a wonderful theory, but rarely results in a meaningful course of ethical action. We engage in ethical connections with others not only because it gives us personal fulfillment but also because it gives our lives meaning, purpose, and direction toward a common good.

> "Another flaw in the human character is that everybody wants to build and nobody wants to do maintenance."
> —Kurt Vonnegut, Jr.
> 1922-2007
> Author, social critic

> "We are what we repeatedly do."
> — Aristotle
> Fourth century B.C.
> Greek philosopher

Real life—yours and mine—involves relationships with others. Born out of the relationship between one person and another, we naturally seek relationships with other human beings. We seek intimacy and relation our entire lives. Relationships are as important to human beings as air, water and food: not options but necessities. So it is with relationships and connections with others. Real life is best lived out in quality interpersonal relationships within a larger community of connections between persons and groups.

Finally, why engage with others by connecting in communities driven by character? Heraclitus said, "Character is our destiny." The Rev. Martin Luther King, Jr. said, "Intelligence plus character—that is the goal of a true education." Martin Buber stated, "Education worthy of the name is essentially the education of character." Get it? Rooted in the Greek language, character has come to mean the "constellation of strengths and weaknesses that form and reveal who we are." (Templeton Foundation, *Colleges that Develop Character*, p.vii). Some say character is what we do when no one is looking. So I ask, **"What shall we do?"**

> "In matters of opinion, swim with the fish; but in matters of principles, stand firm like a rock."
> — Mark Twain
> 1835-1910
> Author and humorist

I propose that you decide to be an ethical person: a person of good character, a principled, engaged, community-minded person who decides this very day to make a difference not only on your own behalf, but for the common good. I want you to see this decision as central to your life today, tomorrow, and always. These values are at the very core of your being and are the cornerstone of civilization. With them, we live together in hope. Without them, we tremble alone in fear. It truly is a matter of life and death, this choice between being alone and being engaged, connected or disconnected. No choice is more essential to our survival than this one! So, which will you lead by? Life or death? Consider that the choice of life means to engage in ethical behavior based on principles of character directed toward the common good. Conversely, the choice of death means to refuse to accept personal responsibility for the betterment of the world. Choose life, connection, character, principles, community!

From the Philosophical to the Practical

Learning to lead with ethics and character means learning to make ethical decisions based on a model that facilitates behavior contributing to the common good. I would now like to share with you a Four-Step Model for Ethical Decision-Making that will help you do just that. It is time to move from the philosophical to the practical, from goal to objective. Assuming I have convinced you "Why" we need to become ethical leaders, let us now consider "How," "When," and "With Whom."

> "No legacy is so rich as honesty."
> —Shakespeare
> 1564-1616
> Poet and playwright

The Four Questions of Ethical Decision-Making

The truth is this: ethical leaders must ask themselves four central questions before engaging in actions that will have an impact upon others. I am indebted to Dr. J. Wesley Robb of the University of Southern California for his understanding of the importance of a model for ethical decision-making. Why do we engage in ethical leadership? Because it is the foundation of a civilized society and world. How do we begin? By finding a model for ethical decision-making and putting it into practice. When do we do this? Now and forevermore. And with whom? With every person who is willing to engage with us in the creation of communities based on character for enhancement of the common good.

For the emerging leader, this process might seem daunting. The process may also seem daunting if you have been the leader of an organization for many years. There are challenges and obstacles along the way of turning a vision into a reality and of leading with integrity, morality, and a steady sense of right and wrong. Whether you have had a successful history or not, the important thing is to get started. You might be wondering:

> "The journey of a thousand miles begins beneath your feet."
> —Lao Tzu in the Tao Te Ching
> Sixth century B.C.
> Father of Taoism

- *How do I follow my voice, my plan, and not the one my parents or guardians laid out for me?*
- *How can I make my mark on the world?*
- *Is there more to life than making money?*
- *How do I make an ethical decision in today's fast-paced world?*

It would be fabulous if I could give you a ready-wrapped answer-to-go for these and many other questions you will ask yourself late in the night. It has been my experience that simple solutions do not fit complex problems. I can, however, share with you a framework that will give you decision-making a system, a plan that will help you develop as an ethical leader. I've also provided a variety of examples to illustrate how to use the following four questions on your way to making an ethical decision.

The Essential Questions of Ethical Leadership:
1. *What is my motive in doing this act? What is my intention?*
2. *What is the applicable law or policy governing this act?*
3. *What are the possible consequences of my actions?*
4. *What are my moral principles regarding this act?*

> "You can live well and prosper by doing what is right."
> —Dr. Will Keim

We can, and must, make a positive impact on the world by making ethical decisions which establish an integrity, a "life-giving" dimension, to our interactions with others. You can live well and prosper by doing what is right, looking out for your neighbor's well-being as well as your own. Below are three examples which demonstrate how to apply the above essential questions to life situations.

Potential Action: Cheat on a test.
- *What is my motive?* To do better on the test and make up for a lack of honest preparation.
- *What is applicable law or policy?* The Honor Code forbids cheating and may demand my suspension if my cheating comes to light.
- *What are the possible consequences?* A better grade or suspension and embarrassment.
- *What are my moral principles regarding cheating?* I am tempted, but I was taught cheating was wrong.

Problem areas include: What if I don't care about being caught? What if I was not taught that cheating is wrong? But these questions prove my point: You can only ignore the fact that cheating is wrong if you are unethical, unprincipled and a person of questionable character. Students sometimes tell me, "There are usually a number of choices that could be ethical and right given a slight reinterpretation of the circumstances." I respond, "You are right...but there is always one choice a little more right than the others."

Another Potential Action: Drop GHB Into Someone's Drink.
- *What is my motive? Is* it intimacy I want? Sex? A relationship? Couldn't these all be better achieved with a conscious and willingly participating partner?
- *What is applicable law or policy?* Drugs are against the law.
- *What are the possible consequences?* I might have sex but I might also be convicted of rape, contributory negligence, or wrongful death; these drugs can cause permanent brain damage or even death after even a single use.
- *What are my moral principles?* It seems like a long time ago, but I was taught to treat other people as I would like to be treated.

Potential problem areas include: What if I wasn't taught basic values, such as treating others as I want to be treated? Or what if I was abused and intend to treat others as I was treated? Again, a lack of character-driven education and unethical choices result in harm for at least one of the parties, proving the point that ethical leadership is needed to teach and make good decisions that do not harm individuals but rather help people to live in community.

Final Potential Action: Feed A Homeless Person.
- *What is my intention?* To help someone out or to put something good on my resume.
- *What is the applicable law or policy?* It is perfectly legal to help someone who is hungry.
- *What are the consequences?* He eats and I feel better about myself.
- *What are my moral principles?* I think it is important to take care of those less fortunate than myself.

Potential problem areas include: What if I think people get what they deserve and since this guy is homeless he deserves to go hungry?

What if I don't really care? What if I only want to put something like "Worked with the homeless" on my resume? There is so much that needs to be done that we cannot afford the luxury of worrying about the motivation behind the good action. If the chooser selects isolation and disconnection, someone gets hurt, once again demonstrating the need for ethical conduct for the common good.

> **"The right thing for the wrong reason is still the right thing."**
> —Dr. Craig Franz
> Christian Monk

The Consistency Factor

The above four-question model works. Becoming a person of character and integrity means narrowing the gap between what you say and what you do and increasing your concern for the well-being of others as well as yourself. And now is the time to make that decision to be an ethical leader. *Why?* Kay Lyons said, "Yesterday is a canceled check; tomorrow is a promissory note; today is the only cash you have—so spend it wisely."

Undoubtedly, the events of September 11, 2001 taught us all how precious life is, how much we should immerse ourselves in the present with our friends and family, and what happens when others choose to act in an immoral, unethical manner. Leadership in the 21st Century demands engagement, integrity and character-driven ethical action. Are you ready? Can you become this kind of leader? The answer, I believe, is a resounding, "Yes!!!" Regardless of your age, position, place of residence (or if you even have one), leadership role, race, religion and the like, I am filled with hope about your potential to enhance your ethical leadership. Becoming a leader with integrity depends upon this understanding.

The Facts of Life

- Say what you mean,
- Do what you say, and
- When you don't, admit it.

> "The probability that we fail in the struggle ought not to detour us from the support of a cause we believe to be just."
> —Abraham Lincoln
> 1809-1865
> 16th President of The United States

No one will ask you to be a saint in order to be a leader. But everyone wants a leader who behaves ethically, who is a man or woman of integrity, whose spirit is governed by character and a deep sense of commitment to community and the common good. And ethical leadership begins with you, right now, right here. Take the first step and begin your journey toward becoming an ethical leader. Do not be immobilized by fear or by the scope of our problems. Do not sleepwalk through history or through your own life. Make your mark by making the decision to care, to hope and to love ... today.

CHAPTER SUMMARY

- The discipline of ethics is concerned with making judgments of good and bad, and right and wrong—as well as—moral duty and obligation.

- Ethical leaders are not born, rather they are made by a series of decisions and the consequences of those decisions.

- Before acting, ask yourself these questions: Why am I doing this? What is the applicable law or policy? What are the potential consequences of my actions? What are my moral principles relevant to my options?

- Real life demands authentic relationships with other people lived out in genuine community.

- Becoming a person of character and integrity means narrowing the gap between what you say and what you do. It means increasing the amount you care about the well-being of others, as well as yourself.

> "Effective leadership is putting first things first. Effective management is discipline, carrying it out."
>
> —Dr. Stephen R. Covey
> Author, co-founder of
> Franklin-Covey organization

Thought Into Action

Identify three people in your life who have exhibited ethical decision making and leadership, and thereby positively impacted your life.

- _____
- _____
- _____

Your assignment is to turn "Thought Into Action" by sending at least one of these people a short note, email, or text telling them about the impact they had on your life. It would be great if you would tell all three, but send a note to at least one!

Ten Characteristics of Effective Leadership

Do you want to be a leader?
Do you want to make a difference?
Then here's how:

Learn to listen ...
> To the voice within and the voices of others. Listen.

Empathy—develop it ...
> For the life history and needs of others. Feel.

Action ...
> Be the director, not the victim, of your life. Get busy.

Delegate ...
> Trust others to help you when you need assistance. Reach out.

Enthusiasm ...
> Get excited about yourself. Don't show up late for your life.

Reflection ...
> Think, meditate, prayer, ponder—pick one! Take time.

Stewardship ...
> Take care of yourself. Treat your life with the respect it deserves.

Humor ...
> Laugh at yourself and with others. Smile and enjoy.

Integrity ...
> Say what you mean, do what you say, and when you don't, admit it. Speak the truth.

Patience ...
> Give yourself and your friends a break. Let go of the past. Live now.

> "When most people talk about 'leaders,' they refer to people who have big titles, like the student-council president or the captain of a team. But true leadership isn't about being president or captain. True leadership is about taking a few minutes each day to lead yourself toward your inner and outer goals. It's about reflecting on your life and making sure that you're headed in the right direction."
>
> —*Mawi Asgedom*
> *Author, The Code*

Citizenship 17

> "We give every appearance of sleepwalking through a dangerous passage of history. We see life-threatening problems, but we do not react. We are anxious, but immobilized.
>
> I do not find the problems themselves as frightening as the questions they raise concerning our capacity to gather our forces and act... Suppose we have lost the capacity to motivate ourselves for the arduous exertions on behalf of the group?"
>
> —Dr. John W. Gardner in On Leadership, 1990
> 1912 – 2002
> Educator, Leader, Activist

Citizenship as a concept was much easier to understand when I was in grade school. We were even graded on it. We received a letter grade on our school work, and a grade for our citizenship. At that time, I figured it meant "behaving myself". My Dad, Jack made it easy for me to understand… "If you get in trouble at school and they have to spank you, you get it again when you get home."

Citizenship = Being Good and Not Getting In Trouble

We are not talking about the 1860's here folks. Rather, we are talking the 1960's. There was truly a sense at school that you were representing yourself and your family and the responsibility to behave was explicity implied. Your actions at school reflected on your family and its role in your neighborhood.

The concept of citizenship has changed and now includes debates and discussions about nationalization versus globalisation, minority and indigenous person rights, feminists' perspectives, health, wealth distribution, and environmental issues. The Stanford Encyclopedia of Philosophy, the Citizenship Studies Journal, and the Citizenship, Democracy, and Ethnocultural Diversity Newsletter are but three of the thousands of on-going dialogues, debates, and discussions about citizenship.

> **Citizenship Defined**
>
> The Dictionary defines citizenship as the state of being vested with rights, privileges, and duties of a citizen. The character of an individual viewed as a member of society: behavior in terms of the duties, obligations, and functions of a citizen.

> "As citizens of this democracy, you are the rulers and the ruled, the law-givers and the law-abiding, the beginning and the end."
> —Adlai Stevenson
> 1900-1965
> Politician, U.S. democratic presidential nominee

The Stanford Encyclopedia of Philosophy states one definition of citizenship: "A citizen is a member of a political community who enjoys the rights and assumes the duties of membership."

Throughout the 20th century, the discussion of citizenship presupposed a sovereign territory, or country, and the essential framework for any discussion of citizenship (*The Stanford Encyclopedia of Philosophy*). Several factors, the SEP reports, have altered the way in which we view citizenship as a concept and impacted our 21st century definition of it:

- Exploding transnational economic exchange
- Competition
- Communication
- Migration
- Social and cultural interaction
- Porous borders

Simply put, is it possible to be a citizen of a specific nation and a citizen of the world at the same time? What is the role of nationalism? Certainly no one is advocating that we do not take pride in our countries, are they? Personally, can I celebrate being an American and at the same time honor my German, Belgian, French, English, and Irish heritage?

Citizenship Studies Journal goes so far as to say that it focuses on debates that move beyond conventional notions of citizenship and "treat citizenship as a strategic concept that is central in the analysis of identity, participation, empowerment, human rights, and the public interest."

Jurgen Habermas in *The Inclusion of The Other: Studies in Political Theory* questions the relevance of sovereign states and talks about 'common humanity as our only bond'. His critics argue that every great social movement that increased the blessings, rights, and responsibilities, of citizenship to the underrepresented and overlooked in the 20th century happened in democratic nations, or was inspired and empowered by them. Nations are relevant today they propose, as important or more important than they ever were.

WHAT DOES THIS MEAN TO THE 21ST CENTURY COLLEGIATE STUDENT?

'All citizens…a perfect equality of rights.'

What about the world? Can we be good citizens of the United States and at the same time be good citizens of the global community? Why does the media insist on making this an either/or situation and choice? One time a student asked me, "Do you believe in evolution or creation?" I said, "Yes." He said, "What do you mean? You have to choose." I offered, "I only have to choose if I believe that the Creator of the universe isn't smart enough to include evolution in the design."

I am going to offer you a personal story that bridges the unnecessary gap between national citizenship and global citizenship: the story of Michael Dunham. It involves New Jersey, Paul Anka's younger brother, the University of Houston, The Grateful Dead, Frank Sinatra, Austin, Texas, Rodney Dangerfield, Willie Nelson, South Padre Island, a surfing angel, recycling, CFC's, the environment, The United Nations, The Montreal Protocol, climate change, capitalism and profit, and seven things you might consider good citizenship. Interested? I hope so, because my meeting with Michael Dunham was the impetus to include a chapter on Citizenship, to help you find pride in your nation and meaning in your world view.

> "The best principles of our republic secure to all its citizens a perfect equality of rights."
> —Thomas Jefferson
> 1743-1826
> 3rd President of the United States
> Author, The Declaration of Independence

> "It was we, the people, not we, the white male citizens, nor yet we, the male citizens; but we, the whole people, who formed the Union … Men, their rights and nothing more; Women, their rights and nothing less."
> —Susan B. Anthony
> 1820-1906
> American civil rights leader

Michael Dunham's Story

ONE MAN'S JOURNEY TO CITIZENSHIP: FROM ENTERTAINMENT TO THE ENVIRONMENT

"CITIZENSHIP . . . How you can make a difference in our world by changing simple everyday behavior."

Michael Dunham
Director, Energy & Environmental Programs
JACO Environmental Member, UNEP Technical & Economic Task Force
2004-2005 Foam End of Life Issues Member,
UNEP Technical & Economic Task Force 2009
Cost Effective methods for handling PU Foam insulation containing Ozone Depleting Chemicals with high Global Warming Potentials (GWP)

> "I have worked toward communicating to others what I had come to believe was the right way to approach everyday life in this everchanging world."
> —Michael Dunham

Like any really good detective or crime scene investigator, I don't believe in coincidence. So when I met Will Keim on an airline flight from Portland, OR to Orange County, CA and he asked me to contribute a chapter on environment in his book, I thought it was an honor. But, our meeting was supposed to happen. After all, since my first days in the entertainment business, I have worked toward communicating to others what I had come to believe was the right way to approach everyday life in this ever-changing world.

I think it appropriate to give you a little background before getting into the many ways we can all make a substantial difference in the world we inhabit and will pass on to our children and future ancestors. It's little things that when multiplied by hundreds of millions, equate to earth-changing outcomes…literally. Currently, I'm an environmental consultant and Director of a company employing over 300 people and grossing $40-50 million each year by saving energy and protecting the earth's valuable resources through responsible appliance de-manufacturing. But this is my second career, and I often refer to the entertainment business as "my former life"…literally.

I grew up in New Jersey where Andy Anka, Paul Anka's younger brother, was one of my schoolmate's and best friend. We often rode to concerts at Palisades Park in the back of stretch limos with hundreds of screaming girls surrounding us. That was exciting for a couple of 12 year old boys and may very well have been the catalyst for why I pursued a life in this business. This popularity came to a screeching halt when my father took a job in Clear Lake City, TX with a new

Stage Four: Aspire Higher ... Citizenship

government entity called NASA. We moved to Houston, where I took up surfing in the Gulf of Mexico, grew my hair long and "colored yella" using hydrogen peroxide, and started listening to the Beatles, Beach Boys, Jefferson Airplane, and other hip bands of our generation. Gone were the songs by Paul Anka, Bobby Ridel, the Shirelles and Roy Orbison.

In 1966 I graduated from high school and enrolled at the University of Houston where my pre-med major changed to engineering and finally ended with sociology with a minor in mass communications. The hair grew longer and the music became a really important part of my education on the campus. I went to concerts religiously and became what is referred to today as a "hippie" with a big moustache and ponytail down to my butt....I had arrived!

> "My father instilled in all of his 5 children that you can accomplish anything in life if you set your mind to it and don't take 'no' for an answer."
> —Michael Dunham

My father instilled in all of his five children that you can accomplish anything in life if you set your mind to it and don't take "no" for an answer. So when a bunch of us were sitting around stoned after a Doors Concert, someone came up with the idea that we should start promoting the concerts ourselves instead of some straight corporate type in a three-piece suit that probably never even heard any of the songs these great artists were performing and certainly didn't live by the lyrics they were preaching. I thought that was the best idea ever and took on the challenge with a vengeance. My friends didn't even remember it the next morning, but I did . . . boy, did I. About six months later, I was sitting in front of Bobby Sakowitz asking for $50,000 to promote a concert with the Jefferson Airplane, the Grateful Dead, the Byrds & Poco. He actually gave my partner and I the money...of course he would control everything but he agreed to finance this concert. The date was October 5, 1969 and I had turned twenty-one just three weeks earlier and that was the start of a thirteen year career that involved over two thousand concerts with everyone from Frank Sinatra to the Rolling Stones and Broadway shows starring Katherine Hepburn/ Christopher Reeves in "A Matter of Gravity" to HAIR...the first play to perform on American stages with full frontal nudity. By this time I had relocated to Austin, TX.....The Music Capital of the World... where I had two nightclubs on 6th Street, and an exclusive contract to produce at The Paramount Theatre on Congress Avenue, a 1,200 seat, fully restored vaudeville house. I spent approximately two hundred days a year on the road for that entire span. In 1982 Rodney Dangerfield agreed to do a US tour after achieving "overnight success" from *Caddyshack*. So he and I

> "This was truly a life changing event which required a year in a wheelchair/crutches and another year in physical therapy."
> —Michael Dunham

travelled the country in Willie Nelson's tour bus with "the Beast" driving and cooking. Willie was over in Hawaii recording his "IRS Tapes" to get out of trouble with those guys. After this Dangerfield tour, I decided to take some down time so went to Padre Island in South Texas for some sun and surf. It was early October and the Gulf of Mexico was churning with six to eight foot waves following a hurricane that had just passed through. I woke up one sunny morning and could see a boat wrecked at the end of a quarter-mile rock jetty just in line of campsite. This looked very serious so I went out to investigate to make sure nobody was on this vessel that needed help. After climbing on and all through every possible nook, it was obvious that the boat was empty and had probably broken loose during the storm. Climbing off was much more difficult than getting on but, I finally made it when a twelve foot monster wave crashed over the jetty and sweep me into the rocks on the other side. I hit with such force it knocked me unconscious for a few seconds, and I could not feel my right leg at all. I was holding onto the boulders for dear life and really thought I had probably lost my leg when the second wave in the set swept me out into the channel where swift currents were taking me out to sea. Since I could feel my lower body by this time and couldn't tread water in rough seas without the use of my legs, I was in serious trouble and sinking fast. Prayers were all I could think of, so I prayed. Miraculously, a lone surfer appeared on the jetty with his board and began yelling to ask if I needed help…which it became obvious I did after disappearing under water several times. The last thing I remember was him throwing his surfboard into the rough surf and diving in to paddle out to help me. I woke up in the South Coast Hospital with a newspaper showing a photo of a helicopter pulling some guy out of the water on a cable….that guy was me. I had undergone an intense surgery to replace my hip, thigh bone and several pins to hold me together. In x-rays, it looks like the Bionic Man and the doctors said it was the most traumatized bone they had ever encountered at that hospital. This was truly a life changing event that required a year in a wheelchair/crutches and another year in physical therapy.

I realized while lying in the hospital that this new condition would put a serious damper on my ability to travel anytime soon. Doctors were not sure if I would ever fully recover and be able to walk without the aid of a cane or walker. Thank God, I did. The next challenge would be to find something to do that would give me the same great satisfaction the music and entertainment industry had provided.

Music was the greatest form of communication in the world and I would only work with those bands and artists whose message I believed in and wanted to put in front of large groups of young people to "spread the word". If I didn't like a band's message, I didn't work with them . . . period.

My decision was to pursue a career in recycling which was a BUZZ word during the 80s and 90s. Tapping into my entrepreneurial spirit, I began small and soon built a company that employed eighty people in five Texas cities. Eventually, we had an opportunity to work with Sears to handle their old appliances. Soon, the direction became totally focused on appliance recycling. Since refrigerators & freezers contained CFCs which are ozone depleting substances (ODS), it required special equipment, training and permits to treat these two household appliances.

In the Summer of 2000, we were contacted by the California Public Utilities Commission, because California was experiencing a severe energy crisis and having to mandate conservation through "rolling blackouts". The plan was to combat this crisis using conservation rather than building new power plants, which are expensive and take years to build. Since the largest drain of electricity in any home is the refrigerator, this was an obvious place to start. Also, 20% of the homes in the US have two . . . one in the kitchen and another in the garage or basement. Typically, the second one is much older and uses three to four times as much as the kitchen unit.

> "The plan was to combat this crisis [energy] with conservation ... since the largest drain of electricity in any home is the refrigerator, this was an obvious place to start."
> —Michael Dunham

So we designed a program to pay homeowners $50 to turn in their old "beer" fridge and we would pick them up free and properly recycle them at no cost to the customer. These appliances also had to be destroyed so they wouldn't end up back on the electric grid. The process we designed separated 95% of the materials that were used to make the appliance so we refer to it as de-manufacturing . . . which is truly the mirror image of the manufacturing process. The process is so efficient that even the foam insulation in the walls was removed and destroyed because it contained CFC-11, a potent ozone-depleting greenhouse gas. This foam was shipped to waste-to-energy plants to actually generate electricity from this material.

JACO Environmental (which is the company that was set up to respond to the California request) was awarded a contract as a result of this program design. We opened a facility in Northern California to handle the 10,000 refrigerators for Sacramento Utility District in 2001. Since then, JACO has expanded across the country to 24 states, 75 utility contracts and has eighteen facilities to handle the 500,000 units we collect each year. We have also created 350 "green jobs" and, each refrigerator collected and de-manufactured in our process is equal to 10 tons of CO_2 or CO_2 equivalent which is like taking 2 cars off the road for an entire year. I often refer to these appliances as 'environmental time bombs', based on their potentially harmful effects. The 1/2 million appliances we collect each year is equal to taking 1 million cars off the road for that year.

This program and process was so unique that JACO was awarded the Stratospheric Ozone Protection award in 2004 and again in 2007 for the Best of the Best, at the 20th Anniversary of the Montreal Protocol in Canada. I was also appointed to a United Nations Environmental Programs Task Force were I continue to serve as an expert in the ODS field . . . particularly foam insulation in appliances & buildings. In this position, I have had the opportunity to travel the world for conferences, meetings and research.

> "The single most asked question is: 'How do you know Global Warming is real?' My reply is 'What if the scientists are wrong?' I think we can all agree that conserving the Earth's natural resources is a wise decision because there's a dwindling supply . . ."
> —Michael Dunham
> UN Task Force Manager

The single most asked question is "How do you know Global Warming is real?" My reply is "What if the scientists are wrong?" I think we can all agree that conserving the Earth's natural resources is a wise decision, because there is a dwindling supply, including fossil fuels like oil, coal and natural gas. We can also agree that burning these fuels pollutes the air we breathe so, the less we use, the better. There is a common misconception that being "green" costs more. JACO's refrigerator program is a perfect example of this being false. The major electric utility companies offer this program because it is highly cost-effective - meaning it is cheaper for them to pay $100 for those old appliances than to generate or buy the same amount of power these appliances would require during their remaining useful life. All the environmental attributes are a bonus and not included in the cost-effectiveness equation.

So what should we do to be considerate to both sides of this Climate Change argument? I believe the reason the world hasn't shifted to alternative energy sources is based on the politics of business or business of politics. We certainly have the technology to tap into renewable energy sources like wind, solar, hydro, geo-thermal and bio-mass. However, there are too many countries, states, companies, and individual jobs depending on the status quo to shift quickly

Stage Four: Aspire Higher ... Citizenship

without causing major problems to the global economy. The transition is coming but it will have to be gradual, not sudden or overnight.

Meanwhile, individuals can make an enormous difference on a personal level just by changing some simple basic habits and buying patterns. Here are just a few:

- Replace the incandescent bulbs in your home and office with CFLs which last five years but use only 20% of the electricity.

- Turn in that old "energy hog beer fridge" in the garage . . . and when replacing any household appliances look for Energy Star logos . . . they will save enough water, gas and electricity to pay for themselves over their useful life

- If you are buying a new automobile, consider either a hybrid, flex fuel or electric car. They get much better mileage and lower emissions. Some states even allow for driving alone in car pool lanes so it saves time as well

- Conserve both hot & cold water by taking showers rather than baths, and use a low flow shower head. A smaller tank on the toilet and turning off the faucet while brushing your teeth will both save water.

- If you unplug the charging devices for your electronics it saves power because they continue to use power even without a device connected.

- Separate your household and office trash into bins for aluminum, plastic, glass and paper. If the city doesn't provide this service, take it yourself to a recycling center . . . most of them will pay for these materials.

> "There is a common misconception that being 'green' costs more. JACO's refrigerator program is a perfect example of this being false."
>
> —Michael Dunham
> JACO Environmental

Believe it or not, every home in the US throws away enough garbage every year to provide enough electricity to completely power it. Again, the technology exists to turn all that garbage in bio-mass to make electricity or bio-fuels, instead of continuing to bury it in landfills. The time is coming so we must be patient but continue to demand better use of our natural resources.

❖ ❖ ❖

Michael Dunham's life changed dramatically on an early October morning with the near paralyzing injuries he incurred trying to help someone in a shipwreck in Texas. I wonder if it always has to be a traumatic event that inspires us to take our life seriously and make our work our vocation, our calling?

You could decide now to be a good citizen of your country and the world. You can do both because you have been blessed with a good brain and a college or university that can help you find your passion and direct you and your life's work toward something that has meaning and will make your nation and the world a better place.

> "You could decide now to be a good citizen of your country and the world."
> —Dr. Will Keim

I am certain there are cynical people who will say it is too late. Dr. John Gardner began our discussion of citizenship with a question about whether we have lost our ability to care for and work for the common good. He kept teaching at Stanford after he posed the question and I am still on the road because I believe this is our time, your time, to make of the world whatever you want it to be. In the past five years I have seen:

- A University of Mississippi student start a school in Africa with money he raised from Ole Miss students and his friends.
- A football player from Wake Forest collect shoes from student athletes and take them to the Dominican Republic for children
- A major corporation, Lenscrafters, send their employees on a 'mission' to South America and hand out glasses they had collected in the United States

I will never forget a story I heard when I spoke to the Lenscrafters and Eye Med professionals. An 8 year old little boy said to George, a Lenscrafters employee fitting him with glasses so that he could see for the first time:

Boy: "Are you God?"
George: "No. My name is George."
Boy: "Are you sure?"
George: "Yes. Why do you ask?"
Boy: "Because my Grandma said only God could make me see again."

If this doesn't move you, then I cannot help you find your unique role as a citizen of your country and the world. Later that day, George fitted the Grandmother with her first pair of glasses and she got to see her grandson clearly for the first time.

> **DON'T TELL ME ITS TOO LATE**
> **TOO MANY PEOPLE ARE DOING TOO MANY GOOD THINGS**
> **RIGHT HERE, RIGHT NOW. THIS IS YOUR TIME!**

For Michael Dunham, it was the environment. He does good work, helps the environment, improves his country and the world, and makes a good living. When you evolve a business like JACO to 24 states, have 75 utility contracts, have 18 facilities, and handle 500,000 units each year, there is room for green (environment) and green (profit).

Michael's Seven Ideas focused on everyday things you can do to improve the environment. Maybe the environment isn't your thing, your passion. That's fine. But what is? What is your passion and what seven ideas can you generate to make yourself a better person, your country a better place, and the world a greater place for its children?

> "Our deepest fear is not that we are inadequate. Our deepest fear is that we are powerful beyond measure."
>
> —Marianne Williamson
> Spiritual activist, author, lecturer, and founder of The Peace Alliance

YOUR PASSION _____

_____

_____

_____

_____

Citizenship involves reason, respect, and responsibility to yourself, your college, your family, friends, city, state, nation, and world. I hope you will let Michael Dunham's journey help you embark on one of your own choosing and design. Michael is looking for a group of students who want to change the world. His contact information is in this book.

SEVEN IDEAS TO MAKE MY PASSION A REALITY

_____
_____
_____
_____
_____
_____
_____

Closing Thought: Do you really believe that the meeting between Michael and me on the Alaska flight was a coincidence? When asked if he thought there was a plan for the Universe, Albert Einstein said, "God doesn't role dice." See the good, work to eliminate the bad, and have faith in the goodness of yourself and others.

Sportsmanship   18

> **"Inappropriate fan behavior disrupts contests and tarnishes the spectator experience. In worst cases it leaves students and fans severely injured and costs institutions and communities thousands in clean-up and restoration dollars."**
>
> —*The NCAA Sportsmanship Report, 2003*

The National Collegiate Athletic Association (NCAA) Sportsmanship and Ethical Conduct Committee has developed and adopted the following definitions for sportsmanship and ethical conduct:

- Sportsmanship is a set of behaviors to be exhibited by student-athletes, coaches, game officials, administrators, and fans in athletic competition. These behaviors are based on values, including respect, civility, fairness, honesty, and responsibility.   (NCAA Bylaw 22.2.4.4)

- Ethical conduct is a set of guiding principles with which each person follows the letter and spirit of the rules. Such conduct reflects a higher standard than law because it includes, among other principles, fundamental values that define sportsmanship.   (NCAA Bylaw 22.2.4.4.)

For the sake of our discussion in this book regarding the role of sportsmanship on the collegiate campus, we will accept these definitions as set forth in the NCAA Bylaw as the governing agency of intercollegiate athletics. We will examine and consider their relevance not only to NCAA sanctioned events, but also to intramural, recreational, and club sport events on campus. Nearly every single student of nearly every campus will be a participant, observer, or fan for an intercollegiate, intramural, recreational, or club sport event. Sportsmanship, or the lack thereof, will ultimately make that experience a positive or negative one.

In my book, *Fan Etiquette*, NBA Star Steve Kerr related the most horrific case of abuse of a player I had ever heard. University of Memphis Head Coach Josh Pastner, one of my former students, had introduced us, and Steve graciously wrote the Forward for the book. He said, "In 1988 when I was a senior at the University of Arizona, I was verbally assaulted before a game by fans in the Arizona State University student sections who stood and mocked me about the death of my father, who had been killed in a terrorist attack in Beirut four years before. I was so shocked and sickened that I sat through the rest of the warm-up session, crying on the bench as my teammates consoled me." He continues, "The story became public and a week or so later I received an unsigned letter from one of the students who had been mocking me. The writer of the letter apologized, but tried to justify his actions saying, 'Do you know how painful it's been to see Arizona athletes being so cocky after beating us over the years?'"

> "What has happened to common decency and civility, at sporting events and in society at large?"
> —Dr. Will Keim

How has the burning desire to win become the desire to burn? What has happened to common decency and civility, at sporting events, and in society at large? Is there anything we can do to make sporting events more humane and enjoyable for all?

Of course, not all students play intercollegiate athletics at the NCAA or NAIA level. A far greater number engage in intramural, recreational, or club sport outings for personal enjoyment, exercise, or pure love of sport. Those who do not play will watch as friends and fans so sportsmanship is an important value across the collegiate campus and merits our concern here.

What do we do when umpires and referees are beaten and screamed at on a regular basis? Professor Jerry M. Lewis of Kent State University states, "Winning has become so significant in college sports that this type of behavior has been institutionalized." Anyone who has witnessed an intramural game at college may have seen the same types of behaviors.

How Bad Is It?

From a booklet called, "'What To Do When They're in Your Face':
'Seven Ways To Develop Thick Skin';
'How To Handle Verbal Challenges';
'When A Fight Breaks Out'; and 'If You're Attacked.'"

From NASO, The National Association of Sports Officials

One student newspaper wrote, "Students at a world-class university should not act like this…this melee of flying garbage, roses, and alcohol bottles absolutely was uncalled for!!! (after a football loss)

We are not advocating for intramural, recreational sports, or intercollegiate athletic events without fans or with those fans sitting in monastic silence. We are proposing that we can play in and attend events and cheer for our team without demeaning the other team. We can practice sportsmanship and ethical conduct and have a great time. We will propose a definition of Fan Etiquette to set the table for good sportsmanship. Co-curricular activities like athletics and sporting events should reduce stress, not create or enhance it!

> **What The Experts Say Regarding the booklet, "What To Do When They're In Your Face" … "It's sad that such a booklet even exists!"**
>
> —Rick Wolff, Chairman
> The Center For Sports Parenting
> & Institute for International Sports

From Major League Baseball

As an NCAA Approved Speaker on Life Skills and Substance Abuse Issues, I wrote in *Fan Etiquette*, "Athletic Directors, coaches, administrators, and the International Association of Campus Law Enforcement Administrators have all identified 'alcohol as a violence escalator'. What role does alcohol play in the behavior you see in stadiums, around intramural fields, and recreational sports facilities? It is time to be honest and address the issue."

> **Fan behavior escalated over the course of my career. At what point did the price of a ticket give fans the right to abuse?**
>
> —Ed Sprague
> 2 time Major League Baseball Champion
> 2 time NCAA Baseball Champion, Stanford
> Olympic Gold Medalist
> Baseball, USA

Time To Be Honest, Time To Be True

What percentage of crazy behavior that you have seen would you say is alcohol related, induced, or escalated?

Are your campus officials concerned? Dr. Eileen Sullivan, Vice President of Student Affairs at Elmhurst College says, "The issues of fan behavior and sportsmanship are of great concern to higher education leaders."

Why Sportsmanship, Why Now?
Athletic Director Mitch Barnhart of The University of Kentucky states, "In today's world the need for someone to establish some responsibilities for fan behavior is long overdue. Dr. Will Keim has spearheaded an effort to define reasonable and sportsmanlike conduct for fans and players."

With this in mind we turn our discussion to Fan Etiquette, the art of sportsmanship.

Fan Etiquette: The Art of Sportsmanship

We affirm the power of play or sport to enhance and change lives. We believe a redirection and reform are needed on behalf of the fans to remember why we were drawn first to play and then to cheer for others playing. All sports have rules and regulations to govern and create fair play. It is time for players, coaches, and fans to do our part.

> "If you're yelling 'cymbals players suck' at a band member, then you have issues."
> —Dr. Will Keim

Etiquette stands for:

Enjoy
Team
Involved
Quiet
United
Excitement
Talk
Treat
Enough

The real player or fan knows that the purpose of the event is to **Enjoy** the event. The contest is a great way to spend time with teammates or friends. I have heard students yell at band members, "Cymbal players suck" and angry fans blurt out to the visiting team, "Go home!" If they went home, you would be watching a practice. When you need to scream at players on the other team, then you have issues. No one should have to suffer second-hand abuse at the hands of the unruly, intoxicated, or rude.

Good fans understand that while they are enjoying the game they should not embarrass themselves but most importantly they should not embarrass their **Team**. Arizona State players were horrified when they learned what their fans had yelled at Steve Kerr. The action should be on the field, court, the ice, or in the pool…not in the stands. If you need to be the center of attraction, got out for the team.

It is great to be **Involved** at the games and events and cheer, support, and encourage your team. How much longer will institutions and the public support events where children in attendance hear a cacophony of profane abuse. If your little brother or sister was on the court, would you be comfortable with someone saying to them what you are saying to someone else's brother, sister, or child?

Experienced fans know the power of **Quiet** in creating an intimidating atmosphere. My friend Dave Jacobs of Whittier College asked his fans to be completely silent during the warm-up and introduction of the visiting team. It was eerie and Dave's teams won 44 games in a row at one stretch. Give the pipes a rest every once in awhile, and use quiet as your weapon.

> "Try the power of silence when the opposing team is introduced. The quiet is very unsettling for them. They're used to getting booed."
>
> —Dr. Will Keim

Fans should feel **United** with their team but should never upstage them. The game is the player's moment to shine. It is the reward for thousands of hours and many years of work. It is ultimately disrespectful to steal their moment in the sun. Players should never have to wait for the naked guy to have his undeserved 15 minutes of shame. When it comes to stealing attention from athletes who deserve it…Just Don't Do It!

Enjoying your team's efforts, being involved in the game, utilizing noise and quiet to create an atmosphere, uniting with thousands of others in a special moment that will never happen exactly the same way again…who could doubt the **Excitement** of this experience? Excitement translates into a positive reward for friends and classmates of those who are doing their very best. You do not need to swear at the opponent to be excited.

Classy fans **Talk** to each other with respect befitting an honored and noble opponent. They do not direct profane or abusive language at

> "Third baseman Emily Keagbine had been hit in the face by a pitched ball. The Pacific Lutheran Pitcher had accidentally hit her. As the Linfield College fans held their breath, Emily spit out two teeth and lay motionless. A PLU Dad said, 'They better not give her 1st base. She walked into that pitch.'
>
> It was all I could do to keep myself from going over and becoming 'That Guy', ... the guy you read about, and I wrote *Fan Etiquette*!
>
> We should all focus on the well being of the players."
>
> P.S. Emily's jaw was broken later Xrays revealed and she finished the game!
>
> —Dr. Will Keim

the other teams or its fans. It might be helpful to remember that you are yelling abuse at an 18-22 year old student who is still working on his or her self esteem, sense of purpose, and place in the world. It is about civility, and respect and you cannot give to another person what you do not have within yourself.

Finally, good fans and friends, in fact, all good people, **Treat** others like they would like to be treated. They know when **Enough is Enough**. If you have had six beers you may have trouble knowing when enough is enough. We do not tolerate harassment of any kind in the classroom. It should not be tolerated in the stadiums, courts, or the playing facilities that great coaches call their classrooms.

The Parable of The Mouth & The Buttocks

If you find yourself yelling at a poorly paid referee, an 18 year old wide receiver, or a cymbal player in the visiting team's band, with your date leaning away from you to disassociate himself or herself with you, with folks referring to you as "That Guy"…listen then, through the haze of the pre-game activities to faintly hear someone saying to you, "Hey, Buddy…sit down and shut up." Listen to them. You are clearly using one part of your anatomy…your mouth…too much…and another part…your buttocks…too little!

One famous football coach told me, "Most fans don't know enough to know they don't know enough." Stay in your area of expertise—cheer loudly and with some class, for your team.

Practice Fan Etiquette. Be a good sport. Enjoy the game for the love of the game. Talk to your Director of Recreational Sports or Intramurals, your Athletic Director, or Director of Student Activities about making your home field advantage a positive experience for your team and for the visiting team or opponent. Without the visiting team, other residence hall's intramural team, or opponent, you would be watching a practice.

***A special thank you to the National Collegiate Athletic Association for their work on Sportsmanship and Ethical Conduct. They have empowered many high school athletic associations to make strong statements on the importance of Sportsmanship, which are making attendance at events enjoyable again for the entire family.

Sportsmanship
    Respect
    Civility
    Fairness
    Honesty
    Responsibility

Ethical Conduct
    Higher Standards
    The Letter and The Spirit
        of the Law
    Fundamental Values

> "I attended a football game at The University of Nebraska versus The University of Missouri. At the end of the game, the Nebraska fans gave the Missouri Tigers a standing ovation for their good effort as they left the field. They do it win or lose. That's Fan Etiquette. That's good sportsmanship. That's ethical conduct befitting a great university!"
>
> *Dr. Will Keim*

To learn more about sport, sportsmanship, and their impact on society, check out:

- National Collegiate Athletic Association
  www.ncaa.org
- Center for the Study of Sport In Society
  www.sportinsociety.org
- National Association of Intercollegiate Athletics
  www.naia.org
- Josephson Institute of Ethics
  www.josephsoninstitute.org
- National Intramural Recreational Sports Association
  www.nirsa.org

A Coach's Perspective

"As an Offensive Coordinator and Head Coach in Division I NCAA Football, I was always focused on how to score on a football field. Much more important than that: How do you score in life? The acronym on this page can serve you well as you navigate your way and help you win the game of life."

- **S**eize the Moment
- **C**onfront Your Weaknesses
- **O**vercome Adversity
- **R**espect Others
- **E**njoy the Ride!

— *Coach Dan Patterson*

S.C.O.R.E.!

❖ ❖ ❖

AUTHOR'S NOTE: "I have known Coach P. for over a decade. He coached for 20 years at Iowa with the legendary Hall of Fame Coach Hayden Fry. They witnessed 14 Bowl games including 3 Rose Bowls and a Number 1 ranking. A West Point Graduate, he flew helicopters for the Army and has been married to Lisa for 30 years. They have a daughter Brooke who is a Doctor of Pharmacy. He coached with Kirk Ferentz, Bob Stoops, Bill Snyder and Barry Alvarez and against Nick Saban, Jim Tressel, and Joe Paterno. 'I lived a blessed life, then I got cancer,' Coach says. His message is a message of hope: 'What's Holding You Down?: Overcoming Life's Obstacles.' 35 radiation treatments and 6 chemos later, he retains his faith, hope, and love for life. He wants every student to score and win in the game of life!"

— *Dr. Will Keim*

Trees of Self-Realization and Self-Defeat

19

John Speaks:

This chapter provides you with the opportunity to design your own personal roadmap for building a meaningful life and an enduring legacy. Your success in this endeavor will bring us great satisfaction and it will also help raise the consciousness level of your family and friends, thus making it a better world for everyone. Our best wishes go out to each of you.

—*Professor John Argeropoulos*

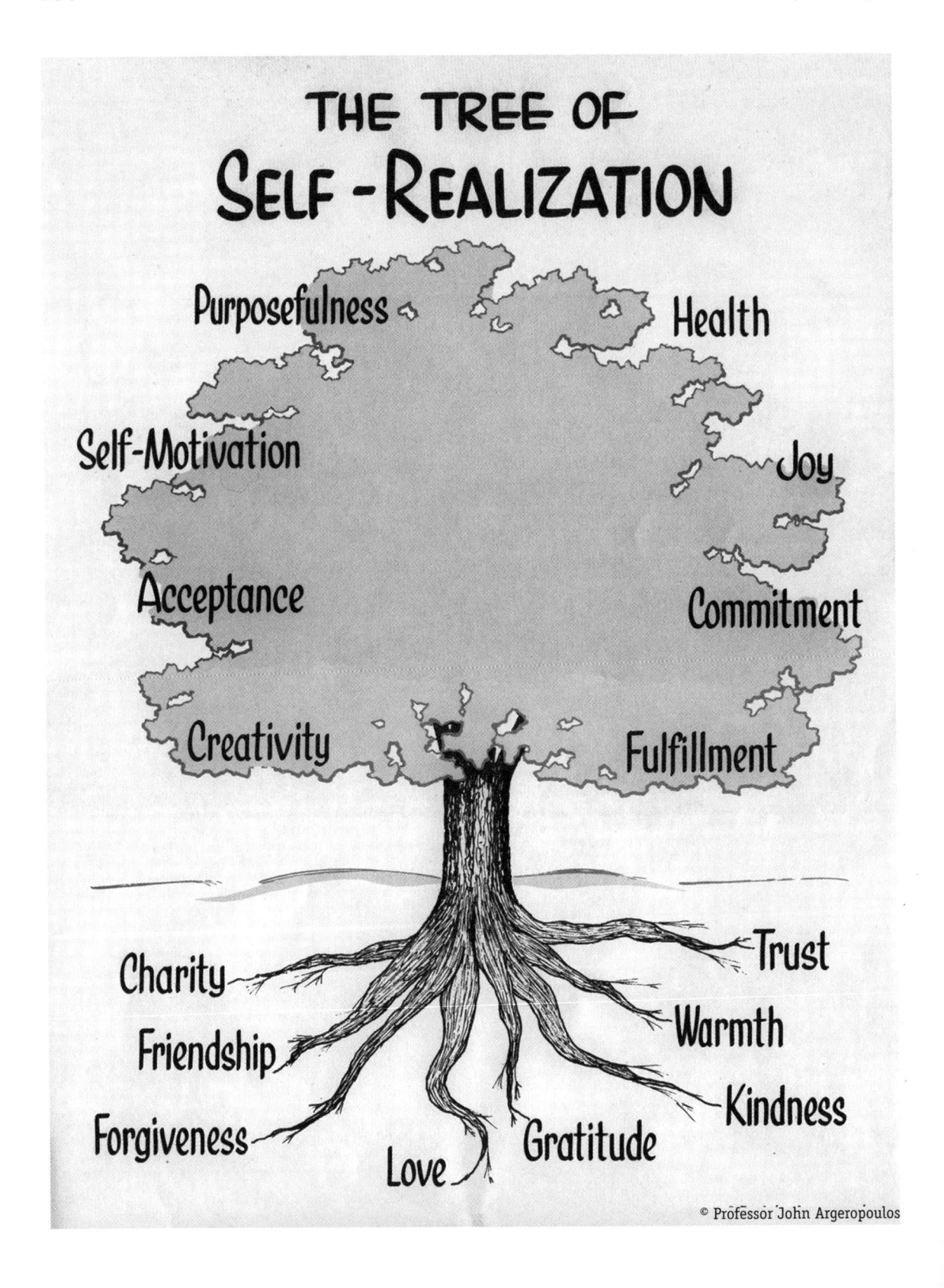

THE TREE OF SELF-REALIZATION

- Purposefulness
- Health
- Self-Motivation
- Joy
- Acceptance
- Commitment
- Creativity
- Fulfillment

Roots:
- Charity
- Trust
- Friendship
- Warmth
- Forgiveness
- Kindness
- Love
- Gratitude

© Professor John Argeropoulos

Stage Four: Aspire Higher ... Trees of Self-Realization and Self-Defeat

THE TREE OF SELF - DEFEAT

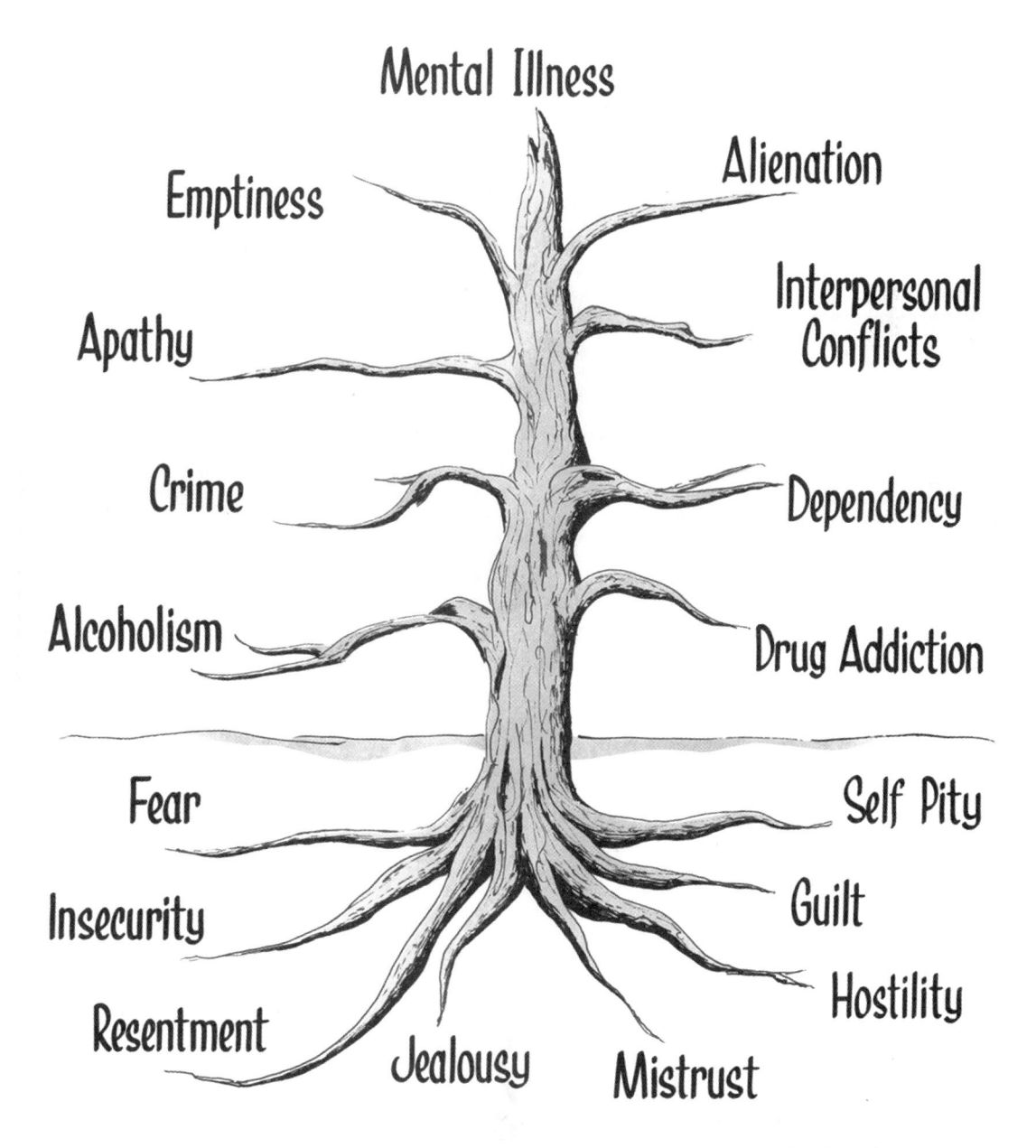

Branches:
- Mental Illness
- Emptiness
- Alienation
- Apathy
- Interpersonal Conflicts
- Crime
- Dependency
- Alcoholism
- Drug Addiction

Roots:
- Fear
- Self Pity
- Insecurity
- Guilt
- Hostility
- Resentment
- Jealousy
- Mistrust

© Professor John Argeropoulos

THE TREE OF SELF-REALIZATION
AND
THE TREE OF SELF-DEFEAT
by John Argeropoulos

Countless books and articles have been written in an attempt to explain the dynamic forces that determine success and failure in our lives. These explanations exhibit a wide range in both their scope and levels of sophistication, and certainly have included many excellent works. Perhaps lacking in the past has been some type of lucid model that can graphically portray these ideas in a parsimonious manner to professionals and lay people alike.

The origin of this model can be traced to the pioneering work of Dr. Hal S., "An AA Doctor's Prescription," which appeared in the July, 1963 issue of *AA Grapevine*. Dr. Hal utilized a rather stark graphic entitled The Tree of Alcoholism to portray the many contributing causes that were at the root of alcoholism and the painfully grim fruits associated with problem drinking. Dr. Harry M. Tiebout was the first psychiatrist to recognize that the philosophy and principles of AA represented an approach to alcoholism of revolutionary significance and he was motivated to develop a more positive companion piece, "The Tree of Sobriety," for the November, 1963 *AA Grapevine*. I did not learn about these materials until 1969 but I immediately grasped the much greater potential inherent in their wisdom. The concept gradually evolved into the idea of a Tree of Self-Realization and a Tree of Self-Defeat in 1970. I shared this new model with Dr. Hal who liked it and gave his blessing as long as his anonymity was maintained. Dr. Tiebout had died in 1966 but Dr. Hal felt that he would have been a strong supporter of the new approach.

The model of a Tree of Self-Realization and a Tree of Self-Defeat represents an evolutionary growth in consciousness that has been calibrated in the range of 480-500 by Dr. David Hawkins on his Map of Consciousness. Work by Dr. Hawkins at the Institute for Advanced Spiritual Research has revealed the existence of subtle energy forces that reflect the level of consciousness of individuals as well as societies. When people are caught up in the self-limiting beliefs of the ego or false self, which are fear based, they exhibit lower levels of consciousness (below 200) and tend to behave as if they are victims with little hope of escaping a life of misery and conflict.

> "Sitting with John Argeropoulos over a cup of coffee, looking out the picture window of his home framing Lake Superior was a very peaceful experience. I asked him to share 'The Trees' with you because I believe they can inspire you toward a higher consciousness and belief in self."
> —Dr. Will Keim

Individuals who are operating from a higher level of consciousness are more concerned with the welfare of others and exhibit greater compassion and unconditional love which serve as attractor forces that are capable of generating growth opportunities which positively impact their lives and the lives of others. It should come as no surprise that these individuals, as a group, enjoy better health, as well as greater success and happiness as a consequence of this enlightened status. Dr. Hawkins has used this model of a Tree of Self-Realization and a Tree of Self-Defeat in his seminars and reported that audiences quickly grasp the dynamics and consequences of the lifestyles they have been living and then realize that they have the power to change. Additional research by Dr. Stephen Post at Stony Brook University and Dr. Harold Koenig at Duke University has demonstrated the positive impact of altruistic behavior on our immune systems.

Extensive research by Dr. Martin Seligman in his book, Authentic Happiness, has shown that optimists and pessimists reveal very specific cognitive patterns that reflect major differences in how they think and in how they interpret their reality. Seligman's work once again demonstrates how The Tree of Self-Realization can impact our health and life satisfaction in a very positive manner while The Tree of Self-Defeat can lead to learned helplessness, victimization, depression, and poorer health. Additional research by Dr. Stephen Post at Stony Brook University and Dr. Harold Koenig at Duke University has demonstrated the positive impact of altruistic behavior on our immune systems.

> "In reality, each of us is involved in relationships with people and activities which are depicted in both Trees..."
> —John Argeropoulos

In reality, each of us is involved in relationships with people and activities that are depicted in both Trees. It is normal and healthy to experience the full range of human emotions because when we try to shut off our negative feelings, we run the very real risk of also inadvertently closing off our positive experiences as an unintended consequence. However, experiencing negative emotions has become a greater problem today as a result of living in an increasingly fast-paced and far more complex world that is changing dramatically every day at almost lightning speed. While clever advertising, highly charged political rhetoric, religious cults and acts of terrorism have always been part of our human history, their negative effects have been magnified by 24/7 cable news and high-tech devices such as cell phones and instant messaging systems. Richard Brodie in his book, Viruses of the Mind, reminds us that words and thoughts can have very powerful consequences because they represent subtle energy sources capable of penetrating and infecting our minds whenever we become vulnerable to incoming erroneous information.

We can learn to protect ourselves from such threats by learning how to discern the intentions of the speaker or writer and also by becoming aware that there is a split-second gap between these negative thoughts and our responses to them during which we can choose positive, constructive behavior from the Tree of Self-Realization instead of reacting reflexively with negative, fear-based emotions from the Tree of Self-Defeat. We thus can create a compelling vision to seek out a successful and fulfilling life by learning to maximize our resources in such a way that we spend the majority of our time and energy reaping the benefits of the Tree of Self-Realization and learning effective coping strategies to minimize the time and energy spent in overcoming the emotional wounds associated with the Tree of Self-Defeat. The true value of this model, however, lies not in the striking difference between the two lifestyles, but rather in the concept of the Tree of Self-Defeat being likened to a dormant tree in real life. Just as a dormant tree comes to life each spring, emotionally wounded individuals can reclaim a life of abundance when they learn to incorporate positive emotions and strategies into their lives.

> "The true value, however, lies not in the striking difference between the two lifestyles, but rather in the concept of The Tree of Self-Defeat being likened to a dormant tree in real life. Just as a dormant tree comes to life each Spring, emotionally wounded individuals can reclaim a life of abundance when they learn to incorporate positive emotions and strategies into their lives."
> —John Argeropoulos

It is tempting at stressful times to seek relief by simply invoking positive affirmations. But positive thinking, magical mantras or moralizing alone will rarely prove sufficient. Many of life's problems are the result of unrecognized but deeply held negative beliefs that lead us into predictable patterns of destructive behavior. The kind of healing process that is required is not a one-time magical solution, but rather an ongoing challenge in dealing with the many dichotomies that assault all of us in our daily lives. Each of us is vulnerable to these dichotomies and thus the challenge is to maintain the courage and the willingness to confront them, instead of retreating into fear and its negative self-defeating behaviors. Dr. Henry Grayson has devised a model for countering these negative core beliefs in his program, *The New Physics of Love*. Grayson utilizes a Five-Step Thought Monitoring Exercise which helps us identify our unique pattern of negative thought constellations, shows how to dismiss such thoughts with a strong action word, and then to replace such thinking with positive affirmations. The successful application of Grayson's approach prepares us for the next step in reclaiming our ability to achieve higher levels of consciousness but much more work remains to be done.

We need a multi-faceted tool-kit from which we can select appropriate resources and strategies that allow us to create a personalized plan of action. The following list of ideas provides a starting point that readers may wish to explore and consider as they move forward with their new goals:

- professional counseling
- personal growth workshops
- specialized support groups
- meditation and prayer
- journal writing
- nature retreats,
- outdoor survival skills training
- tai chi, qi gong, or martial arts training
- strong social network of friends and family

More importantly, we need an informed and concerned citizenry that does not stigmatize and condemn persons in need of treatment. We can attain these higher levels of consciousness once we realize that we are all inter-connected and inter-dependent.

A poignant application of this principle can be found in the somewhat similar challenges faced by our youth and our aged, who often suffer through long bouts of loneliness, boredom, and feelings of helplessness. Involvement in intergenerational endeavors such as school mentoring programs, volunteer and leadership roles in Scouting, Big Brothers-Big Sisters, YMCA activities, Junior Achievement clubs, oral history projects, Make-A-Difference Day programs, and participation in activities with nursing homes that have adopted the philosophy of the Eden Alternative are but a few of the many mutually rewarding ways in which we can express our higher selves. By reaching out in these ways, we will help to create a perceptual shift for ourselves and others that can help create a better world for everyone.

The purpose of the Tree of Self-Realization is to serve as a roadmap that reminds us of what is possible and to serve as a symbol that encourages us to strive for its achievement. The next step is to expand our comfort zone by creating a new image of the person you would like to become and then identifying exactly what it takes to reach that goal by reprogramming your beliefs. To complete the picture, a personal commitment must be made to seek out and pursue a path of lifelong learning that will bring about the necessary changes for the growth and development you desire. Change of any kind typically produces varying degrees of resistance and pain, both internal and external. The internal resistance stems from negative emotions such as doubt, worry, anxiety, and fear of failure. In order to be able to overcome these fears, you will have to learn how to face them, accept them, and then release them because if you hold onto them and keep them in your consciousness, you will build up a strong negative energy charge and fall back into the Tree of Self-Defeat. You may also unexpectedly encounter external resistance from colleagues and supervisors at work, or even from friends and family members who mistakenly try to keep you within their own comfort zones. When this occurs, you will be called upon to tactfully but persistently muster up the courage to be a risk-taker capable of transcending any and all artificial barriers to your goals.

At such demanding times, we all need to be reminded of Carl Jung's sage advice, "What we resist persists." Others have repeatedly observed that what we focus upon expands and thus we need to reach out and develop new friendships with individuals who are operating at a higher level of consciousness as exemplified in the Tree of Self-Realization.

> "John Argeropoulos has graciously created this Resource List to help students understand themselves and The Tree of Self Realization. Thank You John!"
> —Dr. Will Keim

EXERCISE: *Which branch of the Tree of Self-Realization Do you identify with or aspire to? Why?*

_____
_____
_____
_____
_____
_____
_____
_____

> **John speaks:**
> A poignant application of this principle can be found in the somewhat similar challenges faced by our youth and our aged, who often suffer through long bouts of loneliness, boredom, and feelings of helplessness. Involvement in intergenerational endeavors such as school mentoring programs, volunteer and leadership roles in Scouting, Big Brothers-Big Sisters, YMCA activities, Junior Achievement clubs, oral history projects, Make-A-Difference Day programs, and participation in activities with nursing homes that have adopted the philosophy of the Eden Alternative are but a few of the many mutually rewarding ways in which we can express our higher selves. By reaching out in these ways, we will help to create a perceptual shift for ourselves and others that can help create a better world for everyone.
>
> — *John Argeropoulos*

What Volunteer Programs or Community Service have you participated or would you like to serve?

_____
_____
_____
_____
_____
_____
_____

The following reading list of helpful resources is designed to provide a beginning for this journey. As a famous proverb proclaims, *"When the student is ready, the teacher will appear."*

Family Values and Family Enrichment
Allison Christine, *Teach Your Children Well*, Delacorte Press, 1993
Bennett, William J., *Book of Virtues*, Simon & Schuster, 1995
Chapman, Gary, *Love As a Way of Life*, Doubleday, 2008
Cline, Foster, *Parenting with Love and Logic*, 2006,
    www.loveandlogic.com
Covey, Stephen, *Balancing Work and Family*, Franklin Covey Co, 1998

Ferguson, Niall, *The Ascent of Money,* Penguin Books, 2008
Greenleaf, Robert, *Servant Leadership,* Paulist Press, 1977
Jaworski, Joseph, *Synchronicity: Path to Inner Leadership,* Berrett-Koehler, 1996
Kessel, Brent, *It's Not About the Money,* Harper One, 2008
Kinder, George, *Seven Stage of Money Maturity,* Delacorte Press, 1997
Kravitz, Martin, *Fostering Resilience in All Students,* Corwin Press, 1999
Lawson, Douglas, *Give to Live: How Giving Can Change Your Life,* ALTI Pub, 1991
Marx, Jeffrey, *Season of Life (Pulitzer Prize winner),* Simon & Schuster, 2003
Nerburn, Kent, *Simple Truths,* New World Library, 2005
Peterson, Christopher, *Character Strengths and Virtues,* Oxford University Press, 2004
Pollack, William, *Real Boys: Rescuing Our Sons from Myths,* Henry Holt, 1998
Rich, Dorothy, *Mega Skills,* Houghton Mifflin Co., 1992
Salamon, Julie, *Rambam's Ladder: Meditation on Generosity,* Workman, 2003
Satir, Virginia, *Peoplemaking,* Science and Behavior Books, 1972
Search Institute, *Building Community Assets,* www.search-insitute.org
Secretan, Lance, *Inspire: What Great Leaders Do,* John Wiley, 2004

Vocational Guidance and Career Planning

Boldt, Lawrence, *How to Find Work You Love,* Viking, 1996
Bolles, Richard, *What Color Is Your Parachute,* 10 Speed Press, 2004
Bronson, Po, *What Should I Do With My Life?* Random House, 2002
Dikal, Margaret, *Guide to Internet Job Searching,* VGM Career Books, 2004
Edwards, Paul, *Finding Your Perfect Work,* Jeremy Tarcher/Putnam, 2003
Figler, Howard, *Complete Job Search Handbook,* Holt, 1999
Finney, Martha, *Find Your Calling, Love Your Work,* Simon & Schuster, 1998
Gabler, Laura, *Career Exploration on the Internet,* Ferguson Publishing, 2000
Haldane, Bernard, *Employment Websites for Professionals,* Impact Publishers, 2002
Haldane, Bernard, *Career Satisfaction and Success,* JIST Works, 1996
Jackson, Tom, *Guerilla Tactics in the New Job Market,* Bantam, 1993
Jarow, Rick, *Creating Work You Love,* Destiny Books, 1995
Kennedy Joyce Laine, *Joyce Laine Kennedy's Career Book,* VGM Career Books, 1993
Knox, Deborah, *Life-Work Transitions.com,* Butterworth-Heinemann, 2000

Leider, Richard, *The Power of Purpose,* Barrett-Koehler, 1997
Levoy, Gregg, *Callings: Finding & Following An Authentic Life,* Three Rivers, 1997
Taft, Brad, *Boom or Bust: New Career Strategies,* Cambridge Media, 2006
Wolfinger, Anne, *Quick Internet Guide to Career and Education Information,* JIST, 2000

Addiction and Depression
Baker, Dan, *What Happy People Know,* Rodale, 2003
Benson, Herbert, *Timeless Healing: The Power and Biology of Belief,* Schribner, 1996
Black, Claudia, *Changing Course,* MAC Publishing, 1993
Brodie, Richard, *Virus of the Mind,* Hay House, 2009
Brooks, Robert B., *The Power of Resilience,* McGraw-Hill, 2003
Brown, Michael, *The Presence Process,* Beaufort Books, 2005
Dossey, Larry, *Healing Words: Power of Prayer and Practice of Medicine,* Harper, 1993
Dyer, Wayne, *The Power of Intention,* Hay House, 2004
Farber, Maurice, *Theory of Suicide,* Funk & Wagnalls, 1968
Goleman, Tara Bennett, *Emotional Alchemy,* Harmony, 2001
Jampolsky, Gerald, *Forgiveness: The Greatest Healer,* Beyond Works Pub. 1999
Jeffers, Susan, *Feel the Fear and Do It Anyway,* Ballantine, 1987
Jones, Alan and John O'Neil, *Seasons of Grace,* John Wiley, 2003
Kabat-Zinn, Jon, *Full Catastrophe Living,* Delta, 1990
Kaufman, Barry, *Happiness is a Choice,* Fawcett Columbine, 1991
May, Gerald, *Addiction and Grace,* Harper Row, 1988
Miller, Emmett, *Deep Healing,* Hay House, 1997
Miller, Patrick, *A Little Book of Forgiveness,* Fearless Books, 2004
Nerburn, Kent, *Calm Surrender/Forgiveness,* New World Library, 2000
Peck, M. Scott, *The Road Less Traveled and Beyond,* Simon Schuster, 1997
Rubin, Theodore, *Reconciliations,* Viking Press, 1980
Rubin, Theodore, *Compassion and Self-Hate/Despair,* Collier, 1998
Ruiz, Don Miguel, *The Four Agreements,* Publishers Group West, 2000
Seligman, Martin, *Authentic happiness,* Free Press, 2002
Vaillant, George, *Natural History of Alcoholism Revisited,* Harvard Press, 1995
Viscott, David, *Emotional Resilience,* Harmony Books, 1996
Warner, Samuel J., *Self-Realization and Self-Defeat,* Grove, Press, 1966
Wood, Eve, *Medicine, Mind, and Meaning,* Churchill Livingstone, 2004

Did You Know . . .
Beautiful copies of
The Tree of Self-Realization and
The Tree of Self-Defeat may be
purchased online at
www.willkeim.com.
They are color pictures and
suitable for framing as gifts.

Spirituality

Boorstein, Sylvia, *It's Easier Than You Think,* Harper Collins, 1995
Byock, Ira, *The Four Things That Matter Most,* Free Press, 2004
Csikszentmihalyi, Mihaly, *The Evolving Self,* Harper Collins Publishing, 1993
Csikszentmihalyi, Mihaly, *FLOW,* Harper, 1990
Cushnir, Raphael, *Setting Your Heart on Fire,* Broadway Books, 2003
Gongaji, *The Diamond in Your Pocket,* Sounds True, 2005
Grauds, Constance, *The Energy Prescription,* Bantam Books, 2005
Grayson, Henry, *The New Physics of Love,* Sounds True, 2000
Hawkins, David, *Power vs Force,* Veritas Publishing, 2001
Hawkins, David, *Eye of the I,* Veritas Publishing, 2001
Hawkins, David, *Truth vs Falsehood,* Axial Publishing, 2005
Institute of Noetic Science, Shift Magazine, www.noetic.org
Jones, Alan and John O'Neil, *Seasons of Grace,* John Wiley, 2003
Kornfield, Jack, *A Path with Heart,* Bantam Books, 1993
Lesser Elizabeth, *The New American Spirituality,* Random House, 1999
Miller, D. Patrick, *A Little Book of Forgiveness,* Fearless Books, 2004
Moore, Thomas, *Care of the Soul,* Harper, 1992
Myss, Caroline, *Sacred Contracts: Awakening Your Divine Potential,* Harmony, 2001
Osho, *Joy: The Happiness That Comes from Within,* St. Martin's Press, 2004
Post, Stephen G., *When Good Things Happen to Good People,* Broadway Books, 2006
Tamura, Michael, *You Are the Answer,* Star of Peace Pub, 2002
Tolle, Eckhart, *The Power of Now,* New World Library, 1999
Tolle, Eckhart, *A New Earth: Awakening to Life's Purpose,* Dutton, 2005
What Is Enlightenment?, *What is Enlightenment?* Magazine, www.wie.org
Wilbur, Ken, *Integral Psychology: Consciousness and Spirit,* Shambala, 2000
Wood, Eve, *Medicine, Mind, and Meaning,* Churchill Livingstone, 2004
Zukar, Gary, *The Seat of the Soul,* Fireside, 1989

Healthy Aging

Alford, Henry, *How To Live: A Search for Wisdom from Old People,* Twelve Books, 2009
Autry, James A., *The Spirit of Retirement,* Prima Publishing, 2002
Doherty, Dorothy and Mary McNamara, *Out of the Skin and Into the Soul,* LuraMedia, 1997
Berman, Phillip and Connie Goldman, *The Ageless Spirit,* Ballantine, 1992
Booth, Wayne, *The Art of Growing Older,* Poseidon, 1992

Bridges, William, *Transitions: Making Sense of Life's Changes,* Addison Wesley, 1980
Buford, Bob, *Finishing Well,* Integrity Publishers, 2004
Byock, Ira, *The Four Things That Matter Most,* Free Press, 2004
Chopra, Deepak, *Ageless Body, Timeless Mind,* Harmony, 1993
Dychtwald, Ken, *Healthy Aging*, Aspen Publishers, 1999
Dychtwald, Ken, *Power Years: User's Guide for the Rest of Your Life,* John Wiley, 2005
Hayflick, Leonard, *How and Why We Age,* Ballantine, 1996
Hudson, Frederic, *Life-Launch,* Hudson Institute, 1995
Koenig, Harold, *Purpose and Power in Retirement,* Templeton Foundation, 2002
Lyubomirsky, Sonja, *The How of Happiness,* Penguin Books, 2007
Murphy, John, *The Joy of Old: Guide Success for Elderhood,* Geode Press, 1995
Osho, *Maturity: The Responsibility of Being Oneself,* St. Martin's Griffin 1999
Perlmutter, David, *The Better Brain Book,* Riverhead Books, 2004
Rowe, John and Robert Kahn, *Successful Aging,* Pantheon, 1998
Sapolsky, Robert, *Why Zebras Don't Get Ulcers,* W.H. Freeman, 1998
Schachter-Shalomi, Zalman, *From Age-ing to Sage-ing,* Warner Books, 1997
Sedlar, Jeri & Rick Miners, *Don't Retire, Rewire!* Alpha Books, 2003
Silverstone, Barbara, *Growing Older Together,* Pantheon Books, 1992
Smith, Fred, *You and Your Network,* Word Books, 1984
Thomas, William, *The Eden Alternative: Nature, Hope and Nursing Homes,* www.edenalt.com
Vaillant, George, *Aging Well: Guideposts to a Happier Life,* Harvard Press, 2003
Weil, Andrew, *Healthy Aging: A Lifelong Guide,* Knopf, 2005
Whyte, David, *Midlife and the Great Unknown,* Sounds True, 2003
Wood, Eve, *Medicine, Mind, and Meaning,* Churchill Livingstone, 2004

Lifelong Learning Opportunities
Elderhostel (Learning and travel opportunities worldwide), www.elderhostel.org
Generations United, www.gu.org
Institutes for Learning in Retirement (Short term, noncredit courses at local colleges), www.elderhostel.org/ein/intro.asp
Temple University Center for Intergenerational Learning, www.templecil.org/

❖ ❖ ❖

ABOUT THE AUTHOR: John Argeropoulos is an Emeritus Professor of counseling and career development at Northern Michigan University who has extensive experience as a consultant and workshop presenter. Clients have included the U.S. Department of Education, Michigan Department of Education, Michigan Department of Corrections, Michigan Timbermen Association, American College Testing Program, National On Campus Report, The Appalachia Education Laboratory, Western Michigan University Evaluation Center, University of Wisconsin-Stevens Point Wellness Conference, California College & University System, University of Hawaii-Kapiolani Community College, University of Alaska-Anchorage, Ft. Steilacom Community College, Prentice-Hall Publishing Company, McKnight Publishing Company, and the W. K. Kellogg Foundation.

John remains very active with the Northern Center for Lifelong Learning, Elderhostel programs, hiking, nature photography, and The Unsung Heroes Fund, which he co-founded with his wife, Mary, to provide scholarships for self-renewal training that benefits the staffs of nursing homes, hospice, and home care programs in Marquette County.

WILL'S NOTE: I met John on my first visit to Northern Michigan University. He and his wife attended my lecture as part of the Leader Fellows Program. As a Professor Emeritus, he remains engaged and active in the NMU and Marquette, Michigan communities as well as looking out the picture window of his home at the magnificent Lake Superior and eating cookies with his grandchildren. He is the teacher we all wish we had and he introduced the Trees to me during my visit. I knew upon my first look at them that they needed to be shared with students everywhere.

Trees are magnificent and so is a life based in Self Realization and healthy self esteem. You are encouraged to contact Professor Argeropoulos to discuss the Trees via email at jargerop@nmu.edu, or snail mail. Good Reading!

The Secret

20

> **"To love what you do and feel that it matters— how could anything be more fun?"**
>
> —Katherine Graham
> *1917–2001*
> *Publisher, The Washington Post*

Attitude

Olympic gold medalist Carol Schaudt played only one season of basketball at a community college before she came to Oregon State University. "I was totally ignorant of the game," she told me. "The only thing that even got me noticed was my 6'4" frame." Given her lack of knowledge of the sport, she put her faith in her new OSU coach, Aki Hill. Carol remembers thinking: "If I just do what I am told by my coach, I will become successful." One of the first things Coach Hill told Carol was that missing a shot was unacceptable. Make 100 percent of my shots? Carol thought. That seemed extreme to her, but if the coach expected it, then it must be possible.

Carol worked hard at her shooting, doing everything Coach Hill told her to do. By her senior year, she led the nation in both points per game (averaging almost 29), and field-goal percentage (exactly 75 percent). "It was not just about technique; it was mostly about attitude," she says now. "Reflecting back, I realize that I never shot a shot that I didn't think I was going to make. It's true that I fell short of my goal of shooting 100 percent, but do you think I would have averaged 75 percent if my goal had been to shoot 50 percent?"

Is there a better way?

Many people believe that the secret to life is money, power, and possessions. Honestly, if we had to choose between poor and happy or rich and happy, we would choose the latter. But be clear: Money does not make people happy. If it did, then the United States would be the happiest place on earth. Yet we spend more than $150 billion a year on alcohol and import 150 metric tons of cocaine. If life is so good here, why do so many people live it sedated? Is there a better way? We have learned the secret of collegiate life, and we believe it can lead you to happiness and satisfaction with your college experience and beyond.

> **The Secret:**
> Find something you love to do and learn to do it well enough that people will pay you to do it.

Know what you love.
Do what you love.
The Secret to Life.

> **Will Speaks:**
> When I realized at the end of my Sophomore year that there was a major called Communication Arts and one called Religious Studies and that you could Double Major, I thought I had died and gone to Heaven. You can get credit for speaking and for reading inspiring books? Wow. My fraternity brothers used to laugh at me for being a Speech major. "What are you going to do with a speech major? Travel around the country and give speeches?" (Laugh, laugh, laugh, laugh, laugh). I have logged 2 3/4 million miles on Delta Airlines, crossed the country by Amtrak and by car, and have spoken to over 2 million students, faculty, and staff from 2000 collegiate and corporate campuses. Follow your heart and discover the source of your joy. If you can get paid to do what you love, then you will never "work" a day in your life.
>
> —*Will Keim*

> "If one advances confidently in the direction of his dreams, and endeavors to live the life which he has imagined, he will meet with a success unexpected in common hours."
>
> —*Henry David Thoreau*
> *1817 – 1862*
> *Author, poet, philosopher*

Stage Four: Aspire Higher ... The Secret

Choosing A Major: Finding Your Passion

To choose an appropriate major, complete the following chart. The first example is how Will might have filled it out:

What I love	Relevant Major(s)	Potential Job(s)
Speaking *Learning* *Reading Inspiring Books*	*Communication Arts* *Religious Studies*	*Teacher* *Speaker* *Author*

Go through the course catalog with a yellow marker. Highlight all the classes that interest you. See what major they add up to.

> **Will speaks:**
> In college I was ridiculed by two classmates for being a speech major. They were business majors. "Business—that's where the bucks are," one told me. "What are you going to do with a speech major—travel around the county giving speeches"? he added with a laugh. Those guys went to work for Enron. And I, indeed, ended up traveling around the country giving speeches. While I was hanging out with college students, they were hanging out with greedy, future felons. While I was visiting university campuses, they were visiting courtrooms.
> **Do what you love.**
>
> —*Will Keim*

> "Twenty years from now you will be more disappointed by the things you didn't do than by the ones you did. So throw off the bowlines. Sail away from the safe harbor. Catch the trade winds in your sails. Explore. Dream. Discover."
>
> —*Mark Twain*
> *1835-1910*
> *Author and humorist*

Take your own path

Will's story is not meant to belittle business majors. By all means, major in business if you want. But do it because you love it—not because "that's where the bucks are," or because your father wants you to, or because someone else tells you it's hot.

What is the path you are on?

_____
_____
_____
_____
_____
_____
_____

Where would you like to go?

_____
_____
_____
_____
_____
_____
_____

> "The future is not a result of choices among alternative paths offered by the present, but a place that is created—created first in the mind and will, created next in activity. The future is not some place we are going to, but one we are creating. The paths are not to be found, but made, and the activity of making them changes both the maker and the destination."
>
> —John Schaar
> *Futurist and Professor Emeritus*
> *University of California Santa Cruz*

"Sometimes they are wrong"

Despite the objections of many, the actor and director Kevin Costner insisted that the Native Americans speak their own language in his 1990 film *Dances with Wolves,* and be accompanied with English subtitles.

"People will always tell you what to do with your life. That's called conventional wisdom," Costner said when questioned about his decision. "Sometimes they are wrong. Follow your heart."

The movie won seven Academy Awards, including Best Picture.

**Know the Secret.
Find Your Passion.
Create Your Future.**

25,000 Days   21

> "The quality of a person's life is in direct proportion to their commitment to excellence, regardless of their chosen field of endeavor."
>
> —Vince Lombardi
> *1913 – 1970*
> *Coach, Green Bay Packers*

Making every day count

The average life in the world varies from 45 to a little over 80 years. It depends on an accident of birth. That is, where you are born and where you live your life impacts the length of your life. Your genes, the political realities of your country, the ability of your nation to produce and distribute food equitably. War, poverty, famine. Clean water. Disease. Women tend to live a little longer than men in most countries, but the teaching point is: Life is short, life is precious, and we need to get busy making our lives the masterpeaces we want them to be. (And yes...masterpeaces was spelled that way intentionally!) For the sake of our discussion, we have chosen 25,000 Days as the number of days that represents a full life.

> "My best friend gave me the best advice. He said each day's a gift and not a given right."
>
> —Nickelback Song Lyrics
> *"If Today Were Your Last Day"*
> *Canadian rock band*

We all think that we'll be the ones to get a few more years. But think about it: Chances are you know someone your own age who has already died. Ryan White, who was born a hemophiliac, contracted AIDS from a blood transfusion at age 13. He was given six months to live. At the time, the American public understood little about AIDS, and, in the absence of knowledge, fear of the disease prevailed. Ryan was persecuted—school officials tried to bar him from attending, restaurants denied him access, vandals painted "FAG" on his school locker. Ryan defied the odds and lived five years after contracting AIDS. He spent those years working to reduce prejudice against people living with AIDS. He was tireless in his efforts to educate the general public. He became famous. Hollywood made a movie of his life. A recent Google search for "Ryan White" yielded 7.8 million hits, ranging from a national youth conference to a journalism award named in his honor. Ryan died at age 18—52 years short of what he might have expected.

Death denying

Scholars Elizabeth Kübler Ross and Dr. Marcus Borg describe our culture as "death denying." What do they mean? We routinely depict death in movies and television shows, but most of the time death is depicted as a horrific event. In reality, most people die quietly at home. We do not want to think about that, so we throw in a chain saw, ghouls, bats, bees, huge spiders, aliens, and a host of other horrible things that we will most likely never see. The point is this: When we see a huge spider grab a guy we think, "Wow, that'll never happen to me." If we present death as it really is, we would be moved to say, "That is exactly what's going to happen to me."

"Death is the ultimate teacher," said the philosopher Søren Kierkegaard. It should be, and it should keep us busy and moving.

When we avoid death by sending all our old people away to live separately from us or deny it with endless plastic surgeries, we are wearing blinders. When breast, lip and nose jobs become routine, when we label everything "NEW" as if that makes it better, then we are clearly living in a death-denying, youth-focused, elder-phobic society.

> "I look to the future because that's where I'm going to spend the rest of my life."
> —George Burns
> 1896 – 1996
> Entertainer

So what?

You might be inclined to say, "So what? I'm young. What does this have to do with me? I'm just getting ready to start my life."

You may not be as young as you think. Just as "I'll do it later" usually translates to "It won't get done," "I've got all the time in the world" really indicates a lack of understanding the most important point of this lesson:

The day you were born, you had 25,000 days left.

Did you know that 25,000 grains of sand will fit into your two hands? That's not a lot. 25,000 days—that's if you live a full life. If you have prostate cancer, heart disease, or breast cancer in your family, you may get less than 25,000. Singer Selena got 8,744 days. Distance runner Steve Prefontaine got 8,885 days. Ryan White got 6,693 days. My father lived 14,495 days. I never got to meet him.

So, here's the wake-up call:
An 18-year-old has already used up about 6,500 days—that leaves 18,500 days.

How are you going to spend them? If you like the way your life is going, keep on doin' what you're doin'! But if you don't, now would be a great time to make some changes. Why wait? Need help? You've got a whole college or university standing by, including:

- Academic services
- Counseling services
- Tutors
- Health services
- Recreation
- Intramurals
- Food services
- Student activities
- Student involvement centers
- Campus ministries
- Intercollegiate athletics
- Club sports

> "And in the end, it's not the years in your life that count. It's the life in your years."
> —Abraham Lincoln
> 1809 – 1865
> 16th President of the United States

It's all here. The only thing missing is you.

Your Task:
List your thoughts to the following two questions:

1. What are my three greatest accomplishments so far?

1. _____
2. _____
3. _____

2. What are ten things I want to do before I die?

1. _____
2. _____
3. _____
4. _____
5. _____
6. _____
7. _____
8. _____
9. _____
10. _____

Did you know? Head football coaches Lou Holtz and John L. Smith have a list of 100 things they want to do before they die.

> **"Avoiding danger is no safer in the long run than outright exposure. The fearful are caught as often as the bold."**
> —Helen Keller
> 1880 – 1968
> Blind and deaf social activist, author, and lecturer

Make a plan

Now it's time to plan. First, you need to learn the language you will use in your plan.

Dreams: That's the big picture. Think big.
Goals: These are the guidelines to help you actualize your dreams.
Objectives: Specific ways to reach those goals and dreams.
Action Plan: Nuts and bolts. The "How ya gonna do it."
Due Date: Holds you accountable and lets you check your progress.

As you complete the plan on the next page, don't hold back. Be bold. Take a moment to reflect before you begin to write.

What is it you'd *really* like to do?
How can you make it happen?
What do you need to do to make that dream a reality?

Okay, get to it!

The Bucket List: Things to Do Before You "Kick The Bucket." For an interesting take on what is important in life, see the movie *The Bucket List* starring Jack Nicholson and Morgan Freeman.

Your Task:
Make a plan to achieve your dream.

One dream:

_____
_____
_____

Two goals:

_____
_____
_____
_____

Three objectives:

_____
_____
_____
_____
_____
_____
_____

Your plan:

_____
_____
_____
_____
_____
_____

By when:

_____
_____
_____

> **"If you can dream it, it can be."**
> —Walt Disney
> 1901 – 1966
> Creator of the Disney empire

Will speaks:
In one year the fragility and brevity of life were etched forever in my heart and soul. My dear friend Chris Burrus died at our lunch table during our families' vacation together in Hawaii. He looked up and said, "I could use a Parent's nap," layed his head down, and was gone. Neal Pahia told me his back was hurting him during my visit to the University of Redlands in September. Diagnosed with Pancreatic Cancer in February, he was gone in April. He was like the brother I never had. Dr. Tom Shoemaker was changing a flat tire after visiting his parents in Knoxville, Tennessee when an elderly woman hit him and killed him right in in front of his wife. Three good men, husband and fathers, amazing friends and sons gone in the blink of an eye. And all three around 40 years old. My own father died at 41, three months before I was born.

Every day I live I think of the three of them and my Dad. Chris and Neal had young sons and I have tried my best to keep in touch with them and tell them what great men their fathers were. Dr. Tom was making such great strides at the University of Southern Mississippi in getting black and white students to interact and become friends that the Gospel Choir performed at his service and a Plaza was dedicated to him. The Kali'ikoa Leadership Institute continues as an endowed program in honor of Neal Kali'iloa Pahia, and as I write this, my son stayed the night two nights ago with Anderson Burrus McDonough, son of Chris. I have only seen a picture of my father and wonder what it would have been like to know him.

What am I saying to you? Accept your life as a gift. Enjoy it. Live it. Do not take it for granted. Be amazed each morning when your eyes open up and try once more to be the person you always wanted to be. It is not the number of times you get knocked down. Rather, it is the number of times you get up. The good news is that no matter how many times you have been down, you only have to get up one more time than that!

You are stronger than you think! Think…25,000 Days.

```
25,000   Days
-6,500   Days you've already lived
..............................
18,5000  Days to create
         your Masterpiece.
         Or is it "Master Peace"?
         You decide.
```

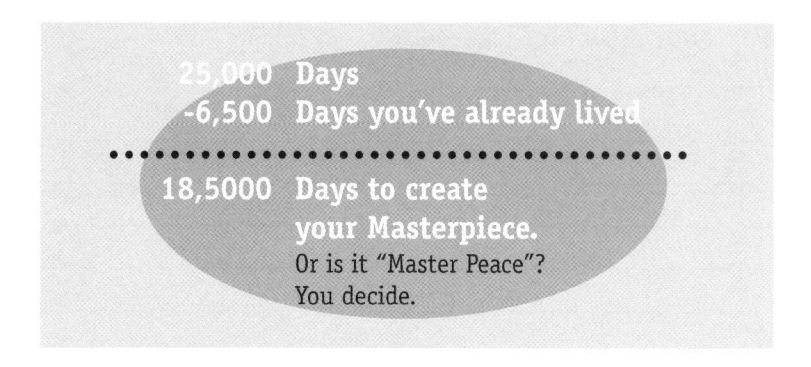

The remainder of your 25,000 days

Your final task for Chapter 21 is to write a Personal Mission Statement on how you envision the remainder of your 25,000 days. We know your mission statement will change over time. So why write one? For the same reason you wash your hands—even knowing they will get dirty again. It's the right thing to do.

Your statement can include, but is not limited to:
- **Your philosophy of life**
- **Intentions**
- **Dreams**
- **Goals**
- **Objectives**
- **Action plans**
- **Timelines**
- **Beliefs**
- **Attitudes**
- **Values**
- **Commitments**

Try starting your Personal Mission Statement with
"I see myself ..."
"I will ..."
"I believe ..."
"I promise to ..."

> "The tragedy of life is not that it ends so soon, but that we wait so long to begin it."

Personal Mission Statement

Date: _____

_____
_____
_____
_____
_____
_____
_____
_____
_____
_____
_____
_____
_____
_____
_____
_____
_____
_____
_____
_____
_____
_____
_____
_____
_____
_____
_____

> "When you were born, you cried and the world rejoiced. Live your life so that when you die, the world cries and you rejoice."
> —Native American saying

Signed: _____

The Commencement Address

Will Speaks

It has been often said that we learn more from our mistakes than from our successes. I find myself learning much more from people who have struggled than from those who lives have wound around a magical thread of "no pain" and "no problems". That is why we have been honest with you about our difficulties, our trials and tribulations. It is called Life Experience, and I sincerely believe that if it does not kill you, it makes you stronger. With that in mind, I offer you a Commencement Address instead of an Epilogue or Final Word. We conclude with my Last Will & Testament (pun intended!) This is just the beginning, and I will always hope that this book has helped you begin your academic journey with an enhanced belief in yourself and your possibilities!

❖ ❖ ❖

I was up late one night after a speech and mentally going over what I said, what I wish I would have said, and frankly, what I wish I had not said. I am my own worst critic, despite my advice to you to cut yourself some slack. My channel surfing brought me to the *Charlie Rose Show*. I became a fan one night some time ago as he talked to Malcolm Gladwell, the author of *The Tipping Point, Blink,* and *Outliers*. These books have changed my thinking about everything and I strongly recommend them to you. As I write this, I am reading his newest effort, *What The Dog Saw*.

Seeing the familiar "Wouldn't he be great to have over for dinner" smile and gentle way of Rose, I then became aware that he was interviewing actress and advocate Carrie Fisher. She will always be Princess Laia for my generation from the first *Star Wars* movies. I have read that her life has been difficult; she has wrestled with substance abuse issues, family issues, and many of the things that have troubled me in my life. She was lively, engaging, and brilliant in her honesty and insight.

I made a mental note when she first spoke, and said to myself, "I've got to remember that." Then, when the next gems came out of her mind and mouth, I got up and began to write them down. When the dialogue between Carrie and Charlie was over, I had a notepad filled with some of the most profound words I had ever heard. Since I no

> "You are only as sick as your secrets."
>
> —*Carrie Fisher*
> *Actress and activist*

> "You've done hard before"
> —Father Tom

longer believe in coincidences, I intuitively knew that these were words I wanted to share with my students and readers. Carrie spoke a hundreds interesting ideas; here are the Top 10 according to me for your consideration as you begin your academic journey.

1. **"You've Done Hard Before"**
   This was a phrase Carrie attributed to Father Tom when she had said to him, "That will be hard." He responded, "You've done hard before". College is not easy. It is at once challenging, disappointing, and thrilling. It is a marathon with several obstacles. It is hard. But you know where I am going. "You have done hard before." You are stronger than you think you are and with a little Sisu (remember Point Seven, Introduction), you can do it!

2. **"You're Only As Sick As Your Secrets"**
   This is the one that got me out of bed and writing on the night stand in the hotel. I realized that it wasn't until I began to share my darkest secrets that I began to get well and like myself. My parent's divorces, infidelity, my problem drinking, sexual abuse as a child...the light of day; that is, speaking them out loud took the big scary things away, or at least made them small enough to look at. Suddenly I found myself surrounded by a huge number of empathic people who not only had experienced their own pain, but could help me cope with my own. If you have problems, see someone, talk to a friend, make an appointment with a counselor. We are only as sick as our secrets.

3. **"The worst thing about drug addiction is the look you put on people's faces."**
   Wow! Promise me you will think about this before you develop a problem with alcohol or a dependence on other drugs. I have seen the faces of two of my dear friends whose daughter is battling drug addiction. Upon whose face can you see the most pain? Your own? Your Mom? Dad? Grandma? Brothers or sisters? No guilt - just think about it and make life giving choices. As Sheryl Garrett so accurately pointed out, Choices Matter!

4. **"If I can claim it, it's mine."**
   There is a freedom that comes from acknowledging a problem as one's own and accepting responsibility for it. No denial. No pointing fingers. Stake your claim on your strengths and weaknesses, then work on minimizing the latter and enhancing the former.

5. **"The point is to find the funny thing in the hard thing."**
   You have to be able to find the humor even in the deepest, darkest sad times. Laughter keeps us sane. If you cannot learn to laugh at yourself, then other people will do it for you. We laugh with people, not at them. It takes many more muscles, and effort, to frown, than it does to smile.

6. **"I came from a place of privilege and ordeal."**
   There is an assumption in our culture than money will make us happy. Being loved and being needed by others is actually what makes us happy. Seek to be rich in heart and spirit. We all have stories we'd rather not share. Do not fear them. We have all had ordeals, but "We've done hard before." (See #1). Coming from a wealthy background does not spare us from life's real pain; and that pain is loneliness and seperation from others. Getting involved on campus and working on community service projects helps to put our own problems in perspective.

> "If you cannot learn to laugh at yourself, then other people will do it for you."
> —Dr. Will Keim

7. **"I want to feel like you seem."**
   Carrie said this to Charlie, and I laughed out loud thinking how many times in my life I wished I was someone other than the only person I can ever be...me! We are often not as we seem, as are many people. Carrie was articulating a real truth that we all aspire at times to be someone else, but the reality is we must invent and become the unique selves we each are. There is no other way. For more on the difference between "finding yourself" and "inventing yourself", please read Marty Catherine Bateson's excellent book, *Composing A Life*.

8. **"I don't want people to look at my house, but rather listen to my furniture."**
   What a great way of saying, "Don't judge me by the externals (house=appearance, clothing, the outside of the situation), but rather listen to what I am really about and what I am trying to say (furniture=my heart, my thoughts and dreams, my story)." Come sit in my living room (my life) and let's talk. You really cannot judge a book by the cover, especially when the book is an analogy for a human being. What is on the inside matters most.

9. **"Say your weak things in a strong voice."**
   You have to speak what you want to happen into existence. Even if you are not sure you really believe 100%. Say it, speak it out loud, in a strong voice. I will succeed. I will succeed. I WILL

SUCCEED. Be bold, be determined, be obstinate in your desire to become the person you have always wanted to be. But first, say it out loud with all your might. Attitude precedes behavior.

10. **"I have problems. Problems do not have me."**

    You are in charge and you can be bold, even obsinate in the face of adversity. I have many problems, but they do not have me. They cannot solve me. I can solve them. I will solve them!

> "No problem can withstand the assault of sustained thinking."
> —Voltaire
> 1694-1778
> French writer and philosopher

Author's Thanks

To PBS for hosting the *Charlie Rose show*. To Charlie Rose for his amazing ability to empower great stories from his guests. To Carrie Fisher for her honesty and willingness to bare her soul and let her life lessons teach us to face our own demons with grace and dignity.

Dr. Will Keim

Last Will & Testament

Your college or university has assembled all the necessary agents for the creation of your life's masterpeace. No one, however, can make you show up. You have to do your part. These 10 Lessons from the life of Carrie Fisher, the 21 Chapters of *Welcome to the Time of Your Life!*, your life experience...you are armed and ready for the battle. And remember...the battle is to find your passion, your vocation, the work you can do and never feel like it is work. Only a warrior can fight this battle, and as you have learned, a warrior is ultimately a man or woman who is no longer afraid to be their real self.

I have always been a fan of Joe Paterno, Head Football Coach at Penn State University. We will conclude this discussion, for now, with two statements he made that I affirm with all my heart. Speaking about the men he coaches, he said, "Every player we have, someone poured their life and soul into that young man. They are giving us their treasure, and it's our job to give them back that young man intact." Many of us have been broken, injured, or hurt. We can with our own effort and the help of others put ourselves back together again, be intact, and help someone else do the same. Joe also said, "What are you going to do about the past? It's over." How true. The past is gone. But right now, right here, the present moment is ripe with possibility. You can create whatever masterpeace you desire. Your spirit is large and in charge. This is your moment. I want it to be a joyous ride toward self-invention, self-realization, achievement, happiness, and service to others. I have given you my very best effort to guide you. I have faith that you will listen and make your own glorious path.

> "What are you going to do about the past? It's over."
> —Joe Paterno
> Head Football Coach
> Penn State University

You do not travel alone. If I can help you, you can always find me at: www.willkeim.com or www.willkeim@att.net.

Aloha, mahalo, and Welcome To The Time Of Your Life!

Dr. Will Keim

Index

Persons, Places, & Concepts Index by Pages

ACPA 52
ACUHO-I 52
ACUI 52
Adam and Eve . . . . .xiii, 144
AFA 52
AIDS 70, 126, 171, 223
Allen, Woody 144
All Hands On Poem 139-140
Americorps VISTA 148
Angelou, Maya 89, 99
Anka, Andy 186
Anka, Paul 185-187
Anthony, Susan B. 185
Archbishop Tutu 149-150
Argeropolous, John . . . . . . .xiii, 170, 203-216, 240
Aristotle 176
Arroyo, Martina 53
Asgedom, Mawi . . . . .xiv, 182
Austin, Texas 185, 187, 240
Baganu, Grace . . . . .xiv, 27
Baha'i Faith 116
Barnes, Rick . . . .xiii, 54, 65-66, 240
Barnhart, Mitch . . . . .xiv, 198
Barrett, Rona 73
Bateson, Mary Catherine . . .86, 233
Beasley-Ross, Valeria . . . . . . .xiii, 90, 133-139, 241
Beastie Boys 102
Beirut, Lebanon 196
Belushi, John 63
Benedict College . . . .xiii, 90-91, 110 115-117, 240
Bennis, Warren 146
Berkowitz, Alan 69
Big Brothers-Big Sisters 209, 211
Blackcoupleitis 135-137
Black History Month 134, 136
Blink 231
Blue Mountain Community College 90, 118, 121-122
Bonsall, Dave . . . . .xiv, xv
Bonsall, Sandy . . . . .xiv-xvi
Borden, Gail 57
Borg, Marcus . . . . .xiv, 149, 224
Boys and Girls Club 143
Bradshaw, Carrie 18
Brown, Jerry 151
Browne, H. Jackson 2, 29

Browning, Christopher R. 129
Buber, Martin . . . .Introduction, 2, 5, 23, 30, 67, 176
Bucket List 226
Buckingham, Lindsey 86
Buffett, Warren 145
Burke, Steven 3
Burns, George 224
Burrus, Chris 228
Bussey, Nikki . . . . .xiv, 2, 15-20, 240
Butler, Gerard 147
Byrds 187
California Public Utilities Commission 189
California State University, Chico 90, 124-126, 241
California State University, San Bernardino . . . . . .xiii, 2, 12, 240
Camas, Washington 143
Canada, Geoffrey . . . . .xiv, 118
Carnegie, Dale 11
Carson, Johnny 68
Carter, Hodding 84
Carvel, Paul 65
Cash Reserves 156-157
Caterpillar Affinity Groups 142
Caterpillar African American Network (CAAN) 142
Caterpillar Armed Forces Support Network (CAFSN) 142
Caterpillar Asian Indian Community (CAIC) 142
Caterpillar Chinese Affinity Group (CCAG) 142
Caterpillar Corporation 142
Caterpillar Experienced Professional Direct Higher Affinity Group (EPDH) 142
Caterpillar LAMBDA Network (CLN) 142
Caterpillar Latino Connection (CLC) 142
Center for the Study of Sport in Society 199
CFCs 183
CFCs 191
Chicago, Illinois 127
Chicano Perspective 119
Children's Miracle Network 148
Chittister, Sister Joan 91, 152
Choices Matter . . .91, 155, 163, 232
Chronicle of Higher Education 51, 128
Churchill, Winston 10

Citizenship, Democracy, and Ethnocultural Diversity Newsletter 183
Citizenship Studies Journal . .183-184
Civil Rights Movement 134
Clark, Ron . . . . .xiv, 119
Clason, George S. 155
Climate Change 185, 190
Clinton, Hillary Rodham . . .113-114
Coleman, David . . .xiii, 2, 36, 41-42, 44, 48, 50-51, 240
Collado, Desiree . . . . .xiv, 33
Colleges That Develop Character .176
Colton, Charles Caleb 69
Columbus, Ohio 133-134
Commitment In Relativism 150
Composing A Life 86, 227, 233
Compound Interest 91, 159-161
Compton, California 125-126
Confucious 116
Coolidge, Calvin 165
Costner, Kevin 221
Covey, Stephen . . .25, 174, 181, 211
Credit Card Debt Exercise 156
Crescent Valley High School 139
Cuomo, Mario 87
Dances With Wolves 221
Dangerfield, Rodney . .185, 187-188
Darwin, Charles 61
Davis, Dr. Bonnie . . . . .xiv, 119
DEA 121
Death Denying Culture 224
Debt Repayment Calculator 164
DeCrane, Gregg 35
Delancey Street 130
Denny, Meagan . . . . .xiv, 2, 240
Disney, Walt 227
Dominican Republic 144, 192
Douglas, Frederick 127
Dr. Laura 175
Dunham, Michael . . . . . . .xiii, 170, 185-193, 240
Duns, Don . . . . . . .xii, xiv, 2, 24, 55
Durein, Tom . . . . . . .xiii, 90, 105-109
Eck, Diana 91, 149, 151
Eden Alternative 209, 211
Edwards, William J. 114
Egan, Ms. 105
Einsohn, Amy 20
Einstein, Albert 94, 159, 194
Elements of Style 20
Elliott, Rebecca 20
Elmhurst College 33, 198

Emerson, Ralph Waldo . . . .Foreward, 3, 21, 78, 95
Etheridge, Melissa 100
Eye Med 192
Fan Etiquette .170, 196-198, 200-201
Fisher, Carrie 231, 234-235
Fitch, Janet 145
Fogg, Piper 128
Four Step Ethical Model 90, 95, 174, 177
Francis, Clarence 32
Frank, Anne 143
Franklin, Benjamin 9,15
Franz, Brother Craig 179
Freeman, Morgan 226
Freire, Paulo 128
Frost, Robert . . . . .xiii, 169
Full Cost/Low Cost 163
Gandhi, Indira 123, 142
Gandhi, Mahatma 30, 96
Garcia-Preto, Nydia 128
Gardner, John . . .170, 173, 183, 192
Garrett, Sheryl . . . . . .xiv, 91, 155-167, 232, 240
Gary, Indiana 134
Gates, Bill and Melinda 145
GED 90, 121-122
Generation X, Y . . . . .xiii, 144
Gibson, Roger C., CFP 159
Giordano, Joe 128
Gladwell, Malcolm 231
God At 2000 Conference 149
Goddard, John 10
Graham, Billy 24
Graham, John 90, 130-131, 240
Graham, Katharine 171, 217
Grateful Dead 185
Greyhound Bus 125
Grisham, John 99
Habitat for Humanity 148
Haines, Michael 62
Hansen, Philip 60
Harlem Children's Zone 118
Hartley, Mark . . . . .xiii, 2, 8, 12, 240
Hartman, Eric 37
Harvard University 78-79, 91, 146, 151
Hawkins, David 170, 206-207
Healthy Aging 214-215
Hemingway, Ernest 15, 22
Hepburn, Katherine 187
Heraclitus 154
Hermiston, Oregon 90, 121

Hill, Aki 217
Hippocrates 75
Historically Black Colleges or Universities 115
Holtz, Lou . . . . .xiv, 5, 146, 226
Imus, Don 175
Institute For Advanced Spiritual Research 170, 206
International Association of Campus Law Enforcement Administrators 197
Islam 70, 116
Jackson, Tondeleya . . . . .xiii, 90, 109-111, 115, 117, 240
JACO Environmental 189-191, 193, 240
Jacobs, Dave 199
Jaime-Diaz, Jesus . . . . .xiii, 2, 118-120, 122
Jamison, Steve 129
Jefferson Airplane 187
Jefferson, Thomas 185
Jesus of Nazareth 97, 116
Jones, Megan 29
Jones, Mona 99
Josephson Institute 32, 201
Kansas City Star Guide 22
Keagbine, Emily 200
Keep It Real Challenge 153
Keim, Mary 91
Keim, Samantha . . . . . .xiv, 29, 90, 105-107, 240
Keller, Helen 11, 33, 171, 226
Kennedy, John F. 49, 132
Kerr, Steve 196, 199
Kimbrough, Dr. Walter .Introduction, xiv, 139
King, Martin Luther, Jr. 84, 176
Klink, Kevin . . . . . .xiii, 54, 82, 241
Klink, Laura . . . .xiii, 54, 80, 82, 241
Kubler-Ross, Elizabeth 224
Kushner, Rabbi Lawrence 91, 149-151
Lao Tzu 4, 94, 177
Leader Fellows Program, NMU . .216
Lenscrafters 192
Lewis, Jerry M. 196
Lifelong Learning Opportunities 209, 215
Lincoln, Abraham 1, 60, 153, 180, 225
Linfield College . . .90, 105, 200, 240
Little Bear , Naomi 90

Lockwood, Jeanie 90, 121
Lombardi, Vince 223
Lyons, Kay 180
Make-A-Difference Day 209, 211
Map of Consciousness 170, 206
Marcia, James 150
Maslow, Abraham 35
Match.com 18-19
Mayer, John xi
McDonough, Anderson Burrus . .228
McGoldrick, Monica 128
Mead, Margaret 31
MEChA Chapter 121
Meier, Golda 93
Mentoring 49, 91, 143, 147, 209-210
Meredith, James 138
Merton, Thomas x
Mills, Billy 91, 151
Modern DeFacto Segregation 120
Montreal Protocol 185
Moses .141
Mother Teresa 146-147
Muhammad Ali 11
NACA 52
NASA .187
NASPA .52
National Association of Intercollegiate Athletics 201
National Association of Sports Officials 197
National Character Partnership . . .32
National Council on Problem Gambling 66
National Intramural Recreational Sports Association 201
National Sexual Assault Hotline . . .64
National Symposium on Character & Leadership . . .32, 130
Native American Saying 171, 230
NCAA 12, 195-197, 201
NCADD 63
NEDA 76
Nelson, Willie 185, 188
New Car/Used Car 91, 162-163
New Jersey 185-186
Nicholson, Jack 226
Nickelback 223
Nobel Peace Prize 150, 159
NODA .52
Northern Michigan University 170, 216
Obama, President Barack 127

ODS 189-190
Old Testament 141
Oprah 175
Oregon State University ..59, 90, 93, 129, 149, 217, 240
Oursler, Fulton 11
Outliers 231
Oxford, Mississippi 135, 138
Pacific Lutheran University 200
Pahia, Neal 228
Palmer, Parker ....xiii, 90, 94
Pappano, Laura 174
Pasqua, Elaine ....xiii, 54, 241
Pastner, Josh 196
Paterno, Joe 235
Peace Corps 148
Penn State University 235
Peoria Magazine 142
Perot, Ross ....xiv, 32
Piaget......................55
Poco 187
Powell, Colin 11
Prefontaine, Steve 171, 224
Presley, Elvis xi
Proposition 8, California 127
Racism 120, 122
Radzvilowicz, Joe ...xiii, 54, 82, 241
RAINN 64
Randall, Semeka 12
Rather, Dan 19
Reeves, Christopher 187
Religioustolerance.org 116
Richardson, Joe ....xiii, 90, 100-102, 104, 241
Robb, J. Wesley 90, 95, 177
Robinson, Travon ..xiii, 90, 124-126, 128-129, 241
Rolling Stones 187
Ron Clark Academy 119
Roosevelt, Franklin D. 23
Rose, Charlie 225, 234
Ross, Charles 90, 133, 137, 139, 241
Rotary International 104, 148
Rudolf, Wilma 91
Run DMC 102

Ruskin, John 15
Ruud, Casey 130
Ryberg, Denny 35
Safire, William 21
Saroyan, William 19
Sawyer, Robin 67
Schaar, John 221
Schaudt, Carol 217
Schweitzer, Albert 149
Selena 171, 224
Shakespeare, William 30, 177
Shakur, 2 Pac 127
Shoemaker, Tom 228
Silbert, Mimi 130
Silva, Father Robert ....xii, xiv
Silver, Dr. Debbie ....xiv, 119
Simpson, OJ 102
Sinatra, Frank 185, 187
Sisu ....xii, xv-xvi, 232
Smith, John L. 226
South Carolina 91, 111, 113-115
South Padre Island 185
Southeastern Conference 170
Spirituality 91, 149-154, 213
Sprague, Ed 197
Stanford Encyclopedia of Philosophy 183-184
St. Jude Children's Research Hospital 148
Stevenson, Adlai 184
Sullivan, Eileen ....xiv, 198
Summitt, Pat ....xiv, 12
Sutherland, Shelley 93
Tao Te Ching 55, 142, 177
Templeton Foundation 176
The Connection Gap 174
The Golden Rule 91, 116, 147
The Millenials ....xiii, 144
The Ohio State University ..133-134
The Richest Man In Babylon 155
The United Nations 185
ThisAmericanLife.org 63
Thoreau, Henry David 218
Tipping Point 231
Title III Education Act 115
Tracy, Brian 8

Trungpa, Chogyam .....xii, 67, 152
Tubman, Harriett 11
Twain, Mark 16, 54, 83, 151, 176, 220
United States Air Force Academy .130
University of Arizona 196
University of California, San Diego .27
University of California, Santa Cruz 221
University of Houston 185
University of Kentucky 29, 198
University of Mississippi 90, 133, 135, 137-138, 144, 192
University of Nebraska 63, 201
University of New Hampshire 83
University of Oregon 93
University of Redlands 3, 12, 28, 100, 146, 177, 228
University of Southern California .71
University of Southern Mississippi 228
University of Virginia 99
Unsung Heroes Fund 215
Valvano, Jim ....Introduction
Vicksburg, Mississippi 134-135
Villareal, Neto 130
Visco, Frank 20
Voltaire ....xv, 234
Vonnegut, Kurt ....xiii, 144, 175
Wakantanka 150-151
Wake Forest University 144, 192
Washington, Booker T. 14
Washington, George 29
Webster's Dictionary 100, 175
What The Dog Saw 231
White, Ryan 171, 223-224
Whittier College 199
Wolff, Rick 197
Women's Initiatives Network (WIN) 142
Wooden, John ....iii, 23-24, 32, 54, 129, 143
Woods, Elle 17
YMCA 209-210

❖   ❖   ❖

Arrive, Survive, Thrive, & Aspire Higher Index

Arrive
1. Scholarship 3-14
2. Writing 15-22
3. Speaking 23-28
4. Character 29-34
5. Relationships 35-52

Survive
6. Stress 55-58
7. Freedom 59-66
8. Health 67-74
9. Eating Disorders 75-82
10. Letting Go 83-88

Thrive
11. Peacemaking 93-98
12. Diversity 99-142
13. Service 143-148
14. Spirituality 149-154
15. Financial Literacy 155-168

Aspire Higher
16. Leadership 173-182
17. Citizenship 183-194
18. Sportsmanship 195-202
19. Trees of Self Realization
    & Self Defeat 203-216
20. The Secret 217-222
21. 25,000 Days 223-230

❖ ❖ ❖

Topical Index By Stages

Stage One: Arrive
Stage One: Arrive Chapters 1-5
   Summary 1-2
Ten Strategic Study Tips 5
Master Syllabus 6-7
Academic Goal Setting 13
"How To Write Good" Parody 20
"Rules For Writers" Humor . . .21-22
Pyramid of Public Speaking 24
UCSD Express To Success 28
Character In The Workplace 31
12 Campus Relationships To
   Foster 37-40
Long Distance Relationships . .47-49
Military Relationships 49-50
National Collegiate Speakers
   Association 51
SpeakeRevolution 51
Dr. Will Keim's Higher
   Aspirations 51

Stage Two: Survive
Stage Two: Survive Chapters 6-10
   Summary 54
50 Stress Busters For Students . .55-57
Stress Test 58
Personal Drinking Inventory 60
The S.A.D. Facts 62-72
Marijuana .64
Problem Gambling 65
Club Drugs & Date Rape 64, 73
Tobacco and Nicotine 65
Dr. Keim's Prescription For
   Healthy Living 68
Making The Case For Sexual
   Abstention 68-69
STDs .70-71
Eating Disorder Facts and Health
   Concerns 76-77
Signs of Eating Disorders 79
Help & Intervention 80
Letter To Parents 85
Letting Go 87

Stage 3: Thrive
Stage 3: Thrive Chapters 11-15
   Summary 90-91
The Big Questions 94
4 Step Ethical Decision Making
   Model .95

Conflict Resolution 96-97
Diversity Perspectives 99-142
Your Diversity Chart 117
Diversity Reading Ideas 128-129
The Power of One Exercise 132
Who Are You? 145
Mentoring 146-147
"I Believe..." Statements 152
24 Hour Activity Chart . . .153-154
Simple Rules of Acquisition 155
Credit Card Debt 156
College Degree and Income
   Chart 158
Compound Interest 160-161
New and Used Cars 162
Choices Matter 163
Small Steps Exercise 164

Stage 4: Aspire Higher
Stage 4: Aspire Higher Chapters 16-21
   Summary 170-171
Leadership: Thought Into
   Action 178-179
Ten Characteristics of Effective
   Leadership 182
Citizenship Defined 184
Sportsmanship Defined 195
Ethical Conduct Defined . . .177-178
Fan Etiquette 198-200
The Tree of Self Realization 204
The Tree of Self Defeat 205
Self Realization Suggested
   Reading 211-215
The Secret of College Life 218
Choosing A Major 219
Making Every Day Count 223
25,000 Days 223-230
Bucket List 226
One Dream Exercise 227
Personal Mission Statement 230
Dr. Will Keim's Commencement
   Address 231-234
Last Will & Testament 235

❖ ❖ ❖

Author's Index: Special Contributors

Dr. Will Keim would like to thank the following special contributors to *Welcome To The Time Of Your Life: 21 Lessons For The 21st Century*. "Your contributions to this work is a gift of your time, knowledge, and expertise, and a testament to the care and love you have for students. I am eternally grateful to all of you for giving so freely of your wit and wisdom." Thank you to:

John Argeropoulos, Professor Emeritus, Northern Michigan University

Rick Barnes, M.A. Rick Barnes Presents and Campuspeak

Nikki Bussey, Graduate, University of Memphis

David Coleman, M.A., Coleman Productions and Coleman Entertainment

Meagan Denny, Graduate, The University of Texas, Austin, High School Teacher, Softball Coach, and Professional Softball Player

Jesus Jaime Diaz, Master's Candidate, Ethnic Studies and Communication, Oregon State University

Michael Dunham, JACO Environmental and UN Commission on Global Warming

Tom Durein, Private Air Travel Industry, and Delta Upsilon Fraternity Foundation

Sheryl Garrett, CPF® Principal, Garrett Planning Network

John Graham, Vietnam Veteran and The Giraffe Project

Mark Hartley, Student Development California State University, San Bernardino

Tondeleya Jackson, M.A. Student Development, Benedict College, South Carolina

Sami Keim, Student and Softball Player, Linfield College

Walter Kimbrough, Ph.D., President, Philander Smith College

Laura Klink, College Student and Gymnast

Elaine Pasqua, Elaine Pasqua Lectures

Joe Radzvilowicz, Nouveau Vie Eating Disorder Clinic

Joe Richardson, J.D. Attorney at Law, Los Angeles, CA

Travon Robinson, M.A. Student Development and Diversity, California State University, Chico

Dr. Charles Ross, Faculty, University of Mississippi

Valeria Beasley Ross, M.A. Student Affairs and Diversity, University of Mississippi

Do you have a younger sister or brother, niece or nephew, cousin, or friend who will need a mentor as they begin to consider going to college? Here are excellent resources you can recommend to them that will jump-start their journey and give you a chance to 'pay it forward'!

Additional Resources Online
petersons.com
collegeview.com
collegebound.net
fafsa.ed.gov
fastweb.com
collegetoolkit.com

A very special thank you and well done to Kevin Klink, Chemical Engineer, my Editor and friend of 25 years. Your work and attention to detail and process made this book possible. Thanks as well to Merry Crain of Central Plains Book, a Division of Sun Graphics for her typing and friendship during this process. The cover was designed by Christa Keim Schmeder, a Master's Candidate in Art Education at Western Oregon University, and made possible through the creativity of Skip Hamilton at Pro Print in Corvallis, Oregon. Photography of Dr. Will Keim by Haugens Photography of Monmouth, Oregon. "Welcome To The Time Of Your Life: 21 Lessons For The 21st Century!" is published by Viaticum Press of Corvallis, Oregon, all rights reserved. Copyright, 2010.